John Robertson McQuilkin

Praise for *Transformed from Glory to Glory*

"This is a remarkable book—well conceived, well done and well deserved. Believe me when I say that this work translates into words not only the mind of this man, but his heart, hands and feet as well. Read this book carefully and read it often, not only to be informed, but also to be challenged and blessed."

—David J. Hesselgrave
Professor Emeritus
Trinity Evangelical Divinity School

"As you read through these pages you will catch a glimpse of what I and so many others have come to know and experience: Robertson's enormous influence on so many leaders (including me) is the overflow of his love and devotion to our Savior. This book you are holding is a tribute to a great servant of the Lord and some of the things he feels deeply about."

—Crawford W. Loritts Jr.
Pastor, Author and Speaker

"This book will mentor you. Something on every page will make you a better person, a stronger leader and a wiser thinker. I confess I've found this book delightful because I know and love Robertson McQuilkin and Columbia International University. But had I known neither, I would still have read every chapter with profit and pleasure. You will too."

—Robert Morgan
Pastor and Author

"Most notable men distinguish themselves in a particular area of life. Robertson McQuilkin is one of those rare individuals who has excelled in multiple areas of academics, missions, writing, speaking, leadership and family life while exhibiting an extraordinary anointing and spiritual depth. This book will continue to bless generations to come as it captures the legacy of his life."

—Jerry Rankin, President Emeritus
International Mission Board, SBC
Director, Zwemer Center for Muslim Studies
Columbia International University

"Robertson McQuilkin crossed my path at a crucial time. I was recovering from a "toxic" church and skeptical of all things Christian. He showed me a new way that combined intellectual rigor with a clear example of compassionate integrity, and in the process helped to set my course forever."

—Philip Yancey
Author and Speaker

TRANSFORMED
FROM GLORY TO GLORY

TRANSFORMED
FROM GLORY TO GLORY

Celebrating the Legacy of
J. Robertson McQuilkin

CLC PUBLICATIONS

Fort Washington, PA 19034

Transformed from Glory to Glory
Published by CLC Publications

U.S.A.
P.O. Box 1449, Fort Washington, PA 19034

UNITED KINGDOM
CLC International (UK)
51 The Dean, Alresford, Hampshire, SO24 9BJ

ISBN (paperback): 978-1-61958-190-6
ISBN (e-book): 978-1-61958-191-3

CONTENTS

CONTRIBUTORS

Ron Barber Jr. is lecturer of Intercultural Studies at East-west College, Gordonton, New Zealand. From 1988–2011, he and his family served in Japan as church planters with TEAM. He holds a BS from the University of South Carolina, an MDiv from Columbia International University (CIU) and a PhD in Intercultural Studies from Trinity International University. He is married to McQuilkin's third daughter, Amy.

Paul Copan is a professor and the Pledger Family Chair of Philosophy and Ethics at Palm Beach Atlantic University. He has a BA from CIU, an MA and an MDiv from Trinity International University, and a PhD from Marquette University. He took Biblical Hermeneutics and Ethics and Sanctification from McQuilkin while at CIU. Paul served with Student Foreign Missions Fellowship (under InterVarsity Christian Fellowship) from 1984–1985, on the pastoral staff of First Presbyterian Church in Schenectady, New York for over six years and as a staff apologist with Ravi Zacharias International Ministries for over five years. He also served as president of the Evangelical Philosophical Society for six years. He is author or editor of about thirty books, including popular-level books such as *When God Goes to Starbucks: A Guide to Everyday Apologetics* (Baker, 2008), *True for You, But Not for Me* (Bethany House, 2009) and *Is God a Moral Monster? Understanding the Old Testament God*

(Baker, 2011). Some of his scholarly books include *Creation Out of Nothing: A Biblical, Philosophical, and Scientific Exploration* (Baker, 2004), *The Rationality of Theism* (Routledge, 2004) and *Philosophy of Religion: Classic and Contemporary Issues* (Wiley-Blackwell, 2007). He has recently coauthored with McQuilkin the third edition of *An Introduction to Biblical Ethics: Walking in the Way of Wisdom* (IVP, 2014).

John C. Crutchfield attended Torchbearer Schools (Capernwray Hall and Tauernhof) and has a BA from Columbia Bible College and an MA from Columbia Biblical Seminary and Graduate School of Missions. After serving as a pastoral intern in the Cleveland area, he completed an MDiv at Trinity Evangelical Divinity School. His PhD is from Hebrew Union College-Jewish Institute of Religion. He served as pastor of Christ Evangelical Free Church in Cincinnati, Ohio and of Fairhaven Community Church in Camden, Ohio. He has taught as visiting professor at New Life Bible College in Moscow and at Lanka Bible College and Seminary in Sri Lanka, and he is currently a professor of Bible at CIU. He is the author of *Psalms in their Context* (Paternoster Biblical Monograph Series, 2011) and a contributor to *What the Old Testament Authors Really Cared About* (Kregel, 2013). He has also written various articles and numerous book reviews.

Ralph E. Enlow Jr. has served as president of the Association for Biblical Higher Education since 2007, following twenty-eight years in service to his alma mater, CIU. His tenure as a CIU student and administrator included the entire twenty-two-year span of McQuilkin's presidency. While earning his bachelors and masters degrees from CIU, he was a student of McQuilkin's in such courses as Ethics and Sanctification and Biblical Principles for Christian Work. He earned an EdD in Higher Education

Administration from Vanderbilt University. He has authored *The Leader's Palette: Seven Primary Colors* (Westbow Press, 2013) and is a contributing author to *Foundations of Academic Leadership* (VTR Publications, 2012). He serves on the editorial boards of *Christian Higher Education* and the *Encyclopedia of Christian Education* (Scarecrow Press, 2014). He is a founding member of the international theological education development initiative Global Associates for Transformational Education (GATE) and has served at length on the governing boards of The Evangelical Alliance Mission (TEAM) and the International Council for Evangelical Theological Education (ICETE).

Hans Finzel and his wife, Donna, spent ten years as missionaries in Vienna, Austria, training church leaders in Eastern Europe with WorldVenture. He served as president and CEO of WorldVenture for twenty years. He has also served on the Board of Trustees of CIU for twenty years, attributing his commitment to the school to his experience as a CIU student and his close relationship with McQuilkin. He and his wife recently founded a new ministry, HDLeaders, devoted to training leaders around the globe. Hans is the host of a leadership podcast on iTunes called "The Leadership Answer Man." He is the author of eight books, including his best seller, *The Top Ten Mistakes Leaders Make* (David C. Cook, 2013). His books have been translated into over twenty foreign-language editions. He has a BA from CIU, a ThM from Dallas Seminary and a DMiss from Fuller Theological Seminary. He can be reached at www.hansfinzel.com.

John D. Harvey is professor of New Testament and Greek, as well as dean of the Seminary & School of Ministry at CIU. He holds a BS from Syracuse University, an MDiv from Columbia Biblical Seminary and Graduate School of Missions and a ThD from Wycliffe College of the University of Toronto. He is an ordained teaching elder in the Presbyterian Church in America and is a member of the Evangelical Theological Society, the Institute for Biblical Research and the Society of Biblical Literature. He has taught in Germany, the Netherlands, Moldova, Zambia and South Africa. He is the author of *Listening to the Text: Oral Patterning in Paul's Letters* (Baker, 1998), *Greek is Good Grief: Laying the Foundation for Exegesis and Exposition* (Wipf & Stock, 2007), *Anointed with the Spirit and Power: The Holy Spirit's Empowering Presence* (P&R Publishing, 2008) and *Interpreting the Pauline Letters: An Exegetical Handbook* (Kregel, 2012).

Roy M. King has been involved in leadership roles in church ministry, with a priority on training leaders, for over forty years. He has provided consulting for over 750 congregations in ten countries and coaching for over 100 church and ministry leaders. He holds a BS from East Tennessee State University, an MA from CIU, a DPhil in Religion and Society from Oxford Graduate School and a DMin with a leadership focus from Fuller Theological Seminary. He has been a professor of ministry studies at CIU's Seminary & School of Ministry since 1997. He is the author of *Time Management is Really Life Management* (LeaderSpace, 2009) and *Remain In Me: Living Through Change with Wisdom and Grace* (IMB, ICEL 2011). He provides resources for life-giving leadership at www.royking.org.

Christopher R. Little has over eighteen years of cross-cultural missionary service in Kenya, Europe, the Asian sub-continent, Mozambique and Jordan. He holds an MDiv from Talbot Theological Seminary, a ThM in Missiology and a PhD in Intercultural Studies from Fuller Theological Seminary. He has served as professor of missiology at the Jordan Evangelical Theological Seminary and, since 2006, as professor of intercultural studies at CIU. He is the author of *The Revelation of God Among the Unevangelized: An Evangelical Appraisal and Missiological Contribution to the Debate* (William Carey Library, 2000), *Mission in the Way of Paul: Biblical Mission for the Church in the Twenty-First Century* (Peter Lang Publishing, 2005) and *Polemic Missiology for the 21ˢᵗ Century: In Memoriam of Roland Allen* (Kindle, 2013), as well as numerous articles on mission in various journals.

Bradford A. Mullen is teaching pastor of Calvary Church, Lancaster, Pennsylvania, where he has served since 2004. He holds an MDiv from Columbia Graduate School of Bible and Missions, a ThM from Trinity Evangelical Divinity School and a PhD from Boston University. He taught theology from 1986–2002 at his alma mater, the Seminary of Columbia International University, where McQuilkin mentored him in the teaching of Biblical Hermeneutics and The Principles of the Christian Life, two courses McQuilkin developed. He collaborated with McQuilkin on the second editions of *Understanding and Applying the Bible* (Moody, 1992) and *Biblical Ethics* (Tyndale, 1995) and coauthored "The Impact of Postmodern Thinking on Evangelical Hermeneutics," published in the *Journal of the Evangelical Theological Society* 40/1(1997): 69–82, a paper he presented at the 1994 annual meeting of the Evangelical Theological Society. He contributed a chapter, "The Legalistic Trap: How to Avoid It," in the volume McQuilkin edited to celebrate the seventy-fifth anniversary of CIU, *Free and Fulfilled: Victorious Living in the Twenty-First Century* (Thomas Nelson, 1997).

Robert J. Priest is G. W. Aldeen Professor of International Studies and professor of mission and anthropology at Trinity Evangelical Divinity School. The son of missionaries Perry and Anne Priest, Robert grew up in Bolivia. He completed a BA at CIU, where he took courses from McQuilkin (his maternal uncle) in Ethics and Sanctification and Biblical Principles for Christian Work. He also has an MDiv from Trinity Evangelical Divinity School, an MA in Social Science from the University of Chicago and a PhD in Anthropology from the University of California, Berkeley. He taught in the seminary at CIU for ten years (1990–1999) and has taught at Trinity Evangelical Divinity School since 1999. He served as president of the American Society of Missiology from 2013–2014. His publications have focused on culture and conscience, race and ethnicity, short-term missions, witchcraft accusations, and megachurches and missions; they include *This Side of Heaven: Race, Ethnicity, and Christian Faith* (Oxford University Press, 2007) and *Effective Engagement in Short-Term Missions: Doing it Right!* (William Carey Library, 2008).

George W. Murray spent thirty years in the world of cross-cultural missions before becoming the president of CIU in 2000, and later its chancellor in 2007. As a missionary practitioner and leader, he served with his family as church planters in Italy for thirteen years, then as the CEO of Bible Christian Union (1983–1993) and TEAM (1994–1999). He holds a BA and an MA from CIU and a DMiss from Trinity International University. At CIU, he has taught courses in missions, leadership and biblical preaching.

Steve Richardson has served as president of Pioneers-USA for the past fifteen years. He was raised in Papua, Indonesia, a story documented in his father's missionary classic, *Peace Child* (Regal, 2011). After receiving his BA and MA from CIU, he and his wife initiated and operated a multifaceted church-planting ministry in Southeast Asia for thirteen years. He has held various leadership roles within Pioneers and facilitated development of its mobilization bases in Australia and New Zealand. McQuilkin has served as a mentor and inspiration to Steve since the early 1980s.

Shirl S. Schiffman joined the faculty of CIU in the last year of McQuilkin's presidency. She served the university as director of instructional development for distance education from 1989 until 2006. During this time, she had the privilege of assisting McQuilkin with the interactive component of *Life in the Spirit* (LifeWay, 1997). She now teaches spiritual formation and Bible teaching in CIU's Seminary & School of Ministry. She has a BA, MS and PhD from Florida State University, and with nearly thirty years as a Christian educator, her passion is to equip leaders for the educational ministry of the global church.

FOREWORD

Over ninety years have come and gone since the founding of Columbia International University. Originally begun as the Southern Bible Institute, it was later named Columbia Bible Institute, and thereafter Columbia Bible College, still known fondly to many today as CBC. To help graduates gain entry into countries potentially hostile to Christian influence, we took the current name of Columbia International University (CIU).

Though CIU's name has changed many times over the decades since six godly ladies prayed us into existence, it has never wavered from its mission. In a very real sense, CIU will always seek to remain CBC: Christ centered, biblically based and culturally relevant.

To understand why CIU, unlike many Christian institutions, has not drifted from its historic mission you must understand one word—one person, actually: McQuilkin. Robert C. McQuilkin served as the first president of CIU for twenty-nine years. His son, J. Robertson McQuilkin, served as the third president for twenty-two years.

This book honors the contributions of the latter McQuilkin, someone I have had the privilege of knowing for almost a quarter of a century. I first met Robertson during my interview to join CIU's faculty. By the time I arrived on campus, he had resigned from his post in order to tend to his beloved wife, Muriel, who could no longer function without his compassionate care. After several years of hearing stories about him, I gathered up the courage to stop by his house to chat—a practice that continues to this day. During these visits he both verbalized and modeled the Spirit-filled life. I would leave him challenged and energized. Little did I realize that years later I would be sitting in his former office, grateful for the powerful way he impacted me.

At my installation service as CIU's sixth president, I told the audience that I would never be able to preach like Dr. George Murray, our fifth president, nor be as intelligent as Dr. Johnny Miller, our fourth president, nor be as godly as Dr. Robertson McQuilkin. Let me be clear that the people who have known Robertson through the years do not worship him, but we do regard him with tremendous respect, honor and adoration. Indeed, our love for him is so great we want others to benefit from knowing him as well.

To this end, I am deeply grateful for this book, as it will not only introduce the reader to this unique servant of God but also to all that he championed during the course of his life. If more would simply emulate his character and live by his teachings, we would be better equipped to face the growing challenges of the twenty-first century. May God be pleased to increase his tribe among us today!

William H. Jones
President, Columbia International University

INTRODUCTION

Christopher R. Little

The name Robertson McQuilkin may not be a household name, but to those who know the man behind the name, it invariably evokes deep emotions of affection, appreciation and admiration. All who know him would acknowledge he is not perfect, but most would insist that they wished to be more like him, to promote all that he stood for. This is what this book is about. Each author has worked in concert to pass on McQuilkin's legacy to subsequent generations of those who desire to take seriously the call to follow in the way of Jesus Christ.

This book is known as a *Festschrift*—German for a work dedicated to the honor of a highly respected individual. But it is not like normal *Festschriften*. Rather than concentrating only on the academic achievements of McQuilkin, which are many, it also explores his life in terms of how he put into practice what he believed and taught throughout his career. In other words, how he walked the talk.

The original idea for the book came in the summer of 2012 when John Harvey and I collaborated in teaching a doctoral ministry course at Columbia International University (CIU) entitled "Acts in Multi-Perspectival Contexts." We were standing in for William Larkin, the course's developer and usual instructor, who was unable to teach that summer because of health concerns. As John was explaining to the class Larkin's approach to interpreting historical narrative, it dawned on me that a fruitful exercise would be to compare and contrast McQuilkin's method for interpreting historical narrative with Larkin's. When I queried John as to whether he knew if this had been done in publication, our conversation unintentionally stumbled upon the idea that, much to my personal dismay, a book dedicated to McQuilkin had never been written. Thus began the process that ultimately resulted in the volume you now hold in your hands.

When I first informed Robertson about this project in the winter of 2013, his response was, "You're making a mistake!"

I replied, "The only mistake here is that such a book hasn't been written yet, and it has fallen upon me to organize it." And, of course, there was clear biblical precedent to do so as we are to "pay . . . honor to whom honor is owed" (Rom. 13:7) and "remember those who led you . . .; and considering the result of their conduct, imitate their faith" (Heb. 13:7, NASB).

The book takes its title from McQuilkin's life verse: "But we all, with unveiled face, beholding as in a mirror the glory of the Lord, are being transformed into the same image from glory to glory, just as by the Spirit of the Lord" (2 Cor. 3:18, NKJV). It is purposefully divided into six parts with two chapters each, covering the specific subjects upon which he concentrated throughout his life. The contributors were asked to use McQuilkin's life and literary works as a springboard to carry forward the conversation in relation to the specific topics under consideration.

Part I, "McQuilkin the Man," launches the book with a lively presentation by Bradford Mullen, who offers the reader an overview of the significant body of literature McQuilkin produced during the course of his ministry. This chapter should be read before any others in order to get one's bearings in McQuilkin's works. Ralph Enlow follows with a personal account of how he witnessed firsthand McQuilkin's putting what he preached into practice. He warmly testifies to how he, along with countless others, is personally indebted to Robertson as a mentor and friend over the years.

Part II introduces the subject of Bible interpretation, an area on which McQuilkin concentrated in earnest. John Crutchfield builds upon McQuilkin's conviction concerning authorial intent and skillfully shows how this concept encompasses the manner in which the entire book of Psalms was organized. William Larkin was originally slated to write on interpreting historical narrative in the New Testament for this section, but upon his retirement in the summer of 2013, he fell sick with cancer and was called home to be with his Lord in the winter of 2014. John Harvey was asked and graciously consented to take on this assignment in Larkin's place. He is the perfect person to do so because he was taught this subject by Larkin, instructed others in it for many years, and also received the materials which Larkin had researched and collected in preparation for writing this chapter before he passed. In his contribution, John very competently highlights various indicators within Scripture that allow an interpreter to know how to properly determine what is normative within historical narrative, particularly in Luke-Acts.

Part III, "Victorious Christian Living," addresses a topic very close to McQuilkin's heart. Shirl Schiffman provides an excellent exposition of this somewhat controversial and widely misunderstood teaching within the evangelical community. If there are any doubts that she faithfully represents McQuilkin's view on the matter, those doubts should be laid to rest as McQuilkin himself, after reading her chapter, confirmed that she had represented him accurately. She commends her presentation primarily to the leaders of the church to faithfully teach and model what the Bible has to say about living victoriously in the power of the Spirit. The second chapter in this section, by John Harvey, builds upon the work of McQuilkin through an exegetical analysis of the different roles of the Holy Spirit throughout the Pauline corpus and specifically in Romans 8. The thoughtful reader of this chapter will be spiritually nourished through all the benefits related to living life in the Spirit.

World missions, something to which McQuilkin contributed both in practice and promotion, comprises Part IV. Steve Richardson shares with the larger missions community the key factors that have led to the sustained growth and health of Pioneers International, an interdenominational missions organization, in hopes of empowering others to achieve organizational effectiveness in a postmodern Western context. My chapter is a contemporary analysis of the missiological landscape as represented in the two schools of thought known as prioritism and holism. Anyone who desires to know what Scripture has to say regarding what the church is called to do in missions would benefit from this chapter.

Part V, "Christian Ethics," addresses another topic upon which McQuilkin put his stamp. In the first chapter, both Robert Priest (McQuilkin's nephew) and Ron Barber (McQuilkin's son-in-law), confess their gratitude to McQuilkin for breaking new ground in the area of contextualization within evangelicalism. They provide a well-reasoned approach to current controlling assumptions and they present formal steps one must apply to the multidimensional task of carefully contextualizing the Christian faith in cross-cultural environments. Thereafter, Paul Copan addresses the notable features of McQuilkin's ethical thought and outlines the parameters for ethics in a postmodern context. His strategy for dealing with ethical issues is something those concerned with honoring the Christian faith in our day should take into serious consideration.

Part VI broaches a topic that McQuilkin effectively exemplified throughout his life—Christian leadership. Roy King invites the reader into a conversation with his son about how to fashion churches in, again, a postmodern context. He colorfully conveys wisdom from his long career of consulting church leaders to empower others to follow the lead of the wild Spirit of God into the vast new territory of the twenty-first century. Dr. Hans Finzel then unpacks some essential leadership qualities gleaned from McQuilkin—qualities which are nonnegotiable for younger leaders for lifelong, fruitful ministry. There are some real spiritual gems in this chapter for emerging leaders to take to heart.

George Murray concludes the book with a discussion of CIU's five core values. He notes that McQuilkin both embodied these values and led the CIU community in articulating them during his presidential tenure. Furthermore, he argues that these values are not only applicable and relevant to the institution McQuilkin led for over two decades but also to any institution that wishes to reflect the truths of Scripture before a conscientious church and watching world.

In conclusion, I have an assertion to make. I cannot prove this assertion, but I do believe heaven will testify to its reality. After editing these chapters, serving on CIU's faculty for almost a decade, hearing from those of you who have known McQuilkin intimately over the years and having known and interacted with the man myself, I have come to the conclusion that the reason CIU is so highly respected and has had such a global impact is due principally to one man—J. Robertson McQuilkin. Of course, it was his father, Robert C. McQuilkin, who laid the foundation, but without Robert's son, the school would never have reached its current widespread recognition and high reputation. Robertson received the mantle at a very challenging time in the school's history, and by the grace of God, he masterfully orchestrated its comeback and expansion. He did not only lead the institution through the courses he taught, the people he impacted, the books he wrote and the sermons he preached. He also led through the countless decisions he made behind the scenes, the people he recruited to serve as faculty and staff at CIU, those he invited to be chapel speakers, the programs and policies he initiated and promoted, the manner in which he conducted himself before peers and pupils, the innumerable prayers he prayed in public and in private that God honored—and much, much more. But if there is one factor that rises above all the others, it can be no other than that God sovereignly placed His hand on Robertson and anointed him "for such a time as this" (Esther 4:14).

Of course, those who know Robertson best know he would never agree to such an assertion. But I find it difficult to see it any other way, and I would surmise there are many, many others who agree with me. If you have not been blessed to know Robertson personally, I offer this book, by which you can come to know and be impacted by this remarkable servant of Christ, and be, like him, "transformed . . . from glory to glory."

Part I

McQuilkin the Man

Chapter 1

The Writings of J. Robertson McQuilkin in Retrospect

Bradford A. Mullen

I t seems easier to go to a consistent extreme than to stay at the center of biblical tension.[1]

There, I've invoked it—the McQuilkin Axiom. And this is likely not for the last time in this volume honoring the life and ministry of J. Robertson McQuilkin. Ask any alum of Columbia International University (CIU), from the McQuilkin era until today, to complete the sentence, "It seems easier . . . " and this axiom will follow as surely as "applying follows understanding" in the McQuilkin approach to interpreting the Bible.

I invoke this axiom to begin my broad-brush retrospect of McQuilkin's writings because it succinctly reveals how he thinks and how he engages every topic on which he wrote. First, he is rigorously *biblical.* What does God say? Robertson champions "functional biblical authority"—the dogged pursuit of applying biblical principles (all of them) to life's issues (all of them). Then, he finds the tension. Biblical principles are many, and though never in conflict, they press in upon themselves. The center of this tension is good. It's the Christian's sweet spot. Our greatest foes are consistent extremes, the consequences of our over-zealous preoccupation with particular biblical principles to the exclusion of others. So "No!" to easy extremes and "Yes!" to *the center of biblical tension*—axiomatic for McQuilkin as it should be for every follower of Christ in any age, from any culture and about any subject.

My retrospective is a tribute to Robertson on behalf of all who have benefitted from his teaching and example. It is shaped by my experience as his student, faculty colleague and friend. My most influential experience of Robertson was coteaching and then teaching solo the courses at CIU he called his "babies"—Hermeneutics and the Principles of the Christian Life. My goal is to present the essential McQuilkin, his big ideas and his abiding influence. I anticipate that my audience is those who have already been introduced to McQuilkin, find him engaging and maybe even compelling and want to learn more.

What kind of man do we meet in the writings of Robertson McQuilkin? In scholarship, he is a bona fide evangelical polymath (i.e., a person whose expertise spans many subjects). Most impressive is not how much he has written, though that is considerable, but the quality and breadth of what he has written. He is a big thinker. Striving to stay at the center of biblical tension has molded him into a skilled synthesizer. In an era valuing specialization, Robertson defies convention to exemplify integrative scholarship. What led him to develop expertise in such an array of disciplines as hermeneutics, ethics, missions and the theology of sanctification? I attribute it to his singular passion to bring everything under the lordship of Christ and to enlist others to share that passion.

In method, McQuilkin is a provocateur. He prods us the way a good educator, evangelist or prophet prods. Some write principally to inform, to explain, to inspire, to comfort or to defend. At one time or another Robertson does all these. Yet he always provokes, and oh so subtly. Robertson is a master of the apt illustration, the probing question and the fresh approach. You feel an urgency when you read him. You say to yourself, "This is important. I've got to deal with this." God has gifted him with a critical thinking apparatus—partly hardwired, partly cultivated by a godly heritage—and a glib, sneak-up-on-you-from-behind style that gets our attention. The man you meet on the page is the man you meet in life—charming, clever and compassionate. So when he challenges cherished ideas or rearranges entrenched priorities with disarmingly clear biblical logic, we don't consider ourselves pestered but provoked.

In overall aim, McQuilkin is a promoter. His agenda is to promote the purposes of God in us—to think and live more biblically, more victoriously, more globally. Robertson writes about the Bible to promote God's independent authority upon our personal and corporate life. He writes about the Christian life to promote pursuing life in the Spirit. He writes about world evangelization to promote an increased flow of divinely called, biblically grounded, fully equipped laborers into God's harvest field.

Robertson often urged me, "Go for it!" The "it"? What God wants! So here's the McQuilkin plan—discover what God wants, go for it and then promote it with all you've got!

In style, McQuilkin is a preacher. He takes you somewhere and then calls for a response. He's not a finger-in-your-face preacher, but a let's-go-on-a-journey-together preacher. In an era that valued verse-by-verse expositional sermons, Robertson gave step-by-step expedition sermons, and he writes the same way.

Diagram a McQuilkin sermon, article or book, and you will retrace his itinerary of discovery. His is not the well-worn pathway. When you arrive at the destination, he expects not "Aha!" but "What now?" Like the best tour guides, he is audience-sensitive. My colleague, Steve Beirn, pastor of missions at Calvary Church, remembers a conversation with Robertson in the 1980s immediately before speaking at our annual missions conference. Robertson asked Steve whether the congregation was anticharismatic or noncharismatic. Steve's answer helped Robertson craft his message.

I present the McQuilkin corpus under four headings: Victorious Christian Living, Functional Biblical Authority, World Evangelization, and the Disciple-Making Church—the last of which is less explicit in his writing but nevertheless vital. Since the 1950s, Robertson has stayed on message. Robertson steered clear, at least in his published writing, of such hot debates as the age of the universe, the *ordo salutis* (i.e., the order of salvation) and eschatological timetables. Robertson bakes his ideas from scratch, so he resists theological systems that come prepackaged. Some theologians write systematic theologies, the arrangement of the Bible's teaching by topic. Robertson's works taken together form a systematic guidebook, the application of the Bible's teaching for life travelers. Consider my retrospective to be a scenic promo.

The Victorious Christian Life

McQuilkin's books are more widely accessible than his occasional articles and contain most of their insights. You may ask, "Where should I begin to read McQuilkin?" You could start with his work on biblical authority, *Understanding and Applying the Bible*, foundational for everything else he wrote. Or read

The Five Smooth Stones and learn much about Robertson's life journey. However, I suggest you begin another place: *Life in the Spirit*, a theology of the Holy Spirit organized around the Spirit's "ten activities," where all Robertson's emphases are brought into dynamic relationship. *Life in the Spirit* is a superb model of the uniting of biblical understanding (how we should think) and life application (how we should act). Robertson's effort to pull the scholarly evangelical community closer to the center of this biblical tension seems to be his greatest legacy.

Life in the Spirit began as a thirteen-week interactive course,[2] appearing later in book form.[3] Try to resist the temptation to read it simply for information. Instead, move through it as Robertson designed—as a manual complete with questions to answer, problems to ponder and activities to practice. Better yet, work through the thirteen-week study with others, perhaps as a family, a small group or an adult church class. Then read and reread the book to keep its principles turning over and over in your mind. This is how to tap into McQuilkin's originality. Let him be your experienced guide, orienting and leading. He never demands or forces. He'll take you to familiar places and show you something new, and he'll take you to unfamiliar places and show you why you need to be there. He is our fellow traveler on a journey he began with his father, Robert C. McQuilkin. To understand Robertson better, read his father.[4] He indeed is Robert's son, both in name and in pursuit of the victorious life God promises us all.

Working through the interactive version of *Life in the Spirit* was a vivid reminder of my student days with Robertson. He gave us handouts of class lectures to be read before class. Class was for probing, deepening, wrestling. This methodology drove some students mad. Highly motivated students wanted good grades, the reward for recalling correct answers to predictable questions. Students returning to school from difficult ministry experiences wanted unambiguous and comforting answers. But Robertson did not dispense bromides or Band-Aids. His treatment included workbooks with exercises, real-life case studies with no easy answers and pop quizzes of questions demanding more than simple recollection of rote responses. He would throw out a challenging question in class, referee the intellectual food fight to follow, and then, in good Socratic fashion, bring biblical order out of chaos. No pat answers! Those who persevered got something better—the tools to think and act biblically.

Robertson's class handout "Overcoming Temptation," a battle plan for confronting temptation, is the gist of "Activity 7— Overcoming." He points the way to victory yet empathizes with those struggling. Working through *Life in the Spirit* leaves you with the impression that the one who wrote it knows you—your struggles, your fears and your hopes. He wants what you want yet he shares your skepticism. He anticipates your reactions.

The book *Five Views on Sanctification* includes a chapter by McQuilkin where he presents an earlier and shorter explanation of the Christian life. The five views span the evangelical spectrum. All the contributors agree that sanctification involves the positional and experiential: the indispensable role of the Holy Spirit, the goal of Christlikeness, the activity of Father, Son and Spirit, the need for growth, the need for divine activity and human responsibility, and the impossibility of attaining perfection before Christ returns. Comparing the views in this book is complicated because each author used his own approach and terminology. The responses are so brief you will need other resources to sort out all the differences.

Robertson would have preferred to entitle his chapter "The Mediating View," because his view draws on distinctive features of each. "The Keswick View," as the title became, is mediating nonetheless. Keswick is a scenic region of western England in which an annual conference promoting "The Victorious Christian Life" (among other names) has been conducted since the 1870s. The speakers span an array of evangelical denominations and theological positions. The Keswick five-day methodology reveals its message—sin and need, Christ's full provision, consecration to God, life in the Spirit, and servanthood (particularly evangelization). "Triumphalistic" is the common criticism of the Keswick approach. Yet did not Christ come to triumph?

Because "it seems easier to go to a consistent extreme than to stay at the center of biblical tension," some passionate Keswick adherents, like those found among all traditions, wrongly turn sanctification either into morbid introspection or frenetic works-sanctification. McQuilkin is keen to correct that caricature of the Keswick movement as a whole.

In *Five Views on Sanctification*, McQuilkin responds to critics of triumphalism by drawing two sets of distinctions. First, he clarifies what the Bible says about a believer's two natures. McQuilkin asks, if it is true that the "old nature" inherited from Adam always sins and the "new nature" given at the new birth is always righteous (the view of John Walvoord, then president of Dallas Theological Seminary), who decides which nature prevails? A third nature? Which nature grows? Neither? The application of this teaching alarms Robertson most; he remarks, "As a result of this distorted teaching, a whole genre of higher-life, deeper-life teaching has developed, a genre that advocates a do-nothing, let-Jesus-do-His-thing kind of passive Christian existence."[5] A second distinction Robertson identifies to rescue biblical sanctification from misunderstanding is the difference between "deliberate sin" and "unconscious sin."[6] Anthony Hoekema, representing the Reformed view, resists this distinction and thereby leaves little place for the present victory the Bible promises.

The ever-quotable McQuilkin opens his chapter with a memorable first line, "Average is not necessarily normal." The normal Christian life, normal by biblical standards, is not the average, often abnormal, experience of Christians. Biblical faith for McQuilkin is more than a momentous decision. It is a present dynamic. I think I've heard Robertson reference Second Corinthians 3:18 more than any other verse. It compactly declares our new potential in Christ. We are being transformed (passive voice). And the Lord is actively, continuously transforming us by His Spirit. The result is increasing glory as we exercise continuous and increasing faith (see Rom 1:17).

Free and Fulfilled: Victorious Living in the Twenty-First Century, a book conceived and edited by McQuilkin, contains what he calls "powerful expositions of what a normal victorious life of freedom and fulfillment is, and it describes how it can be one's daily experience."[7] I was honored to contribute a chapter on the danger of legalism. Robertson chose to write "Imperfections: How Perfectionist is 'Victorious Life' Teaching?" to tamp down the unfair criticism that those who promote a victorious life in Christ are really perfectionists in disguise. The general posture of *Free and Fulfilled*, however, is constructive, not polemic.

An Introduction to Biblical Ethics is the older kissin' cousin of *Life in the Spirit*. Both grew from CIU courses taught by Robertson—Ethics and Sanctification (undergraduate) and The Principles of the Christian Life (graduate). For McQuilkin, understanding sanctification must lead to applying sanctification, or ethics. In *Biblical Ethics*, McQuilkin boldly goes where many evangelicals dare not go. Staying at the center of biblical tension when applying biblical principles to ethical dilemmas requires rigor, both to remain biblical and to resist following the crowd. Critiquing revered Western culture and challenging popular evangelical sensibilities is not calculated to win or keep friends.

Biblical Ethics is where McQuilkin defines, identifies and applies God's law, or the moral law, as distinguished from the Mosaic law. The moral law is a description of God's moral character and His communicable attributes, the standard of godliness. Christ's forgiveness saves us from the guilt for violating the standard and failing to meet it. Christ's life by the Spirit restores us to that standard. We are free from the law as a means of salvation, but not as an expression of its end. Legalism is not recognizing a place for law in godliness. Could the apostle Paul have been clearer when he said that Christ came, died and now lives, "in order that the righteous requirement of the law might be fulfilled in us, who walk not according to the flesh but according to the Spirit" (Rom. 8:4)? Neither is legalism giving attention to the letter of the law as well as the spirit of the law. God expects us to do both. Legalism is seeking to fulfill the law in the flesh. We go to "a consistent extreme" when we contrast law and love. Robertson chose his opening chapters, "Love" and "Law," to coexist in biblical counterpoise. As the quotable McQuilkin was fond of saying, "Love is not lawless; and Law is not loveless."

In *Biblical Ethics*, McQuilkin discourses so broadly on ethical subjects and says so much to challenge prevailing evangelical culture that just about everybody can find something with which to disagree. For example, McQuilkin disturbs most dispensationalists by defending the Sabbath as "a law rather than a recommendation," "a special day of rest, worship, and service to the Lord" that never has and never will change.[8] Is Robertson's claim palatable that "the Bible nowhere directly condemns polygamy and nowhere directly affirms monogamy as the only legitimate arrangement"?[9] Would you agree with his borderline un-American proposition, "Capitalism is for freedom, socialism is for equality; neither economic freedom nor equality is very pronounced in Scripture"?[10] Robertson would rather you follow his lead in seeking to faithfully and rigorously apply the Bible to all life's issues than to arrive at his exact conclusions. House-trained evangelicals just won't do! Ambiguity, even disagreement, is okay. Failing to obey Scripture or going beyond Scripture never is.

Don't misunderstand! *Biblical Ethics* is not about being controversial, even less confrontational. Sure, where else can you find conservative evangelicals talking about animal rights, multinational corporations and civil disobedience? But McQuilkin's real goal in *Biblical Ethics* is to show how it is possible to bring all of life under the functional authority of Scripture. Challenges and surprises await a close and fair reading. Personally, I have made good use of his chapter "Root Sins and Virtues." Particular sins need to be traced back to their root. There can be no proper remedy without accurate diagnosis. Likewise, his explanation of the three primary "ego defenses"[11]—rationalization, suppression and projection—has for me become an invaluable diagnostic tool. Robertson remains sensitive to today's issues. A 2014 edition of *Biblical Ethics,* written with coauthor Paul Copan, is on the horizon.[12]

A Promise Kept is destined to be a classic. If *Biblical Ethics* displays the complexity of applied sanctification, *A Promise Kept* reveals its simplicity. It's a must read, not just because it is touching, but because it is exemplary of his method (apply all the Bible to all of life) and his heart (God first). *A Promise Kept* is still talked about as being so selfless, so caring, so rare! But for Robertson, it was so simple. How does a victorious Christian respond to the ravages of Alzheimer's on the love of his life? I had a ringside seat at an evening episode in the McQuilkin love story. Robertson accepted an invitation for him and Muriel to dine with my wife, Noel, and me at our home. Robertson told me it was the last time they dined out with friends. I don't remember what we talked about. I don't remember what Noel served, though her cooking is always superb. I do remember the love, the ease and the joy. I understood better why, when frequently asked about the challenge of caring for Muriel, Robertson would contentedly reply, "I don't have to, I get to!"

Functional Biblical Authority

In terms of theology, McQuilkin is not easy to categorize. Boilerplate labels don't fit. It is easier, however, to categorize him epistemologically. His hermeneutic is straightforward—interpret the Bible the way God gave it! The historical-grammatical approach uncovers what Scripture means; functional biblical authority points to how Scripture is lived. The "tension" created by the mix of biblically-derived principles with real-world challenges is, well, the stuff of life. On a few topics, very few and relatively insignificant, I see things differently than Robertson. He welcomes the engagement of ideas. But be prepared! His first question will be as predictable as a winter cold: "According to what biblical authority?"

Measuring the Church Growth Movement, Robertson's first book, asked that very question in its subtitle: *How Biblical Is It?*[13] He concludes, about the biblical soundness of necessity of measuring church, "Yes!" The young McQuilkin tested a hopeful world evangelization strategy by Scripture. His analysis shows more than consistency and fairness. It shows his hope that this movement might be used to make great strides to fulfill the

Great Commission. The jury was out then as to whether the movement would produce the great influx of believers its adherents predicted. Functional biblical authority was never a club Robertson sought to use to slay enemies. Rather, he wanted it to be a tool for discovering God's will and God's way.

Defining and defending the inerrancy of Scripture was the focus of much late twentieth-century evangelical scholarship. Did the biblical authors advocate it? Has the church consistently held to it? Does the nature of language allow it? Robertson chose to pursue the practical implications of inerrancy. How do we maintain the spirit and letter of functional biblical authority in our lives through God's inerrant Word?

Understanding and Applying the Bible is Robertson's hermeneutics primer with a twist. Robertson's title is revealing. "Applying" not only gets equal billing with "understanding"; it is the essential end to which understanding is the means. Unlike most hermeneutics textbooks, where application gets scant mention, Robertson uses the same rigor in applying the Bible as in understanding it. For McQuilkin, understanding the Bible accurately is not enough. God designed His Word so that by it He would reign in life.

Like *Life in the Spirit, Understanding and Applying the Bible* grew from an introductory course on hermeneutics McQuilkin taught at CIU. Students took the principles he taught and tried them out in workbook exercises—first on a few easy examples, then on advanced, more difficult examples, which are the ones we commonly confront in the real world of biblical study. Robertson wants new believers out of the hothouse as soon as possible. Why is it that the older Robertson gets, the more young people are drawn to him? It's because he is dauntless in the face of challenges, and the archenemy of easy answers.

Understanding and Applying the Bible has undergone two revisions, the most recent in 2009. Robertson asked me to work with him on the first revision in 1992. The publisher was open to minor additions, so Robertson used the opportunity to expand his explanation of how an existential approach robs Scripture of its authority. About the same time we coauthored a more substantive critique of relativism, which was becoming, increasingly evident in evangelicalism, in the article "The Impact of Postmodern Thinking on Evangelical Hermeneutics."[14] I presented the substance of this paper at the annual meeting of the Evangelical Theological Society (ETS) in 1994. Robertson supplied the intellectual heavy lifting. Our critique and warning about postmodern trends is no less relevant today:

> Ours is the age of subjectivism, of freedom and personal autonomy, of undogmatism and tolerance, and of other reinforcing or conflicting currents. In Protestantism, existential approaches have dominated the theology of the last half of this century. Did postmodernism thinking create these, or is it merely part of a larger flow? Whatever the sources, we seem to be in the process of losing any assurance of certainly about knowing and communicating objective reality. And many evangelicals are becoming at least moderate relativists.[15]

Robertson wrote about the threat of postmodernism, before the term came into vogue, in his analysis of cultural relativism. Always with a moist finger sensing the winds of change in evangelical core principles, he engaged and provoked the evangelical scholarly community with his article "The Behavioral Sciences under the Authority of Scripture."[16] To be functionally authoritative, only the Bible may limit its own authority. Anthropology and psychology, for example, can give insight into Scripture,

but cannot be used to interpret Scripture in a way that contro-
verts Scripture.

The following year, 1978, Robertson presented a paper at
ETS entitled "Biblical Authority Made Functional." Its thrust is
captured in the last two chapters of *Understanding and Applying
the Bible*. Two flowcharts outlined his strategy for identifying the
audience God intends and the response God desires. The first
chart moves from the Bible to life,[17] the second from an idea
or activity to the Bible.[18] These charts are a visual example of
Robertson's skill as an original thinker—scholarly without being
stuffy, accessible without dumbing down.

He continued to champion the preservation of biblical authority in the face of cultural relativity in "Limits of Cultural
Interpretation"[19] and "Problems of Normativeness in Scripture:
Cultural versus Permanent" in *Hermeneutics, Inerrancy and the
Bible*.[20] Culture, Robertson agreed, is useful for illumination and
communication but deadly when used to contradict or set aside
the plain teaching of Scripture. He considered various scholarly attempts to ground authority—reproducing the responses
to God found in the Bible, discovering universal norms in the
Bible, regarding biblical principles (not specifics) as normative,
seeking norms from nature or creation, looking for repetitions
from the Old Testament in the New—but concludes that they
all, in one way or another, ultimately appeal to an extrabiblical
authority. God's Word is not only its own best interpreter, but
also its own authority for whether, or when, what it asserts may
be limited.

World Evangelization

The Great Omission reveals Robertson's ultimate ministry
goal—world evangelization! It is arguably the best mobilizing

tool for world evangelization apart from the Bible. Its subtitle, *A Biblical Basis for World Evangelization*, lifts its argument above the trendy or cultural. He peppers us throughout with questions. It's not that the questions are hard to answer; it's that their answers indict us. Robertson has street cred. He has mobilized. He has strategized. He has sacrificed. Robertson's many articles on specific issues related to world evangelization are found in the bibliography at the end of this book. Each one is a vector pointing to his target, obeying and fulfilling the Great Commission, the subject of *The Great Omission*.

Robertson always keeps world evangelization in his sights when thinking about other matters. When believers live victoriously and function biblically, they will evangelize globally. Beware: don't read *The Great Omission* unless you are prepared to become unsettled, likely convicted. This book is preacher McQuilkin at his provocative best.

The big question, the premise for the book, was posed by a student attending a session Robertson led at an Urbana missions conference, "How come?" Robertson skillfully directed attention away from the student to God, who has been asking "How come?" for two millennia, without getting a satisfying answer. "With so many unreached people, how come so few are going?"[21] In five chapters Robertson offers five answers to that question: we don't care that much, we don't see very well, we think there must be some other way, our prayer is peripheral and someone isn't listening.[22] *The Great Omission* is a quick read, but will take considerable time to digest. A fresh rereading has caused another one of McQuilkin's questions to worm its way into my thinking, "Do people have to be nearby for me to love them?"[23]

Robertson wrote *The Great Omission* to mobilize laborers for the harvest, whether as goers or senders. Revealing are his two appendices. Appendix 1 is a draft contract with God, a "Disciple's Pledge," complete with dotted line for signature and confirmation date. I might have placed Appendix 2— seventeen obstacles or objections that might interfere with our commitment—before Appendix 1. Perhaps he ordered them this way to emphasize that our first responsibility is to respond to God's call. Only after saying "Yes!" to God can we properly confront obstacles.

Robertson's response to the disquieting question of a new Japanese convert is a great example of the conjunction of theology and life. The convert wanted to know, "What about my ancestors?" Robertson said, "We are not called as judge—either of God whose ways we do not fully know nor of man whose destiny we are not called upon to settle. Rather, we are commissioned as His representatives to find the lost."[24] His nuanced thinking is a lesson in how to find the tension and be content to live there. He refuses to be authoritative where Scripture doesn't go. He refuses to shrink from declaring what Scripture unequivocally declares. Read *The Great Omission*, if you dare.

The Disciple-Making Church

To the three core areas of truth, Victorious Christian Living, Functional Biblical Authority and World Evangelization, Robertson adds a fourth—the Disciple-Making Church. The full demonstration of the first three concepts can only be found in a church that lives by the fourth.

The Five Smooth Stones: Essential Principles for Biblical Ministry is Robertson's handbook for leading functional biblical churches. Robertson loves the church in part because of what God has made it to be, "central to all God's plans for redeeming a world."[25] Because Robertson is multidenominational, evangelically pluralistic and global, you might think he would fix his attention on the universal church. But for him the local church is where the action is. It is *the* place in which disciples serious about the lordship of Christ are made and from which evangelists entrusted with the gospel of Christ are sent.

As God equipped the future King David with five smooth stones to wield against Goliath, so God has given five well-worn principles to confront the giants of our day, or any day, that threaten to thwart God's purposes for His church. Robertson here is at his most reflective—part ministry testimony, part ministry workshop. You sense you are following him on his quest for and discovery of the principles that make or break ministry. His search began with a nagging question: "At the end of seven years of formal theological education, I began to wonder: why were the solid academic disciplines sealed off from the practical ministry departments? Sealed on both sides of the divide, I noted."[26] Perhaps his passion for uniting theory and practice in each of the three core areas—hermeneutics, sanctification, evangelization—began with his quest to unite the biblical picture of the church with the gloomy snapshots he experienced.

In the face of recent waves of pragmatic self-help approaches to church and discipleship drawn from consumer models, Robertson identifies five bedrock principles of classic theology which, when faithfully followed, produce functioning churches that please God. (It isn't surprising that empirical data supports his claims!) The five principles are as follows: The Bible—Making It the Functional Authority, The Church—Aligning the Congregation with All of God's Biblical Purposes, The Holy Spirit—Releasing His Energizing Power, The Plan of Redemption—The Mission of Every Disciple, The Lordship of Christ—Gauging Servant Leadership. Get a copy of *The Five Smooth Stones*. Better yet, get your church and its leaders to use Robertson's text as a handbook. The biblical principles might transform you as they transformed Robertson. I have wondered while reading *The Five Smooth Stones* how much Robertson influenced me to split my life's ministry between seminary teaching and local church pastoring.

I know Robertson takes disciple making seriously. He discipled me, and so many others, not in a discipleship program, as useful as some might be. He discipled by example, encouragement and exhortation. Most precious of all that Robertson has written has not been published nor likely ever will be—personal letters, e-mails, handwritten notes, book dedications and the like. Personalized copies of *A Promise Kept* to my wife, Noel, and of *Life in the Spirit* to me remain cherished possessions.

The McQuilkin body of work will age well. Future generations will face different issues than his. Robertson provides a model for addressing them. His work will endure because he writes so well. There are many who have his or her favorite McQuilkinism. Robertson's knack for the quip, the unexpected, the turn of a phrase make him eminently quotable. But the granddaddy aphorism of them all, the one with which I began this too-cursory retrospective, is this: "It seems easier to go to a consistent extreme than to stay at the center of biblical tension." What remains so impressive to me is how consistently, over six decades of teaching and writing, Robertson has modeled for us the wisdom, the grace and the beauty of a life lived "at the center of biblical tension."

Chapter 2

Personal Reflections on the Life of J. Robertson McQuilkin

Ralph E. Enlow Jr.

D uring the summer of 1968, I received a letter that would change my life. It came from Columbia Bible College, the institution where I had been accepted to enroll as a freshman that fall. The letter, distributed to the college's entire constituency including incoming students, was apparently the first official communication from J. Robertson McQuilkin. It was my earliest introduction to the man who assumed office as Columbia's third president. Frankly, I suspect that, like most seventeen-year-olds, I made my decision to attend CBC with neither knowledge nor concern about who was the institution's president. Back then, I was oblivious to the significance of that role. Today, forty-five years later, I marvel and swell with gratitude at the felicitous providence that led to the intertwining of my life and career with that of Robertson McQuilkin.

We first became acquainted through my involvement in student ministry teams that frequently accompanied Robertson on weekend speaking engagements. Conversations with Robertson during those weekend travels were wide-ranging, disarming, engaging, unpretentious, edifying, jovial—sometimes hilarious—but never aimless or frivolous. I didn't know it then, but he was watching me, generously and optimistically assessing my gifts and leadership potential as well as gently and persistently stimulating, prodding, admonishing, cultivating and encouraging me. And I was watching him, consciously and unconsciously, and observing, reflecting upon, savoring and internalizing his ideas, dispositions, priorities and leadership patterns.

I should be clear. At no time in my life have Robertson and I engaged in a formal, mutually acknowledged discipleship or mentoring relationship. Yet I regard Robertson to be my most influential lifelong ministry model and mentor. How so? There has been a great deal more mutual intention in our relationship than there has been mutual interaction about it. I have been studiously watching and listening to Robertson for over four decades, and he—despite varying and sometimes vast geographical and relational distances—has invested his heart and mind in me, sought soul-stretching and gift-expanding opportunities for me, risked his reputation for me and, above all, interceded for me. And those are only the things I know about.

In sports, the term "coaching tree" has come to be associated with individuals whose philosophy, ideas, strategies, values and character commitments are evident in the careers of multiple individuals who follow in successive generations of the coaching profession. In the American context, individuals with extensive "coaching trees" include Sid Gillman, Tom Landry and Bill Walsh (football); Red Auerbach, Jim Boeheim and Pat Summit (basketball); and Ned Hanlon, Bobby Cox and Mike Scioscia (baseball). Even if you don't know these individuals, and care nothing for sports, you get the idea. A person's legacy is incarnated in others, and for some, including Robertson, it vastly exceeds their present renown and will endure for generations after their careers have concluded.

Robertson often quotes John 15:16 as a life verse: "You did not choose me, but I chose you and appointed you so that you might go and bear fruit—fruit that will last—and so that whatever you ask in my name the Father will give you" (NIV). I can attest that Robertson's life has borne fruit that nourishes and lives on in me and many, many others.

Robert Clinton is a fellow Columbia alumnus and student contemporary of mine. His intellectual legacy in leadership emergence theory and his career leadership progeny at Fuller Seminary are widely acknowledged. Clinton developed the following taxonomy of mentoring:

Type	**Central Empowerment**
Discipler	Habit Formation
Spiritual Guide	Directional Evaluation
Coach	Skill Development
Counselor	Advice
Teacher	Knowledge
Sponsor	Promotion, Protection
Contemporary Model	Values
Historical Model	Inspiration[1]

With reference to Clinton's taxonomy, I would say that Robertson's primary modes of mentoring exercised toward me and others would include teacher, sponsor, model and guide. It occurs to me that these represent an illuminating framework through which to reflect upon Robertson's leadership legacy.

Robertson the Teacher

From the outset of his tenure as CBC's president, Robertson insisted on teaching courses. And not just any courses. He staked out Hermeneutics, Biblical Personal Ethics and Biblical Principles for Christian Work as the curricular territory upon which he was determined, by the Spirit's enabling, to leave an enduring mark. Somehow, despite the staggering and ever-expanding demands of his local role as college president and his global engagements as missionary statesman, he persisted in teaching these three courses for most of his twenty-two-year presidential tenure.

Teaching hermeneutics was the most direct means by which Robertson could imbed the core conviction into the thinking and practice of every graduate that the Bible—the whole Bible and the Bible alone—must function as sole authority for faith and practice. His own seminary experience had taught him that an equivocating embrace of Scripture's infallibility and authority is typically enabled by hermeneutical methods that further undermine those commitments. In hermeneutics, he argued, we learn to embrace and employ the interpretive principles and practices that ultimately determine whether Scripture actually functions as the sole authority for what we believe and how we live.

Biblical Personal Ethics was the vehicle by which Robertson sought to make the doctrine of sanctification practical, helping students discover the Spirit's wisdom and grace to confront cultural relativism, to embrace biblical moral purity and to pursue spiritual growth. Asserting that persons "must first hear the thunders of Sinai before they can appreciate the sweet grace notes of Calvary," he led students through the Ten Commandments, penetratingly examining the root sins and virtues represented by each. In matters of ethical ambiguity and disputed practices, he insisted that the true nature of biblical liberty is not the freedom to do what we want but the liberty to do as we ought. He maintained that the average Christian experience relative to temptation and sin is by no means the normal experience described in Scripture as a life of Spirit-empowered living characterized by consistent victory over temptations to sin and transformational growth into ever-increasing Christlikeness.

His course entitled Biblical Principles for Christian Work grew out of the long quest, which began in his early missionary career in Japan, to integrate theology into ministry practice. Robertson's historical research into great spiritual movements over the centuries yielded the conclusion that there was no connection between those movements and conformity to particular apostolic methodologies described in the New Testament. He discovered that there was, however, a marked similarity among historical stirrings of God's Spirit to revive and grow the church. These spiritual movements shared five core theological principles: functional authority of Scripture, vital church alignment with biblical purposes, reliance upon the Holy Spirit by prayer and faith, the engagement of every disciple in the mission of world evangelization, and leadership that reflects and promotes the lordship of Christ.[2] By means of the course he developed to teach these principles, Robertson challenged and equipped students to distinguish their methodological preferences and convictions from biblical mandates and to seek a balance of unity and purity under the authority of Scripture in matters of methodological divergence and disputed interpretation.

Robertson's approach to teaching reflected his critical brilliance and playfully contrarian intellect. A prodigious reader, he keeps himself well-informed of biblical and theological dialogues in both the academy and the church. He is nothing if not a voracious learner. I often observed him making notes of student questions so he could ponder them more thoroughly and address them more fully in future courses. In a posture of humble yet biblically insistent inquiry, he took on the ideas and trends that were sweeping the evangelical imagination at the time, subjecting each one to intense yet balanced biblical scrutiny. This approach is reflected in his 2007 book *The Five Smooth Stones*, in which he expounds the Essential Principles for Biblical Ministry he taught in the classroom over many years. In *Five Smooth Stones*, he takes on cultural orthodoxies uncritically imbibed by most contemporary evangelicals, such as therapeutic theology, the gospel as a social mandate, wider hope and emerging mission paradigms, to name a few. With his students, he preferred posing provocative questions to offering neat, note-friendly lectures that yielded page after page of preformulated answers. He exposed his students to contrary views through a variety of assigned readings. In many areas of theological and methodological controversy, he offered a biblical corrective to sweeping contemporary currents. In teaching as in life, he refused to counter extreme and polarizing positions with extreme and polarizing rigidity. Generations of students can quote his aphorism: "It is much easier to move to a consistent extreme than to remain in the center of biblical tension."

Robertson's teaching was by no means limited to the college and seminary classroom. He not only taught formal college and seminary courses but also leveraged the chapel platform as a teaching venue. The required daily chapel and monthly prayer day regime at CBC afforded a dozen or more President's Chapels each year. On many of those occasions, I observed that Robertson clearly intended to address a wider audience that included not merely students but especially the key stakeholder groups of faculty, staff, alumni, trustees and, in some cases, constituent churches. He taught on such subjects as discipleship, moral purity, biblical authority, prayer, Sabbath keeping, faith and financial provision, evangelism, the missionary mandate, spiritual gifts, biblical separation and biblical stewardship. He frequently subjected near-sacred institutional traditions to intense yet loving and respectful biblical scrutiny. Even when he did not occupy the pulpit, I often marveled at the display of his teaching through extemporaneous commentary on current events or the controversial actions and remarks of others. On one such occasion, the campus was abuzz with controversy when a revered alumnus from the developing world railed against his alma mater's scandalous decline into ungodly materialism, as evidenced by what he regarded to be lavish campus facilities, dining hall food and dorm room amenities. Rather than dodging the issue, Robertson addressed the issue the next day, deftly and disarmingly inviting examination of this brother's presumptive judgment without letting anyone's conscience off the hook. He placed three volumes on the podium, representing a continuum of sorts from poverty to riches. "In the matter of biblical attitudes and practices toward material things," he said, "our brother is clearly here [gesturing to his left] and McQuilkin is clearly here [gesturing to his right]." Positioning a Bible in various places from extreme left to middle to extreme right, he quietly asked, "The question is, where is Jesus on this continuum?" The controversy was quelled, the room was quiet, but no thinking observer felt exonerated.

Robertson also taught through his prolific production of institutional philosophy and policy documents. These documents offer a glimpse into how an institution can implement a commitment to operate under the authority of Scripture in everything from student admissions to curricular programs to student development to employee compensation to faculty promotion and tenure, to name a few. This is not to suggest that the Bible speaks definitively, much less exhaustively, to all such issues; only that where the Bible speaks by precept or principle, we must seek to understand and submit. He insisted that erroneous attribution of biblical authority to institutional policies and rules—the realm in which institutional traditions flourish—undermines biblical authority every bit as much as ignorance of biblical principles or disregard of biblical mandates. He taught that many, if not most, institutional policies may only be justified on rational and pragmatic grounds and are therefore subject to review and revision as circumstances warrant. The residue, though not the full substance, of most of Robertson's policy articulation efforts may be recognized in some of Columbia's employee handbooks and policy documents to this day.

Particularly in the latter stages of his career, Robertson sustained and extended his teaching through his publications. It is easy to recognize that three of his books—*Understanding and Applying the Bible, An Introduction to Biblical Ethics* and *The Five Smooth Stones*—correspond to the three courses he taught consistently during his presidential tenure. Other works cluster around these core convictions, calling for critical reexamination and return from theological erosion, cultural accommodation or methodological ambiguity in light of the authority of Scripture.

Robertson the Sponsor

One of my favorite biblical leaders is Joseph of Cyprus—whom we know as Barnabas—because he epitomized encouragement. A key aspect of Barnabas' leadership by encouragement was his bent toward sponsorship. It was Barnabas who risked his reputation and vouched for Saul, the dubious and dangerous new convert whom the Jerusalem elders regarded skeptically. Assigned to join the pastoral staff of the exploding Hellenistic church in Antioch, Barnabas personally recruited Saul to join the leadership team (see Acts 11:25–26). Later, his insistence upon risky sponsorship of young John Mark forced him to part paths with Paul (see 15:36–41). Paul later, however, seems to acknowledge the profound worth of Barnabas' sponsorship by affirming and calling for John Mark during his imprisonment (see Col. 4:10).

When people ask me to tell the story of my life and career, I frequently joke (with apologies to Bill Bright) that "Robertson loved me and had a wonderful plan for my life." After completing most of my master's degree course work, I was weighing several ministry opportunities when Robertson called me. "Don't accept any offers until I talk to you," he urged. And so began a lifelong pattern of Robertson's active and astute sponsor-shepherding. Like Barnabas, one of Robertson's key legacies is his bent toward recognizing potential and taking risks in developing and deploying people for kingdom impact.

From the beginning of my career to the present day, Robertson was observing my abilities and inclinations, fueling my growth, and anticipating—perhaps even maneuvering me into—roles and responsibilities he believed would suit me and strengthen the Lord's work at Columbia and beyond. He astutely observed, long before I had much self-awareness of it, that I am an initiator, not a maintainer. When he detected in me the restlessness that comes with cresting a horizon and shifting from reaching forward into routine, he was uncannily ready to propose a new challenge, if not a new role. He prodded me into doctoral studies in higher education, made costly provision for my studies and pushed open doors for me to enter into senior educational leadership roles. I shudder to think of the risks and ridicule to which Robertson has exposed himself in sponsoring me. I know this: I was by no means always a credit to him. Within hours of the greatest rupture and failure of my career, Robertson contacted me to assure me that he was standing by, steadfast in his friendship, eager to support and guide me toward a new season of fruitfulness and flourishing.

I am by no means the only one who has been the object of Robertson's pattern of sponsorship over the years. I could easily name at least a score of others. There must be hundreds of us. I have never seen them, but I am told Robertson maintained extensive lists of people he was watching—including prospects for specific roles—projecting future options for expression of their giftedness and expansion of their leadership calling. And although he was jealous and zealous to identify, develop and retain leaders for the work at Columbia, he consistently exhibited a kingdom mind-set and extended a graciously open hand in recommending and releasing leaders to other ministries.

Robertson the Model

I have never known anyone who "walked the talk" more consistently than Robertson. His long life of Spirit-empowered authenticity and fidelity stands as a prophetic rebuke to a culture—sadly, even our evangelical culture—enamored by image and celebrity and beset by scandal. His steadfast refusal of self-gratification and self-aggrandizement exposes and explodes the false gospel of self-indulgence masquerading as self-actualization. His resolute nonconformity to the ways of this world surely illustrates what is meant by Romans 12:2: "Do not conform to the pattern of this world, but be transformed by the renewing of your mind. Then you will be able to test and approve what God's will is—his good, pleasing and perfect will" (NIV).

I think most of us who know him would conclude that modeling is perhaps Robertson's most impactful mentoring modality. In what specific areas has Robertson mentored by modeling? The list could be endless, but I offer comment on just seven of the most illustrative.

Personal Intimacy with God

Robertson is neither by nature nor persuasion particularly self-divulging. He talks freely and believably, however, about his love relationship with Jesus and his deep conviction that God desires our intimate companionship above all else. Without boasting, he speaks often of the vital and nourishing nature of his daily communion with the Lord involving Bible reading, worship, and prayer. Moreover, you do not have to be around him long before you hear him speak of his pattern of periodic withdrawal "to the mountaintop" in spiritual retreat, seeking the Lord in more extended and intimate sessions of study, worship and prayer. Robertson testifies that such mountaintop retreats have been a key factor in virtually every major life transition, crisis and spiritual breakthrough.

Simple and Sacrificial Living

Robertson has waged a lifelong war against the acquisitive, materialistic bent of our culture. He has done so much more loudly and persuasively by life than by lip. He and Muriel agreed they would pursue a simple, sacrificial lifestyle and they did. Robertson frequently wore used clothing, rode his bicycle, repaired his own shoes and appliances, and drove jalopies—despite the ample justification, if not entitlement, of his office to the contrary. To this very day, Robertson lives in a very modest home he inherited from his parents. During some seasons of his life, he even determined to live on half his modest income in order to practice sacrificial biblical generosity. He openly testified that though many of the choices he and Muriel made were painful at first, they did not lead to misery, want and worry. Instead, they yielded freedom, joy and thanksgiving. Despite his personal commitment to and commendation of simple and sacrificial living, I have never heard Robertson utter words of judgment concerning the lifestyle choices of his godly friends. His life offers more than adequate cause for sober self-reflection.

Learning and the Life of the Mind

I have known few people more committed to deep inquiry, rigorous reading and critical reflection than Robertson. He confronted every problem and controversy as an opportunity to learn. He committed himself to studying a wide range of cultural, intellectual, theological, educational and missiological trends, asking colleagues and peers to recommend the best resources. Year after year, he would choose a subject to study in depth, reading extensively and focusing many of his speaking and writing opportunities on the topic. Over the years, he sought to acquire a deeper and more biblical grasp of such subjects as church growth, biblical inerrancy, divorce, gender, abortion, distance education, postmodernism, therapeutic theology, spiritual warfare, social science in missiology and contextualization, to name a few. Chapel and guest lecturer rosters demonstrate that he was prepared to welcome, engage and learn from scholars and practitioners with whom he disagreed. He also vigorously promoted and stimulated learning and professional development among his colleagues. At the outset of his presidential tenure, he insisted on allocating a $250 book allowance for each classroom and administrative faculty member—an outlandish commitment in those days in light of the institution's financial state and budget size. Arguing that the institutional budget is the most profound philosophical statement an institution can make, he insisted on robust commitments to informal professional development as well as formal educational advancement studies for his colleagues.

Servant Leadership

No one would mistake Robertson for a weak, passive leader. He is proactive, assertive and courageous. He believes that leadership in family, church and society involves divine authority mediated through humans. Nevertheless, he has consistently espoused and embodied the kind of servant leadership commended in Scripture and demonstrated by the Lord Jesus. The leadership he invariably modeled before me and others was characterized by, among other things: accountability—exercising authority under authority, promoting leadership plurality, practicing personal restraint and respect for all; accessibility—loving by listening to the least, cultivating inclusion and ownership; and humility—deflecting honor and respecting criticism and correction. Robertson has provided an exposition of his views on servant leadership in his book *The Five Smooth Stones*.[3] I can testify that he has practiced what he preaches.

World Christian Engagement

Robertson believes that the call of every true disciple of Jesus involves devoted embracement of and engagement in the Great Commission. The biblical case for this conviction is laid out most clearly in his books *The Great Omission* and *The Five Smooth Stones*.[4] The contours of Robertson's life and career consistently correspond to his passionate preaching, teaching and writing on the subject. Although he began his career as a missionary church planter, he has validated his "world Christian" convictions perhaps even more convincingly as a college president, speaker, author and "homemaker." (Even under the severe constraints of his role as the primary caregiver to his Alzheimer's-stricken wife, Muriel, his contributions to Great Commission thinking, intercession and mobilization were sustained.) His prayer life and his checkbook illustrate this commitment more authentically than his stature as a missionary statesman, influencing the Lausanne Movement, many key aspects of mission strategy and missiological thinking. To borrow a military term, he has been a "force multiplier" in a global gospel endeavor. His persistent, fervent intercessions that the Lord of the harvest would thrust laborers into His harvest have been accompanied by a lifelong legacy of mentoring and mobilizing the brightest and best of his acquaintance into missionary service and leadership. That branch of his "coaching tree" towers above all the others.

Loyalty

Robertson has a penchant for loyalty. I have had a front row seat from which to watch him practice it consistently in the context of institutional routines and in the face of unjust criticism and personal betrayal. He deliberately sought diverse personalities, perspectives and persuasions within the board, leadership team and faculty. He insisted upon, indeed fostered, healthy debate among colleagues at every level. Once decisions were made, however, he practiced and expected unity and solidarity. In the case of one rather profound and protracted policy difference between him and the board, he told them, "I can implement the policy, but I cannot defend it biblically." Nevertheless, I never heard him speak publicly or privately about his disagreement with the policy nor disparagingly of the board. It was years later that I learned his personal convictions on the matter profoundly differed from the institutional policy over which he was honor-bound to preside. His commitment to loyalty was severely tested when a wealthy and influential board faction conspired against his leadership and, after the board majority exonerated him, resigned en masse. Early in their marriage, he and Muriel had made a pact: the absent are safe with us. He honored that pact at great personal cost. He not only refused to speak against the defectors, he sought and gained personal reconciliation and ministry repatriation with most of them. Later, a key leader to whom he had entrusted an enviable and exhilarating initiative that was dear to his heart humiliatingly betrayed his trust and torpedoed the project. Yet again, he resolutely refused to take any path toward vengeance or vindication.

Living by Vows

Perhaps Robertson's most singular modeling imprint has been his decision to forsake his career at its zenith in order to devote himself to full-time care for Muriel. Over nearly a decade, signs that his beloved had been stricken with early-onset Alzheimer's had become more and more apparent. He had told the board that when her condition dictated she needed him full time, she would have him. I'm not sure they believed him. I still vividly remember the day he stood before a packed Shortess Chapel audience and announced he was stepping down from the presidency he had held for twenty-two years. It is no surprise that his announcement that day has reverberated for over two decades in the life of everyone who heard it. More surprising—and significant—is the fact that it has reverberated around the world. Perhaps Robertson should be known as a brilliant and godly leader, innovator, educator, theologian, missiologist and missionary statesman. He is all of these. Nevertheless, he is and will be better known for his commitment to lay aside all these pursuits in order to fulfill, in the manner he was persuaded was required of him, the vow of faithfulness to Muriel "in sickness and in health." In this, his model most clearly resembles his Savior, who "loved the church and gave himself up for her" (Eph. 5:25).

Robertson the Guide

Surely Robertson has mentored many through his teaching, modeling and sponsoring. He also, however, has exercised profound influence through the spiritual guidance he has rendered to many of us. In his final season of life, when his strength has diminished to the point that he has withdrawn from public speaking ministry, this spiritual guidance continues to flourish. I am one of many who have been deeply enriched and empowered by Robertson's counsel at life's most critical intersections. A few, including his presidential successors, have sought and enjoyed the privilege of more regular counsel and coaching.

An astute listener and relentless questioner, Robertson's guidance is as likely to feel like a barb as it is a balm. Columbia's sixth president, Bill Jones, affectionately but aptly refers to Robertson as his "tor-mentor." Ever one to provoke the brethren to love and good deeds, Robertson has guarded and guided without interference or manipulation. He rarely states his opinion or gives explicit direction. Instead, he probes and parries, offering impressions, ideas and inclinations, and gently shepherding his mentees away from danger and toward the biblical fidelity and fruitfulness for which he prays.

Like John the apostle, I testify that what more could be written could fill many books. Indeed, much more follows in this book. Even more will be revealed at the judgment seat of Christ where I have no doubt Robertson's most richly deserved reward will be flung at the feet of the Savior he adores. In the meantime, these reflections have been as edifying for me to write as I trust they have been for you to read.

Part II

Bible Interpretation

Chapter 3

Authorial Intent and the Redaction of the Book of Psalms

John C. Crutchfield

It is a personal privilege to contribute this essay to a volume honoring J. Robertson McQuilkin. As a student at CIU during his presidency, I benefited immensely from many lunch conversations in the cafeteria when he would agree to meet with several close friends and me to answer our pressing questions. I can also remember many impromptu conversations around campus and countless after-chapel discussions that impacted me. And on at least one occasion, I was the beneficiary of some of his well-chosen, gentle, but firm words.

Although I never had McQuilkin as a professor, I have been trained and mentored by two teachers whom McQuilkin strongly influenced—Jack Layman and William Larkin. From McQuilkin, through these mentors, I learned of at least two vital truths in relation to hermeneutics: (1) the importance of meaning in the interpretation process, and (2) the important role authorial intent plays in meaning. In this essay, I will seek to expand the concept of authorial intent to include the compiler or editor of a biblical book—in this case, the book of Psalms.

McQuilkin and Authorial Intent

McQuilkin is certainly not the only defender of the primacy of authorial intent in the hermeneutical task, but he is consistent. In fact, his first hermeneutical principle reads as follows: "Since the Bible was written by human beings, it must be treated as any other human communication in determining the meaning intended by the writer."[1] Later, when discussing "Understanding Human Language," he writes:

> Successful communication depends on both the sender and the receiver of the communication. The sender of information must accurately put into words his own thoughts, and the receiver must accurately understand those words. In the case of Scripture, God is the sender through human transmitters. We are the receivers, and our task is to make sure of the human author's intended meaning. That is what interpretation is all about.[2]

Authorial Intent Today

A brief survey of evangelical works on hermeneutics reveals that the concept of "authorial intent" remains an important goal in the task of interpretation. In their recent manual on hermeneutics, Andreas Köstenberger and Richard Patterson write: "Every document has an author, and the resulting text is shaped by his or her intention. It is this authorial intention the interpreter must aim to recover."[3] J. Scott Duvall and J. Daniel Hays discuss the importance of communication in the hermeneutical process:

> The issue of communication, therefore, lies at the heart of one's decision about how to interpret a text. If you, the

reader, see the text as a communication between the author and yourself, then you should search for the meaning that the *author intended*. If, however, you as the reader do not care to communicate with the author, then you are free to follow *reader response* and interpret the text without asking what the author meant. . . . In biblical interpretation, the reader does not control the meaning; the author controls the meaning. This conclusion leads us to one of the most basic principles of our interpretive approach: *We do not create the meaning. Rather, we seek to discover the meaning that has been placed there by the author.*[4]

Grant Osborne, longtime professor of New Testament and hermeneutics at Trinity Evangelical Divinity School, agrees: "The goal of evangelical hermeneutics is quite simple—to discover the intention of the Author/author (author = inspired human author; Author = God who inspires the text). . . . I want to encourage you to get and use the tools that enable us to bridge the gap back to Bible times and authorial intention."[5] Elsewhere Osborne, expressing indebtedness to Kevin Vanhoozer, notes, "Meaning is the 'embodied intention' seen 'in a stable verbal structure' that is 'enacted' by the author in order to be shared with the readers."[6] Lastly, Jeannine K. Brown, assistant professor of New Testament at Bethel Seminary, comments, "In a nutshell, the communication model I propose is this: Scripture's meaning can be understood as the communicative act of the author that has been inscribed in the text and addressed to the intended audience for purposes of engagement."[7]

This respect for authorial intention extends beyond the evangelical camp. Carolyn J. Sharp, professor of Hebrew Scriptures at Yale University, writes sympathetically:

I have always been willing to concede that authorial intention is tricky to discern and may only ever be partially and imperfectly known. I also concede that the ways in which we reconstruct authorial intention are always shaped by our own predispositions and assumptions. But texts were produced by real people whose voices, expressed through the choice of rhetorical strategies and artistic decisions within their texts, should be listened to in any responsible ethic of reading.[8]

However, authorial intent has fallen on hard times, especially in the academy. In the mid-twentieth century, W.K. Wimsatt and Monroe Beardsley's essay "The Intentional Fallacy" launched "New Criticism"—a movement that "privileged the autonomy and formal unity of the text rather than the personality or biography of the author."[9] The "locus of meaning," according to New Criticism, is the text with its various genres and structures, not the author. But the locus of meaning can be shifted another step, from text to audience. This movement from author to text to audience has spawned a veritable explosion of approaches to interpretation, each with its own set of presuppositions, agendas, concerns and goals. A partial list includes: Reader-Response Criticism; *Tendenz* Criticism; Reception Theory; Ideological Criticism; Marxist Criticism; Mimetic Criticism; Psychoanalytic Criticism; Deconstructionism; Postmodern Criticism; Structuralism; Cultural Materialism; Feminist Criticism; Queer Theory; Race, Class, Gender and Postcolonial Criticism; *Mujerista* and Womanist readings; and Childist Interpretation.[10]

It is against this background of hermeneutical chaos that McQuilkin's commitment to authorial intent makes an important contribution. His consistent assertion of the author's role in interpretation has helped preserve the authority of Scripture in an age of relativism, deconstruction and personal moral autonomy.[11]

Authorial Intent and the Redaction of the Book of Psalms

I'd like to suggest an expansion to the definition of "author" in an author-centered hermeneutic. I want to propose that McQuilkin's hermeneutical understanding of authorial intent should be expanded to include not only the writers of Scripture but also the redactors or editors of Scripture, particularly with reference to the book of Psalms.

In the last thirty years or so, Brevard Childs' work in the area of canonical criticism has reenergized the study of the book of Psalms.[12] For most of the twentieth century, scholars sought to interpret psalms as individual poetic works by analyzing their historical setting, their literary form, the setting in the cultic worship of ancient Israel or their linguistic context in light of the Ugaritic tablets (a collection of texts from the ancient city of Ugarit in present-day Syria). All of these approaches had serious problems. For example, reconstructions of a psalm's historical setting were almost totally hypothetical; many psalms do not fit a recognized literary form; we know very little about how temple worship was actually done; and, although Hebrew and Ugaritic share a great deal of lexicography, we should not assume that the worldviews and theologies of the Hebrews and the northern Canaanites were similar enough to draw solid conclusions between the two.

While still accepting all the conclusions of standard critical scholarship on the Old Testament, Childs sought to respect the final shape of individual books. When applied to the book of Psalms, this emphasis on final shape prompted new questions. Instead of looking at each psalm as a poem in literary isolation, perhaps the interpreter should look at the context in which the particular psalm appears, and at the location of the psalm in the book of Psalms as a whole. These new and interesting questions have led to discussions on the purpose behind the current structure of the book of Psalms.

Evidence for a Purpose behind the Structure of the Book of Psalms

Recent studies have argued at length for a purposeful redaction of the Psalter.[13] I will attempt here to present a summary of the most repeated arguments used to build a case for purposeful redaction.[14]

I begin with what is probably the weakest point. In an attempt to establish the idea that collections of (religious) poetry in the Ancient Near East (ANE) were gathered with particular intentions in mind, Gerald Wilson appealed to ANE collections of hymnic material. He laid the methodological groundwork in his 1985 dissertation entitled *The Editing of the Hebrew Psalter*.[15] I call this a weak point because the kind of purposeful redaction he finds is only that some collections of hymns in the ANE were organized according to author, genre or the divinity addressed. I know of no one who has argued that a broad theological agenda governed the organization of these collections. All we can say at this point is that some collections of ANE hymns were organized by some guiding principles. Nevertheless, today scholars wrestle with the idea that a broad theological agenda *is* at work in the redaction of the Hebrew Psalter.

Second, the book of Psalms seems to have a clear introduction: Psalms 1 and 2 introduce the Psalter as a whole and together cast a hermeneutical grid for its proper interpretation.[16] This contention is supported by the many correspondences between these two psalms and the observation that these are the only two structurally prominent anonymous psalms in Book I of the Psalter (Psalms 1–41).

Some have argued against this claim by noting that psalms 1 and 2 probably have very different dates and origins.[17] But this objection fails to understand that the point is not that the two psalms share authors and/or origins but that the two psalms were placed at the beginning of the Psalter intentionally. This is a literary claim, not a claim about the authorship and provenance of the two psalms.[18]

Third, the book of Psalms seems to have a clear conclusion: Psalms 146–150 place an emphasis on praise that exudes a sense of finality.[19] Certainly in Psalm 150 the call to worship reaches an apex, and on that note, the Psalter ends.

Fourth, scholars have recognized four doxologies placed at several points in the book of Psalms (see 41:13; 72:18–19; 89:52; 106:48), which divide the Psalter into five books: Book I = Psalms 1–41, Book II = Psalms 42–72, Book III = Psalms 73–89, Book IV = Psalms 90–106 and Book V = Psalms 107–150.

If the above observations are correct, the book of Psalms has an introduction, a conclusion and internal book divisions. Once these points are acknowledged, other phenomena about the book of Psalms begin to add increasing evidence to the contention that the book of Psalms was redacted with a specific purpose in mind. For example, as Wilson noted, the presence of royal Psalms at the "seams" between the different books of the Psalter reinforce a hermeneutical framework that includes a royal ideology.[20] Also, as numerous studies demonstrate, adjacent psalms contain lexical and thematic links, which indicate that they were placed side by side and were intended to be read together.[21]

Not everyone is convinced. Several have raised their voices in objection. Norman Whybray remained unconvinced that there was sufficient evidence for a "Psalter-wide" redaction.[22] John Goldingay is also dubious: "The process of [the book of

Psalms'] development means that the Psalter as a whole does not have a structure that helps us get a handle on its contents, as the structure of Genesis or Isaiah helps us grasp the whole and the parts. . . . The Psalter does not work like Genesis or Isaiah."[23]

In his recent review of Psalms scholarship over the last twenty years or so, J. Kenneth Kuntz listed me among those who doubt that a comprehensive agenda has been found, and this is true, to some extent.[24] It is frustrating to see scholars put forth mutually exclusive agendas for the Psalter's redaction instead of benefiting from the work of others and forging a plausible all-encompassing theory for the message of the whole book. So, although I formally criticized the attempts of others, I am, at least at this point, on board for searching for such a comprehensive proposal. Much work still needs to be done. But it is difficult to deny the many helpful observations others have made about the structure of the book of Psalms, especially the degree of lexical overlap between adjacent psalms, as demonstrated by David Howard, Robert Cole, Robert Wallace and others.

In summary, then, despite a few voices of objection and the difficulty of the task, the above observations are generally accepted now in Psalms study as valid arguments for some kind of editorial or redactional activity behind the canonical shape of the book of Psalms.

The Hermeneutical Significance of the Psalter's Shape

The impact of these arguments for some kind of intention behind the shape of the book of Psalms has been to push interpreters to examine a given psalm's "Psalter context" when doing exegesis. I think it should be accepted that indeed the compilers structured the book of Psalms intentionally. Unfortunately, at present there is no consensus as to what that intention actually is. My suggestion, argued elsewhere,[25] is that the introduction and conclusion to the book of Psalms provide a hermeneutical framework within which we should understand the book as a whole and its constituent parts, i.e., individual psalms. The book of Psalms is an earthy book, acknowledging the presence of pain, fear, rage, enemies, sickness and death, as well as beauty, teaching, fellowship with God and His people, thanksgiving, joy and worship. The editor(s) of the collection as a whole recommend a way of living in such a world. The wisdom theme in Psalm 1 allows us to read individual psalms for personal edification; part of living in such a world involves living wisely. The eschatological theme of Psalm 2 creates an expectation of prophecy; part of living in this world also involves waiting for God to establish His kingdom and bring justice. The worship theme of Psalm 150 leads the entire collection to its ultimate purpose: divine adoration.[26] Therefore, a necessary component of psalm exegesis is to consider its themes in light of the whole Psalter and its hermeneutical framework.

Examples of Psalter-Context Reading

Having argued that editors intentionally redacted the book of Psalms and that the introduction and conclusion of the book provide a hermeneutical framework for its interpretation, I will offer a few examples of how this kind of reading includes this editorial intention as part of the "author's intent."

Psalms 109–110

Psalm 109 is almost universally recognized as a psalm of lament. Its central section, involving imprecations (109:6–15, maybe extending all the way to 19), has troubled interpreters. One suggestion prefers to see in verses 6–19 an extended quotation of the psalmist's enemies, not the words of the psalmist toward his accusers.[27] This suggestion makes sense of the internal logic of the psalm. In verses 1–5, the psalmist begins to paint a picture: he has offered friendship to people who have rejected him, slandered him and repaid good with evil. In turn, the psalmist did not resort to violence or revenge but rather appealed to God in prayer. Imprecations follow, which seem to prove his point that he is being slandered and victimized. Verse 6 refers to an "accuser" standing at the right hand of the accused. The major transition in the psalm occurs in verse 21, where the writer appeals to God and asks God to treat him differently than his enemies have. He continues to make his case by demonstrating his own pitiful state, and he asks God for vindication. Although the outcome of this situation remains hidden, the psalmist ends on a triumphant note in verses 30–31. He says he will one day praise God before a large crowd, because—and this is key—God stands at the right hand of the needy.

In summary, Psalm 109 presents a Davidic figure ("of David"[28]) who extends friendship to his own people, but these same people respond by rejecting and slandering him publicly. The psalmist responds to this abuse by appealing to God's character and by presenting his own pitiful state before God. He ends his plea with confidence, being assured that God will stand at his right hand to defend him.

Psalm 110 is the most quoted psalm in the New Testament.[29] Interpreters have rightly called attention to the two "lords" (one, the divine covenant name, "YHWH"; the other, "Adonai"), but few have noted the connections with Psalm 109. Just as Psalm 109 deals with enemies, Psalm 110 promises deliverance from enemies (see 110:1, 5–7). Just as Psalm 109 ends with a reference to "right hand" (109:31), so Psalm 110 begins with a reference to "right hand" (110:1). Just as Psalm 109 ends without a clear resolution to the psalmist's plight, so Psalm 110 announces divine vindication to David's "Lord."[30]

Other considerations made Psalm 110 popular in the early church. The literature is immense, but several interesting points stand out. The psalm clearly echoes Psalm 2, an eschatological psalm which discusses God's "anointed one."[31] Psalm 110 also alludes to eschatological warfare, the theme of resurrection (compare 110:3 with Isaiah 26:19, which clearly alludes to resurrection[32]), and the absolute sovereign rule of the Lord, "Adonai," from Mt. Zion. But when read in conjunction with Psalm 109, a compelling picture emerges: a Davidic figure who comes to his people, suffers rejection at their hands, appeals to God and is vindicated (by resurrection?) over his enemies, takes up priestly duties and will return in the eschaton to judge the nations of the earth, crush rebellious kings and rule as sovereign under God's mighty power. It is no wonder that early followers of Jesus, taking the lead from Jesus Himself (see Matt. 22:41–46), saw in Psalm 110 significance for His person and work.

The point here, however, is that the pattern we see in the life and ministry of Jesus is present as well in the Psalms, but only by reading them together, not as individual poems, does one come to recognize this. It is difficult to deny that Psalms 109 and 110 were placed together intentionally and were meant to be read together.[33] If this is true, we are including the intention of the editors of the book of Psalms in our interpretation.

Psalms 118–119

Psalm 118 brings to a climax several themes of Psalms 107–117. The celebrant of Psalm 118 takes on a Mosaic mantle, leading a new people through the "gates of righteousness" in a new exodus. When an interpreter considers all that is affirmed about the celebrant in Psalm 118, it is hard to resist the idea that the Messiah is being described. There may have been pre-Christian messianic interpretations of Psalm 118[34] and certainly the "crowds" interpreted it this way in the Gospels.[35] The Messiah will be a righteous figure who, though rejected by His people, leads His followers in a new exodus. It is interesting, in this regard to note the placement of Psalm 119 immediately after a psalm celebrating a new exodus.

Psalm 119 is one of the torah psalms, and, given its length, it is perhaps *the* torah psalm. Although the original author of the psalm is unknown to us, it is likely that his purpose was somehow to demonstrate faithfulness to God by his prolonged meditation on torah. The psalm itself contains elements of wisdom psalms, lament psalms, thanksgiving psalms and praise psalms. The psalm, then, is a mixed genre.[36] Nevertheless, the presence of torah (or one of the several synonyms for divine revelation) dominates nearly every verse of this poem.

The placement of Psalm 119 immediately after Psalm 118 invites thought. Is there an intentional progression from the Moses figure and the new exodus to the torah? Is the editor of the book suggesting that those who follow the Messiah of Psalm 118, joining a new exodus, share in the receiving of a new torah?

When read eschatologically, the juxtaposition of Psalms 118 and 119 echoes the hope of the prophets that there will be a future in which God so works among His people that His torah is written on their hearts. The pattern of Mosaic figure and exodus followed by receiving of torah repeats the pattern of events within the torah itself; in the context of the Psalter, it takes on an eschatological tone.[37] One day, God's Messiah will lead a people who will obey Torah from the heart. Psalm 119, therefore, may be the Psalter equivalent of Ezekiel's "heart of flesh" (Ezek. 11:18–20; 36:26–27) or Jeremiah's torah "written on the heart"

(Jer. 31:33). The author of Psalm 119 demonstrates what that will look like in a future follower of the Messiah. In this way, the author of Psalm 119 represents the relationship between torah and a messianic disciple—devotion to the divine will, as embodied in Scripture, will be central to one's internal life.

This reading of Psalms 118 and 119 also combines two important themes from the Psalter's introduction: torah piety (see Ps.1) and eschatological expectation (see Ps. 2). The Messiah leads His people in a new exodus, and those people have, like the author of Psalm 119, torah on their hearts.

The Psalter Narrative and the Kingdom of God

Another kind of observation that may arise from viewing the order and structure of the Psalms as indicating meaning stretches across entire books of the Psalter and sees a large narrative at work. Books I–II of the book of Psalms (Ps.1–72) contain mostly individual laments. Book III (Ps. 73–89) contains many corporate, or national, laments. Wilson has made the suggestion that the message of the Psalter to that point is that the Davidic office of kingship has failed and that Book IV, opening with a psalm (or two) by Moses and emphasizing God's rule, calls the nation back to a theocratic, premonarchical structure of authority.[38]

But more can be said on the placement of these psalms. Instead of seeing Book III as an indictment on the failure of the office of kingship, perhaps we should see Book IV, with its emphasis on the "kingship of YHWH" psalms, as an introduction to the coming eschatological kingdom of God.[39] The point is not failure, but patience; the kingdom is coming, despite the painful history of the house of David and the horrors of the exile.

This broad narrative of exile followed by coming kingdom may inform what we find in the New Testament. It is noteworthy that both John the Baptist and Jesus began their ministries preaching about the kingdom of God. The Gospel of Matthew devotes great space to Jesus' teaching about the kingdom of heaven. I am suggesting that at least one of the sources for both John the Baptist's and Jesus' contention that the kingdom of God/heaven had arrived was the narrative progression of the book of Psalms: after the national pain of the exile (Book III), God will establish His kingdom (Book IV) through His eschatological Messiah (Book V).

These three examples demonstrate that the consideration of the final edited form of the Psalter is an important interpretational step in determining the meaning of individual psalms and the book as a whole.

Conclusion

We have attempted here to honor McQuilkin's contribution to an evangelical hermeneutic of Scripture by suggesting that the intention of the editors of Scripture should be included in the concept of "author." We used the book of Psalms as an example of what this approach would look like. In our exegesis of individual psalms, we as interpreters should include in our interpretation a consideration of how a particular psalm interacts with adjacent psalms and with the broader structure of the Psalter as a whole. This consideration respects the intent of the editor(s) of the collection.

Chapter 4

Recognizing Normative Content in New Testament Narrative, with Special Attention Given to Luke-Acts

John D. Harvey

I n the preface to his textbook on hermeneutics, *Understanding and Applying the Bible*, J. Robertson McQuilkin writes,

> Throughout church history there has been a grave omission in scholarly biblical hermeneutics—the development of guidelines for applying Scripture authentically. The effort given to understanding the meaning of Scripture has been immense, but few evangelicals . . . have given themselves to developing principles for establishing the significance of Bible teaching for faith and obedience today.[1]

Especially in his early writings, McQuilkin framed the discussion of application in terms of what is normative.[2] Of particular concern were: (a) the extent to which culture might possibly limit application of those beliefs and behaviors,[3] and (b) the factors that might limit the application of beliefs and behaviors found in Scripture. His conclusion on the former issue is that "the cultural context is normative unless Scripture treats it as limited" (318). In his discussion of the latter issue, however, he takes the approach that "the historical context is normative only if Scripture treats it that way" (318).

The question naturally arises: what are the indicators found in Scripture that enable the interpreter to determine which beliefs and/or behaviors recorded in historical narrative should be understood as normative? To put it another way: how do we determine whether a belief or behavior found in biblical narrative is normative for us today? Although his writings do not address the literary genre of narrative in detail, McQuilkin's approach lays the foundation for identifying normative teaching present in biblical narrative because it proposes basic levels of authority in dealing with that genre. This study will seek to build on his foundation by probing for indicators of normative content in the book of Acts.

McQuilkin's Approach to Recognizing Normative Content

Understanding and Applying the Bible is divided into four basic sections: presuppositions, distorted approaches and basic principles (chapters 1–6); guidelines related to human authorship (chapters 7–14); guidelines related to divine authorship (chapters 15–18) and guidelines related to application (chapters 19–20). It also includes specific chapters on the literary genres of parable (13), poetry (14) and prophecy (18). Although he identifies historical narrative as a separate category of communication, McQuilkin folds the discussion of that genre into chapters 19, "Identifying the Audience God Intended," and 20, "Identifying the Response God Desires," where the discussion of normative content also occurs.[4]

The premise undergirding McQuilkin's entire discussion of normative content is that "every teaching of Scripture is to be received universally unless the Bible itself limits the audience, either in the context of the passage itself or in other biblical teaching" (307). The strength of this premise lies in the priority it gives to Scripture. It establishes Scripture rather than the interpreter as the ultimate authority in the hermeneutical task. It also differs significantly from approaches that see history, science, culture or other factors as limiting the application of principles and practices that occur in Scripture.

How, then, does Scripture set limits on normative content? McQuilkin identifies two primary ways: the immediate context and subsequent revelation. The immediate context limits a teaching when the author or speaker designates a specific audience (308). For example, Peter's statement at Pentecost appears to be universal when he says, "For the promise is for you and your children and for all who are far off," but he qualifies the promise with the next clause, "as many as the Lord our God will call to Himself" (Acts 2:39, NASB).[5] Whatever position we might hold on the relationship between divine sovereignty and human responsibility, Peter's statement limits the application of God's offer of forgiveness of sins to those whom God calls to Himself (see 2:38).

The immediate context also limits a teaching when it is directed to a specific individual or group (310). A simple example occurs in Acts 9:11 when the Lord says to Ananias, "Rise and go to the street called Straight, and at the house of Judas look for a man of Tarsus named Saul." Another example occurs in Acts 10:5 when an angel instructs Cornelius to "now send men to Joppa and bring one Simon who is called Peter." In neither instance does the specific instruction apply to anyone other than the person addressed. As McQuilkin notes, however, taking this latter guideline to its consistent logical extreme would eliminate every teaching Christ directed to His disciples (e.g., Acts 1:8). For that reason he concludes, "We must take the teachings of Christ . . . as universal in their application and normative for us today, because that is the way the early apostles took those teachings" (311).[6]

Subsequent revelation can also limit an entire class of teachings or a specific teaching (311–312). Peter's vision of the sheet let down from heaven in Acts 10:9–16 is an example of subsequent revelation setting aside a class of teaching, in this instance the Old Testament dietary laws. In Luke's Gospel, Jesus Himself sets aside one of His own specific teachings. Although He had previously told His disciples not to take purse, bag or shoes with them when He sent them out on mission (see Luke 9:3, 10:4), He later tells them, "'But now if you have a purse, take it, and also a bag; and if you don't have a sword, sell your cloak and buy one.'" (22:36, NIV). Subsequent revelation and immediate context, therefore, are the primary ways in which Scripture sets limits on normative content.

McQuilkin's Approach to Historical Narrative

Because he views it as a separate category of communication, McQuilkin takes a different approach to recognizing normative content in historical narrative. While the teachings of Christ, the New Testament letters and the Old Testament Psalms must be received as normative unless limited by the immediate context or by subsequent revelation, events, behaviors or beliefs recorded in historical narrative may be adopted as normative under certain circumstances. From McQuilkin's perspective, much of Scripture is "simply a record of history" (309). What Scripture records, it records accurately, but the fact that a passage provides an accurate record "does not necessarily make [the event, behavior or belief recorded] a revelation of God's universal will."

Because he recognizes that historical events always have implications (331), McQuilkin suggests that passages of historical narrative have three levels of authority as sources for contemporary application (334):

1. When Scripture evaluates an event, behavior, or belief and gives a reason for the evaluation, that event, behavior, or belief may be considered *normative*.

2. When Scripture evaluates an event, behavior, or belief but does not give a reason for the evaluation, that event, behavior, or belief may be used as the basis for developing a *principle*.

3. When Scripture does not provide an evaluation, an event, behavior, or belief recorded in historical narrative, the verses may be used to *illustrate* truth clearly taught elsewhere.

In other words, it is the designation by an authorized spokesperson for God that establishes an event, behavior or belief recorded in historical narrative as normative (308).

Jesus, of course, is the authorized spokesperson for God *par excellence*. When He commends the actions of the Queen of Sheba and the citizens of Nineveh in Luke 11:29–32, therefore, we can be confident that their examples of seeking wisdom (see 1 Kings 10:1–10) and responding to preaching with faith and repentance (see Jon. 3:1–10) are models for behavior that should be universally adopted. In both instances, Jesus also includes the reason for His evaluation (see Luke 11:31, 32).

Although Jesus' own actions and words need no evaluation by others, His celebration of Passover in Luke 22:14–23 provides another example. When Paul uses Jesus' words as the basis for his instructions on the Lord's Supper (see 1 Cor. 11:23–34), he provides a reason for observing the sacrament on a regular basis (see 11:26), thereby reinforcing the normative nature of the observance implicit in Jesus' command, "Do this in remembrance of me."

Explicit references to events recorded in the book of Acts are comparatively rare in the New Testament letters, but three passages from Paul's letters might prove helpful. In two passages from First Corinthians, Paul reflects on his ministry among the members of that church (see Acts 18:1–21). He mentions baptizing Crispus (see 1 Cor. 1:10–17; Acts 18:7–8), and he discusses his practice of bivocational ministry (see 1 Cor. 9:3–18; Acts 18:1–4). Paul provides no evaluation of his practice of baptizing, which potentially locates that behavior at the lowest level of authority (illustrative). He evaluates and provides the reason for his practice of bivocational ministry in First Corinthians 9:17–18, which establishes that model of church planting as normative.

Paul also reflects upon his time in Thessalonica in his first letter to the church in that city (see 1 Thess. 2:1–12; Acts 17:1–9). He describes several aspects of his ministry positively but does not provide specific reasons for his evaluation. From that passage, therefore, it is possible to derive several principles for ministry, including the importance of being bold in the face of opposition (see 1 Thess. 2:2), maintaining pure motives and conduct (see 2:3–6, 10), genuinely caring for the individuals to whom you are ministering (see 2:7–8, 11–12), and sharing the gospel without being a financial burden on others (see 2:9). These examples from Jesus and Paul serve to illustrate McQuilkin's approach to applying events, behaviors or beliefs recorded in historical narrative. As noted, McQuilkin's discussion of historical narrative occurs in his explanation of application (chapters 19–20). There are, however, at least four guidelines in his section on divine authorship (chapters 15–18) that undergird his approach: compare Scripture with Scripture; base doctrine on the entire Bible; give greater weight to teaching that is often repeated; and reflect Bible emphases. These guidelines reflect McQuilkin's commitment to respecting the unity of Scripture and the coherence of truth. That commitment rests on the presupposition that the Bible is human/divine communication (28). Although there might be diversity among the human authors of the Bible, the active participation of the divine Author insures the unity and coherence of the Bible's teaching (see 2 Pet. 1:20–21).[7]

In light of this presupposition and these guidelines, it is worth considering whether it might be possible broaden McQuilkin's approach to interpreting historical narrative. For example, if when comparing Scripture with Scripture and taking into account the context of an entire narrative book, there appears to be a repeated pattern that the biblical author seems to emphasize, could that pattern also be indicative of a potentially normative belief or behavior? Is it possible that the Holy Spirit has guided the human author in the selection, repetition and/or placement of an event, behavior or belief to present truth and/or provide guidance for His readers? Further, if the teachings of Christ and the authors of the New Testament letters should be received as normative, and if divinely authorized spokespersons provide the key to establishing normative content, should the teachings of Spirit-filled speakers in Acts also be received as normative? Finally, is it possible to establish a case for understanding biblical narrative as theologically interpreted history?[8]

Taking the last question first, two pieces of evidence may be considered in seeking an answer to the question of the theological nature of biblical narrative. The first comes from the historian Lucian in his work *How to Write History*, where he identifies two purposes in writing history: to present truth and to provide guidance.[9] The second comes from Luke, who explicitly sets out the purpose for each of the volumes of his double work. In Luke 1:1–4 he writes, "Inasmuch as many have undertaken to compile an account of the things accomplished among us . . . it seemed fitting . . . to write it out . . . in consecutive order . . . so that you might know the exact truth about the things you have been taught." The phrase "the things accomplished among us" (τῶν πεπληροφορημενῶν, *ton peplerophoremenon*) would naturally seem to include events as well as beliefs, and "the things you have been taught" (ὧν κατηχήθης, *hon katechethes*) would suggest behaviors as well as beliefs. In Acts 1:1, Luke writes that his "first account" (i.e., Luke) was "about all that Jesus began to do and teach," with the implication that his second account (i.e., Acts) is about what Jesus continued to do and teach through His followers as they were empowered by the Holy Spirit (see Acts 1:5, 8). Acts, therefore, is about more than what the apostles taught; it is also about what the apostles did. It would seem natural to expect that Luke writes to provide guidance as well as present truth.

What about the speeches in Acts? From the perspective of New Testament scholarship, I.H. Marshall notes that the speeches are often highlighted as the chief medium through which Lucan theology is communicated.[10] Similarly, C.K. Barrett writes about Peter's Pentecost speech, "The speech then contains Lucan theology, and the *Lucan* way of preaching the Gospel (probably, that is, the theology of the church as it was known to Luke)."[11]

These conclusions, however, are essentially philosophical. Is it possible to identify a textually based key that might lead us to consider the speeches as sources of normative content?

McQuilkin specifies Jesus' teachings as normative but leaves aside other spoken discourse recorded in biblical narrative unless it is commended (or condemned) by an authorized spokesperson for God.[12] The speeches in Acts, however, are all spoken by three individuals—Peter, Stephen and Paul—each of whom is described as "filled with the Spirit" (2:4; 6:5; 9:17). Such a narrative clue suggests that the teachings of these speakers might potentially be received as normative as well.[13] It would also seem logical to extend the same thinking to other speeches in Luke-Acts that are similarly qualified (e.g., Zacharias in Luke 1:67–79 and Simeon in Luke 2:27–32). Although space prohibits further discussion of this subject, it would seem worth exploring whether there might be other potential clues to assessing spoken discourse in historical narrative elsewhere in the New Testament.

Among others, David Peterson has noted the common features in the speeches of Luke-Acts. A repeated pattern emerges in the speeches, consisting of seven elements: scriptural warrant, messianic suffering, messianic resurrection, call to repentance, promise of forgiveness, universal offer, and method and power. Those seven elements are also present in Luke's commissioning account (Luke 24:46–49), which serves as the model for the speeches. The following table sets out the elements as they appear in the commissioning and the five longest speeches in Acts (references in parentheses are inferred from the context):

PASSAGE	LUKE 24:46-49	ACTS 2:14-40	ACTS 3:12-26	ACTS 10:34-43	ACTS 13:16-41	ACTS 26:1-29
AUDIENCE	Disciples at the Ascension	Jews at Pentecost	Jews in the Temple	Cornelius in Caesarea	Jews in Pisidian Antioch	Festus and Agrippa
ACCORDING TO SCRIPTURE	24:46	2:16-21	3:18, 22-25	10:43	13:27, 29	26:22
CHRIST SUFFERS	24:46	2:22-23	3:13-15	10:39	13:28	26:23
CHRIST RISES FROM THE DEAD	24:46	2:24-36	3:15, 26	10:40	13:30-37	26:23
CALL TO REPEN-TANCE	24:47	2:37	3:19	(10:42)	13:40-41	26:20
PROMISE OF FOR-GIVENESS	24:47	2:37	3:19	10:43	13:38	26:18
UNIVERSAL OFFER	24:47	2:39	3:25	10:43	13:39	26:23
METHOD AND POWER	24:48-49	2:32, 38	3:16	10:36, 39	13:31-32	26:16

Both the repeated elements within Acts and the connection to Jesus' own teaching suggest potential avenues for approaching the question of establishing normative content found in historical narrative. The next section will explore some of those potential avenues.

Probing for Indicators of Normative Content in Acts

McQuilkin has already identified two indicators of normative content in biblical narrative. Framed as questions related to the author, they are:

Does the author limit the belief/behavior in the immediate context?

Does the author provide a positive or negative comment on the belief/behavior?

A third indicator may be based on McQuilkin's guideline that Jesus' teaching should be taken as normative unless specifically limited. The above discussion of the speeches in Acts suggests that a similar indicator may be applied to teaching or preaching sections outside the Gospels:

Does the author incorporate the belief/behavior into an authoritative preaching or teaching section?

In other words, when an author presents spoken discourse as teaching by an authoritative spokesperson for God, the beliefs and/or behaviors addressed in that teaching may potentially be received as normative. In addition to these three indicators, the following suggestions may be offered as helping to establish normative content in historical narrative.

Narrative Clue

The discussion above described the qualifier "filled with the Spirit" as a *narrative clue* that applied to all three of the speakers in Acts and designated them as authoritative spokespersons. This concept is similar to what Peterson calls a "key term," a repeated word or phrase that indicates thematic significance. He continues, "Sometimes related terms occur with surprising frequency in a particular context, indicating that this is a theological focus of the section, where Luke may also be explaining and commending certain behavior to his readers."[15] Framed as a question, this potential indicator is:

> *Does the author provide a narrative clue to the importance of the belief/behavior?*

The phrases "filled with the Spirit" (see Acts 2:4; 4:8, 31; 9:17; 13:9, 52) and "full of the Spirit" (see 6:3, 5; 7:55; 11:24) occur ten times in Acts and align with Luke's emphasis on the Holy Spirit as the promised power for witness (see 1:8).[16] For example, the occurrence of this particular narrative clue in 4:31 commends both believing prayer and witness, when Luke writes of the Jerusalem believers, "And when they had prayed, the place in which they were gathered together was shaken, and they were all filled with Holy Spirit and continued to speak the word of God with boldness." Similarly, Luke commends Barnabas' ministry activities in Antioch, when he describes Barnabas as "a good man, full of the Holy Spirit and of faith" (11:24).[17]

Key Theme

The concept of tracing key themes is closely related to the previous indicator. In his essay on writing a theology of Acts, Marshall concludes, "The study of themes is manifestly legitimate, provided that we pay attention to the intricate interplay of numerous themes and do not hitch our wagon to a single star."[18] The question to ask in connection with this indicator is:

Does the author connect the belief/behavior to a key theme that runs throughout the book?

In addition to *spirit* (πνεῦμα, *pneuma*), which occurs seventy times in Acts, other key themes include *salvation* (σῴζω, *sozo*; σωτηρία, *soteria,* twenty-four times), *witness* (μάρτυς, *martus*; μαρτυρία, *marturia*; μαρτυρέω, *martureo,* twenty-five times), *church* (ἐκκλησία, *ekklesia,* twenty-three times), and the *miraculous* (σημεῖα, *semeia*; τέρατα, *terata*; δυνάμεις, *dunameis,* twenty times). Tracing these themes can help locate Luke's theological emphases and potentially identify beliefs and/or behaviors that are important within his narrative. For example, by tracing the theme of salvation in Acts, it becomes clear that the Lord saves (see 2:21), through grace (see 15:11), based on faith in Jesus (see 16:31). These beliefs are part of the theology Luke commends to his readers.

Use of the Old Testament

Among the authorial techniques Peterson presents is the use of Scripture. He notes that characters "cite Scripture at strategic points in the argument to explain and justify what has happened."[19]

Framed as a question, this potential indicator is:

Does the author use Scripture to explain or clarify the belief/behavior?

Five brief examples demonstrate that passages from the Old Testament can commend (or correct) both beliefs and behaviors: Psalm 16:8–11 validates a belief in Jesus' resurrection (see Acts 2:24–28), Psalm 110:1 validates a belief in His ascension (see Acts 2:33–35), Isaiah 66:1 corrects a Jewish belief in the importance of the Temple (see Acts 7:48–50), Isaiah 49:6 justifies

Paul's action of expanding his ministry beyond the Jews to include the Gentiles (see Acts 13:44–49) and Amos 9:11–12 validates the decision of the Jerusalem Council (see Acts 15:13–21).

Placement

Most commentators recognize the presence of summary statements at key points in the narrative of Acts (see 2:41, 47; 4:4; 5:14; 6:7; 9:31, 42; 11:21; 12:24; 13:48; 16:5; 19:20; 28:31).[20] As Peterson notes, many of these statements speak of growth or progress after the resolution of a conflict or the end of some sort of persecution.[21] For example, Luke's comment in 6:7 that "the word of the Lord kept on spreading; and the number of disciples continued to increase greatly in Jerusalem, and a great many of the priests were becoming obedient to the faith" follows the choosing of the seven (see 6:5–6). His comment in 16:5 that "the churches were being strengthened in the faith and were increasing in number daily" follows the delivery of the Jerusalem Council decree (see 15:30–35; 16:4). In both instances, the summary statements comment on events in the immediately preceding narrative and provide Luke's implicit commendation. When an event occurs in the context before a summary comment, therefore, its placement might well indicate its importance. The question to ask in connection with this indicator is:

> *Does the author place the belief/behavior in a context that indicates its importance?*

Underlying Teaching

William Larkin suggests three factors in deciding whether Luke intends a historical event to have normative value: (1) a positive statement in the immediate context might show that Luke would like his readers to imitate the behavior, (2) the principle behind an action might be present in a teaching portion elsewhere in Luke-Acts and (3) an unambiguous pattern might indicate that the action became a sustained practice.[22] The first echoes Mc-Quilkin's basic approach and has been discussed above; the third will be examined in the next section. The second may be framed as this question:

> Does the author use the belief/behavior to illustrate an underlying teaching found elsewhere in Scripture?

A simple example, cited by Larkin, is the early church's practice of prayer (see Acts 1:14; 2:42; 6:4; 14:23), which illustrates Jesus' teaching in Luke 18:1–8. Another example is the way in which Peter and John's Spirit-filled defense before the Sanhedrin (see Acts 4:5–12) illustrates Jesus' teaching in Luke 12:11–12: "And when they bring you before the synagogues and the rulers and authorities, do not become anxious about how or what you should speak in your defense, or what you should say; for the Holy Spirit will teach you in that very hour what you ought to say." Both behaviors should be considered normative because of the clear teaching that lies behind them.

Consistent Pattern

In an unpublished paper, Larkin proposes three levels of detail in historical narrative.[23] An *inaugural* detail, such as the tongues of fire on the day of Pentecost (see Acts 2:3), is not normative because it is unique and unrepeatable. A benchmark detail, such as the apostles speaking in other tongues (see 2:4), establishes a reference point to which the subsequent narrative refers (e.g., 10:45; 19:6). A precedent-setting detail, such as the apostles' Spirit-filled witness (see 2:4), can be established as normative if it is repeated consistently. The concept of a consistently repeated pattern suggests a final indicator:

Does the author present the belief/behavior as part of a consistently repeated pattern?

Evaluation of a potentially precedent-setting belief or behavior requires careful tracing of the pattern throughout the entire narrative. The question often arises, for example, of whether the sequence of details recorded in connection with the founding of the church in Samaria (see Acts 8:5–17) should be considered normative. That sequence—conversion, baptism, a time lapse, the laying on of hands, the gift of the Holy Spirit and speaking in tongues—seems to support the experience of a "second blessing." Can it be demonstrated that such a sequence occurs consistently in Acts? The following table sets out the details of four passages. (The numbers at the top of the cells identify the sequence in which the details are recorded, and references in parentheses are inferred from the context.)

PASSAGE	ACTS 8:5-17	ACTS 9:1-19	ACTS 10:34-48	ACTS 19:2-6
AUDIENCE	Multitudes in Samaria	Saul in Damascus	Cornelius in Caesarea	Disciple of John in Ephesus
PROCLAM- ATION OF THE GOSPEL	1 8:5	1 9:4-6	1 10:34-43	1 19:4
RESPONSE OF FAITH	2 8:12	2 (9:8)	2 (10:44)	2 (19:5)
BAPTISM	3 8:12	6 9:18	5 10:48	3 19:5
TIME LAPSE	4 8:14-16	3 9:9		
LAYING ON OF HANDS	5 8:17	4 9:17		4 19:6
GIFT OF THE HOLY SPIRIT	6 8:17	5 9:18	3 10:44	5 19:6
SPEAKING IN TONGUES	7 (8:18)		7 10:46	6 19:6

Not only is at least one of the details missing in the other three passages, the sequence of details is not the same in any of them. The lack of a consistent unambiguous pattern, therefore, means the sequence of events recorded in Samaria is not normative for all believers in all ages. In contrast, however, the consistent inclusion of each of the elements in the table of speeches above suggests a normative pattern of essentials of the gospel that should guide all followers of Christ as they share the good news with others.

Conclusion

McQuilkin has proposed three levels of authority when dealing with biblical narrative. Those levels of authority lay the foundation for the task of recognizing normative content in such books as Luke and Acts. His articulation of guidelines related to the divine authorship of Scripture and the possibility of establishing a case for understanding biblical narrative as theologically interpreted history suggest that it is possible to identify authorial indicators of normative content. Probing the book of Acts for such indicators leads to nine questions that might profitably be used in that task. Hopefully, this exercise makes a small contribution to addressing McQuilkin's concern that evangelical scholarship has done little work on the task of establishing the significance of Bible teaching for faith and obedience today. Perhaps it will also serve as the basis for others to pursue that same task.

Part III

Spiritual Living

Chapter 5

Victorious Christian Living:
J. Robertson McQuilkin's View of Sanctification

Shirl S. Schiffman

"Therefore, if anyone is in Christ, he is a new creation; old things have passed away; behold, all things have become new."
(2 Cor. 5:17, NKJV[1])

S
o when I was saved, I became a completely new creation? What exactly does that look like? Reading the Bible? Praying? Being in a good church? Becoming more loving, joyful, peaceful, patient? Finding strength to cope and helping others along the way? Witnessing?

How would you respond if asked those questions? Before answering, consider how the Bible portrays those of us who have become new creations in Christ (see 2 Cor. 5:17). Paul says that "sin shall not have dominion over [us]" (Rom. 6:14), and though we were once "slaves of sin," we're now set free to be "slaves of righteousness" (6:17–18). Peter sees us as believer-priests who have an incredible ministry: "But you are a chosen generation, a royal priesthood, a holy nation, His own special people, that you may proclaim the praises of Him who called you out of darkness into His marvelous light" (1 Pet. 2:9; see also 2:5). Jesus described the relationship He would have with His disciples as one that could not be closer or more loving (see John 15:4–5; 15:15). Unless these passages are simply rhetorical flourishes, it sounds like the Christian life is supposed to be something far beyond natural human existence. It sounds like it is supposed to be something very different—something supernatural!

This essay is an appeal to give very careful consideration to the view we hold concerning what God's people should expect postconversion, especially those of us who have the privilege to preach, teach or disciple others—and that includes all of us! The saints need to understand how they were forgiven and justified. So too, they need to know what it means to be regenerated and sanctified.

Explaining Justification, Regeneration, Sanctification

Justification may be more familiar than regeneration or sanctification to many in the church because we tend to talk about it more. Justification is an unfathomable miracle and yet, thanks to Old and New Testament teaching (particularly Paul's), it can be explained with considerable precision—and needs to be. It occurs in a spectacular moment, orchestrated by a sheer act of God's grace and power through the atoning death of His Son. In a legal transaction, a holy God lays the sinner's guilt on Christ and lays the righteousness of His perfect Son on the one redeemed! In the eyes of the Father and Judge, the penalty of death we should have paid is cancelled. Our only part is to receive God's free gift (see Eph. 2:8–9). Unbelievable, but true!

Regeneration is a second miracle that occurs in that cosmic moment. The Holy Spirit of the risen Christ literally takes up residence in a previously corrupted sinner, breaking the grip of sin and imparting a new, divine nature. This action brings dead hearts alive, making them capable of being conformed to the image of Christ. In this amazing union, the Spirit does not suppress, but rather transforms all the potential, beauty and eternal fruitfulness each believer was created to have.

Then there is *sanctification*. Instead of a moment, sanctification takes a lifetime. It's a process rarely free from problems, pain and suffering. It's messier than justification and regeneration because we are active participants. Right off the bat we have a conundrum: to be justified and regenerated is to be instantly sanctified (already) and in the process of being sanctified (not yet). Two verses capture this divine paradox: we "are new creations" (2 Cor. 5:17) while we are being transformed into Christ's image (see 3:18). In other words, God chose for us to respond to His grace by daily working out what He has already worked in us (see Phil. 2:12). Speaking of the interrelationship of the core doctrines of justification, regeneration and sanctification, James Wilhoit says:

> Much of our failure in conceptualizing spiritual formation comes from our failure to keep the gospel central to our ministry. Too often people see the gospel as merely the front door to Christianity, or worse, "heaven's minimum entrance requirement." A bifurcation of salvation into a grace-filled regeneration followed by a human-striving sanctification leads to so many spiritual sorrows. The gospel is the power of God for the beginning, middle, and end of salvation. It is not merely what we need to proclaim to unbelievers; the gospel also needs to permeate our entire Christian experience.[2]

Challenges to Teaching Sanctification

What should the saints be told to expect on the journey of sanctification? Here we have some disagreements. One tension relates to the interplay of divine sovereignty and human responsibility. Rightful concern is expressed that sanctification should not be understood (as Wilhoit noted) as Christians trying hard to be more like Christ; Scripture renders that an impossibility and an affront to the gospel. At the same time, repeated exhortations to put into practice who we are already in Christ make it clear that God both commands and empowers believers to be holy as He is holy (see Lev. 11:44–45; 1 Pet. 1:15–16). Somehow we must counter any suggestion of a works-based sanctification while at the same time not minimizing the active role we're meant to have as we walk in the Spirit (see Gal. 5:25). As Steven Barabas notes,

> It is a grievous mistake . . . to suppose that the sanctification of the believer is a matter of course, and that he need not trouble himself about it. For one thing . . . this position ignores the whole question of backsliding, which is not only possible but quite common among Christians. Moreover, it fosters carelessness of Christian living, for if sanctification will proceed automatically without our doing anything about it, then why be concerned about it?[3]

Another tension relates to just how holy, how much like Christ, those in the process of being sanctified can actually become on this side of eternity. No one wants to discourage or embitter Christians by promising more victory over temptation and sin than is possible. At the same time, neither do we want to abet the mind-set that very little needs to be changed or will change in our lives before heaven.

Resolving such concerns with biblically accurate explanations of what we can expect as new creations in Christ represents one of the challenges in teaching about sanctification. Another is recognizing that knowledge about sanctification must be integrated with opportunities to put that knowledge into practice. Only in this way can the doctrine of sanctification be understood as the living, breathing, moment-by-moment, supernatural experience it is meant to be. My hope and prayer for this essay is that it will encourage more teaching on sanctification, teaching that is vibrant, biblical and transformational.

Searching for a Definition of Sanctification

An important step forward is to find a biblically and experientially accurate definition of sanctification. Definitions are important; they convey in few words the essential nature and scope of what is defined. They help us know what to expect and what to look for. Good definitions paint word pictures that describe and inspire. Mission and vision statements, for example, are definitions that describe the heart and core functions of an organization, announcing, "This is who we are. This is what we stand for. This is what we dream to accomplish." Knowing a definition is not to fully know what it defines, but good ones say a lot in a little, point in the right direction, and, ideally, build motivation for going there.

A good definition of sanctification would be biblically substantiated. It would point God's people toward the wonder and adventure of what it means to live a Spirit-filled, Spirit-led, Spirit-empowered life. It would capture the transformative language of the New Testament yet be real for twenty-first century believers. In relatively few words, it would paint a picture of what it means to be "in Christ." Against those criteria, how would you rate this very small sample of definitions?

> Sanctification is a progressive work of God and man that makes us more and more free from sin and like Christ in our actual lives.[4]

> Spiritual formation for the Christian refers to the Holy Spirit-driven process of forming the inner world of the human self in such a way that it becomes like the inner being of Christ himself.[5]

> Sanctification is the work of God's free grace, whereby we are renewed in the whole man after the image of God, and are enabled more and more to die unto sin, and live unto righteousness.[6]

> Spiritual formation is the divinely ordained transformational process by which the Holy Spirit leads believers to embrace the Lord Jesus Christ through the Word of God, and by that relationship become progressively more free from sin and more like Christ. The Spirit's formative work occurs in the context of a vital engagement with a community of believers.[7]

These definitions are helpful. They show sanctification as a process, the Spirit as the agent of divine change, sin as a barrier to that change, being like Christ as the desired outcome. They serve well the purposes for which they were written.

For teaching purposes, however, we need more. First, we need language that is theologically accurate but not dispassionate lest we invite a tepid reaction to God's stunning, amazing grace. Second, several vitally important elements are not addressed in these definitions. Finally, phrases like "becoming more like Christ" need further illumination to be truly instructive, as noted by theological educators Stephen and Mary Lowe:

It is our contention that until we have a clear, biblically-shaped view of the target of faith formation we will never achieve the intended outcome of whole person transformation into the image and likeness of Jesus Christ. This includes a biblically-explicated concept of what must be included in the phrases whole person transformation and the image and likeness of Christ. There are many references to Christlikeness in the literature on Christian spirituality. There is very little in this literature that goes into great detail to explain exactly what this phrase means.[8]

My own search for an accurate and compelling view of what it means to "become like Christ" led me to the work of Robertson McQuilkin. Along with books on missions, hermeneutics, ethics and church leadership, McQuilkin has made a significant contribution to the literature on sanctification and the work of the Holy Spirit.[9] His approach is shaped by his heritage (including his father's leadership in the Victorious Life Movement, with roots in the US and British Keswick conventions[10]) and his personal, passionate pursuit to know and love Christ. Also, Spirit-filled living, historically called "Victorious Christian Living," is one of the five core values of Columbia International University, where McQuilkin led as president for twenty-two years.[11]

As both author and speaker, McQuilkin has a great ability to communicate deep theological truth in relevant, colorful, accessible language. This is nowhere more evident than in the paragraph below, which presents his view of the Christian life. In just three sentences, McQuilkin describes the transcendent, fruit-bearing, love relationship with Jesus that is the birthright of the redeemed:

What glorious good news! No matter what may or may not have occurred in the past and no matter how inadequate my understanding, if my relationship to God is one of unconditional surrender and confident expectation that He will keep His word, I can experience a life of consistent victory over temptation and growth toward His own likeness. I can see His purpose for my ministry supernaturally fulfilled, and above all, I can daily experience loving companionship with my Savior.[12]

The remainder of this essay will elaborate on this definition point by point, but in reverse order, so that we begin with the greatest gift of all.

"And above all, I can daily experience loving companionship with my Savior."

The phrase "and above all" reminds us that among created beings, humans alone were uniquely made in the image of the Creator to be loving members of His family (see Gen. 1:26–28; Heb. 2:10–13). God so lavishly loved us that He became like us, suffered and died for us so that we could share an intimate, loving relationship with Him (see John 3:16; Rom. 5:8; 1 John 3:1). Other definitions may omit this, but McQuilkin grounds his in the loving oneness we are meant to have with the triune God. When asked the greatest commandment, Jesus, quoting from the *Shema*, did not say we were to worship, obey or glorify the Lord our God but that we were first to love Him with everything we are and have (see Deut. 6:5; Matt. 22:37). Clearly, worship, obedience and bringing glory to God—all essential responses—spring most authentically and spontaneously from hearts full of love and gratitude. McQuilkin's choice of the words "daily... loving companionship" reflect this foundational truth. They draw on Jesus' metaphor of the vine and branches (see John 15:1–8), and His unforgettable statement that He, the soon-to-be crucified, resurrected, glorified Messiah, would not call us servants who are excluded from the Master's business, but friends who are the Master's partners and confidants (see John 15:15)! What does it mean to be related to Christ? Many things for sure, but for McQuilkin it means this:

> Incredible as it may seem, God has planned my life around Himself, uninterrupted companionship with the greatest Lover who ever lived! No getting an appointment a month in advance. No taking a number and waiting my turn. He doesn't just tolerate me. Outrageous mystery—God actually desires my company! In fact, He wants to be best friends. That's what it means to be "in Christ" and for Christ to be "in me"—a new relationship that defies analysis or description. While we wonder about the mysterious physical aspect of my body as a residence for God, and while we exult in that mystery, let's be sure to focus our attention on the relationship between the two of us.[13]

God, of course, is also holy, righteous, and just, and this will be dealt with below. For now, whatever else we teach about sanctification, let us frame it within the love-based union we have with our Savior whose Spirit lives within us. The truth is, "Sanctification is not something Jesus Christ puts into me: it is Himself in me."[14] John Piper speaks movingly of one of his professors who helped him grasp this point:

> One of the most memorable moments of my seminary days was during the school year of 1968–69 at Fuller Seminary. . . . A group of us were huddled around James Morgan, the young theology teacher who was saying something about the engagement of Christians in social justice. I don't remember what I said, but he looked me right in the eye and said, "John, I love Jesus Christ." It was like a thunderclap in my heart. A strong, intelligent, mature, socially engaged man had just said out loud in front of a half dozen men, "I

love Jesus Christ." He was not preaching. He was not being recorded. He was telling me that he loved Jesus. . . . There are a thousand things I don't remember about those days in seminary. But that afternoon remains unforgettable. And all he said was, "John, I love Jesus Christ." James Morgan died a year later of stomach cancer, leaving a wife and four small children. His chief legacy in my life was one statement on an afternoon in Pasadena. "I love Jesus Christ."[15]

Father, teach us to love You more and more, and to experience Your love for us more and more. May our loving companionship bring You great joy, and may knowing You be our greatest joy.

"I can see His purpose for my ministry supernaturally fulfilled . . ."

A second distinctive of McQuilkin's definition is to make explicit not just an upward but also an outward dimension to sanctification. After stating the greatest commandment, Jesus quickly added that "the second is like it: 'You shall love your neighbor as yourself'" (Matt. 22:39). God's people have always been called to respond to His extravagant love not just in personal devotion to Him but also in relating to others as His representatives (see Gen. 12:1–3; Lev. 19:33–34; Ps. 67:1–2; Matt. 28:18–20; Acts 1:8). Yet it is not uncommon for books, courses and definitions on spiritual formation to exclude mention of ministry, no doubt viewing it as a separate subject. In fact, in a special theme issue of the *Journal of Spiritual Formation & Soul Care*, M. Robert Mulholland speaks of a "perennial tension between the contemplative life and the active life, between spiritual formation in Christ and mission with Christ,"[16] and thereafter argues:

> Being formed in the image of Christ integrates believers into God's mission for the redemption of all creation, not

simply as a specific role in a particular mission, but as a life hid with Christ in God that incarnates God's redemptive activity in the midst of the world as it is. Spiritual formation in Christ and mission with Christ are the inseparable components in our participation in God's redemption of all creation.

McQuilkin agrees, describing the inseparability of knowing Christ and making Christ known in *The Great Omission*:

> "Man's chief end is to glorify God and to enjoy Him forever," the Westminster Shorter Catechism assures us. As a summary of a human being's proper view of reality, this statement is illuminating and authentic. But how does man fulfill this chief end? Surely by adoring and worshiping his Creator; certainly by obedience, as one is recreated by the Spirit after the moral pattern of God Himself; indeed through the building up of God's church. But the human event that brings greatest glory to God and satisfaction to His heart occurs when a prodigal returns home, when one immigrates out of the kingdom of darkness into the kingdom of His dear Son. Human redemption is the focal point of God's purpose in this world.[17]

Sanctification means becoming like Jesus in all He was, including His mission. As we listen to His Spirit, we increasingly see His global, redemptive purpose as our purpose. We realize that God is most glorified when receiving the worship and love of an ever-growing family of sons and daughters. We understand that all saints are ministers (see Eph. 4:12), that we are royal priests (see 1 Pet. 2:9; Exod. 19:6). We take seriously the privilege and responsibility of pointing others—unbelievers *and* saints—ever closer to Christ. Assignments, locations, gifting and calling will vary, but we unite in passionately longing for the expansion of His kingdom. We learn that ministry which is not supernatural is not truly ministry. Only when we abide in the Vine can God supernaturally work in and through us.

Father, we open our hearts and our lives so that You, through Your Spirit, can carry on Your Son's work through us as His body in the world.

"I can experience a life of consistent victory over temptation and growth toward His own likeness . . ."

Here McQuilkin confronts the problem of sin head-on. The God of perfect love is also the God who is perfectly holy. Sin barred us from His presence before redemption; we continue to face temptation and sin after redemption but with a new nature and power. It is here, as previously noted, where some evangelicals disagree—a matter too complex for this essay.[18] For his part, McQuilkin seeks a biblically mediating position between extremes of expecting chronic failure in the face of temptation or expecting sinless perfection. He states his position this way:

> The Bible makes clear that God doesn't expect absolute perfection in this life, though He does promise just that when we reach heaven—"We shall be like him, for we shall see him as he is" (1 John 3:2). In the meantime, what can we expect? What does the Spirit mean by speaking of our being more than conquerors (Rom. 8:37) and always caused to triumph (2 Cor. 2:14)? As we have seen . . . *when we live in the Spirit we can expect to*
>
> • consistently win over temptations to choose wrong and
>
> • grow steadily toward greater likeness to Jesus in our attitudes and actions.[19]

Note the phrase italicized above. McQuilkin teaches two mutually reinforcing truths about dealing with sin. First, we can expect, *only through the Spirit,* to consistently (not perfectly) find growing strength to stand against temptation to commit willful, deliberate sin. Second, we can expect, *only through the Spirit,* to grow steadily to be more like Jesus. As our attitudes and what we do and say become more like Him, we're less drawn to things He would not think, feel or do because our minds are increasingly set on things above (see Col. 3:2). We can never let down our guard. Our adversary walks about (see 1 Pet. 5:8) plotting our defeat, but we no longer have to face him on our own. Instead, we appropriate power through the Spirit from the Word, prayer and the support of other believers to make choices that bring God glory. With each victory we spiral upward toward greater likeness to the Savior. Each failure drives us to Him in repentance, finding the mercy and forgiveness we are promised (see Heb. 4:15–16; 1 John 1:9; Rom. 8:26).

With whatever nuancing we feel necessary, may our explanation of sin engender appropriate resolve among the saints so that they never feel the pursuit of holiness is hopeless:

> [to] fall back on the idea that "Christians aren't perfect, just forgiven," in a way that dampens the zealous pursuit of holiness would be to pit one biblical truth against another (i.e., "be holy" versus "God loves me even though I am a sinner"). Maturing Christians will be eager to detect and resist such simplistic "solutions," and to do their best to embrace the whole message of God's Word.[20]

The gospel is indeed needed at the beginning, middle and end of our spiritual journeys. Take care, though, that believers don't think of the gospel as a concept, something only to believe, or a message for the unsaved. No, it is the power of God for salvation—the same power that brought Jesus to life and the power Jesus promised we would receive when the Holy Spirit came (see

Acts 1:8). It is the life and power of the triune God that makes victory over sin possible.

Father, continue to teach and convict us, in a deeply biblical and personal way, what it means to be holy as You are holy.

"If my relationship to God is one of unconditional surrender and confident expectation that He will keep His word . . ."

McQuilkin here addresses our role in partnering with the Spirit in our sanctification. While even the desire to respond to God is of His grace, we have choices to make. Jesus Himself prefaced many of His calls, as McQuilkin did above, with the word "if," as seen in: "If anyone desires to come after Me, let him deny himself, and take up his cross, and follow Me" (Matt. 16:24). Consider the most well-known commandments carved in stone by the finger of God. They state what is true of God's character and glory, and what will be true of those who choose to love and honor Him. Yet no one, on either side of Calvary, has been forced to obey them by the One who had the right and power to do so. In relation to this, Wilhoit sometimes refers to the "invitations" of Scripture instead of the "commands," defending his practice by saying, "I do not intend to soften the language of command, but rather to recognize that Jesus is inviting us to a certain way of living. He is not content to simply order us to do such and such; he wants 'us' far more than our actions. He wants all of us."[21] McQuilkin agrees, and notes two prerequisites for ongoing spiritual growth: unconditional surrender and banking on the promises of God. Or, as he often referred to them even more simply: "yield and trust."[22]

Yield. Asking formerly self-centered, self-focused people (i.e., all of us) to yield or surrender is asking for a lot of counter-cultural humility. Even the word "surrender" may sound more like weakness, compromise and failure "we had to surrender our position"—than strength, courage or victory. "Unconditional surrender" sounds even worse—and impossible. But is it? Did Jesus ask the impossible when He told those who wanted to follow Him to deny themselves? Obviously not, but it takes more than good intentions to crucify our "flesh with its passions and desires" (Gal. 5:24). Like everything else on the journey of sanctification, we need (and have!) the power of the indwelling Holy Spirit to be victorious in laying down our lives. In his book *Absolute Surrender*, Andrew Murray reminds us of the importance of prayer in this process:

> I am sure there are workers who often cry to God for the Holy Spirit to come upon them as a Spirit of power for their work, and when they feel that measure of power, and get blessing, they thank God for it. But God wants something more and something higher. God wants us to seek for the Holy Spirit as a Spirit of power in our own heart and life, to conquer self and cast out sin, and to work the blessed and beautiful image of Jesus into them.[23]

In addition to prayer, our growing, loving companionship with Jesus also fuels surrender. His sacrificial, unconditional love for us makes our grateful, unconditional surrender to Him increasingly more spontaneous and joyful, less dutiful or painful. The more we know Him, the more we love Him. The more we love Him, the more we want to obey Him. The more we obey Him, the more we want to know Him, and on and on it goes.

Trust. The only way to know the unchanging, unfailing character of our great God is through the pages of His Word. It is there we learn that He always has fulfilled His promises, and this builds the confident expectation that He always will (see 2 Cor. 1:18–22). The saints must be equipped and encouraged to read, understand and live out the Word of God. Those with the privilege and responsibility for preaching and teaching on sanctification should also take seriously these words from A.W. Tozer:

> Sound Bible exposition is an imperative must in the Church of the Living God. Without it no church can be a New Testament church in any strict meaning of that term. But exposition may be carried on in such a way as to leave the hearers devoid of any true spiritual nourishment whatever. For it is not mere words that nourish the soul, but God Himself, and unless and until the hearers find God in personal experience they are not the better for having heard the truth. The Bible is not an end in itself, but a means to bring men to an intimate and satisfying knowledge of God, that they may enter into Him, that they may delight in His Presence, may taste and know the inner sweetness of the very God Himself in the core and center of their hearts.[24]

Father, help us respond to You lovingly, humbly and unconditionally. Help us study and teach Your Word in a way that You are known and trusted more.

"No matter what may or may not have occurred in the past and no matter how inadequate my understanding . . ."

This short preamble reminds us that regardless of past or present human sins, failures or limitations, a holy and merciful God is constantly at work through His Spirit drawing the unregenerate to salvation and the regenerate toward deeper oneness with Himself. On this topic, Robert C. McQuilkin noted: "A lost sinner must hear the gospel, the good news that Christ has died for his sins. The background of this glad news is the sad news that he is a lost sinner, deserving eternal death. So [too] a Christian must know the good news of God's provision for victorious living. This is good news for one who is facing his own defeat and failure."[25] In other words, the gospel—the unleashed power of the crucified, risen Son of God—holds victory for sinners and saints regardless of where they are, or what they know or don't yet know. The gospel shatters our utter inability to help ourselves, but it must be received by faith. Why? "Faith is needed because God is needed."[26] Our hope is built on the sovereign work of the God who seeks, saves and sanctifies. Oswald Chambers exhorts us to remember that "the final thing is confidence in Jesus. Believe steadfastly on Him and all you come up against will develop your faith. . . . Faith is unutterable trust in God, trust which never dreams that He will not stand by us."[27]

Father, even when we still struggle, even though we still see only as in a mirror dimly, we praise and thank You for Your abundant grace and truth poured out on us!

"What glorious good news!"

How fitting that such a rich, vivid definition of sanctification begins with praise, since there is so much to praise God for! What did Jesus mean in John 10:10 when He said, "I have come that they may have life, and that they may have it more abundantly"? He meant that victorious, growing saints would share daily, intimate, loving fellowship with Him and with other saints. He meant that they would have lives of purpose and adventure as they carried on His work in millions of creative ways around the world through His Spirit. He meant that they would see themselves grow (not perfectly, but consistently) to have an amazingly strong familial resemblance to the Father, Son and Spirit. And He meant that they would one day see Him face to face and dwell with Him for all eternity.

Oh Father, thank You for this truly glorious good news!

Conclusion

With McQuilkin's viewpoint in mind, my prayer is that those who lead and teach God's people will paint a picture of sanctification that is biblically clear and compelling, one that shows life in Christ after salvation as a magnificent work of God carried out "for His good pleasure" (Phil. 2:13). Let's teach the saints (including ourselves) that they can experience growing victory against temptation and sin through Christ (see 1 Cor. 15:57). Let's encourage and model what it means to experience loving companionship with Jesus through His Spirit. Let's not fear overselling this essential doctrine, nor fear challenging the saints and ourselves to go deeper and higher in knowing Christ as Paul wanted to (see Phil. 3:10). Rather, in the authority of Christ, and in the power of the Holy Spirit, as revealed in the Word of God, may "we all, with unveiled face, beholding as in a mirror the glory of the Lord, [be] transformed into the same image from glory to glory, just as by the Spirit of the Lord" (2 Cor. 3:18).

Father, thank You for Your sovereign, supernatural work of sanctification. Help us and our fellow saints experience life "in Christ" as the adventure it is meant to be. May all that we do be to the praise and glory of our Lord and Savior Jesus, Amen.

Chapter 6

Life in the Spirit According to McQuilkin and Paul

John D. Harvey

The important place the Holy Spirit holds in J. Robertson McQuilkin's thought and life can be seen in his publications. His introduction to biblical hermeneutics highlights the Spirit's role not only in ensuring that the original intent of the human authors is communicated but also in enabling us to understand that intent.[1] The Spirit naturally plays a key role in McQuilkin's presentation of the Keswick perspective on sanctification because the fourth day of the traditional Keswick Convention focuses on Spirit-filled living.[2] The closing chapter of his introduction to biblical ethics places special emphasis on the Spirit's role in guiding believers as we navigate areas about which God has not given direct revelation.[3] The energizing power of the Spirit is the third of five principles he sets out in his book on effective biblical ministry.[4]

Of course, McQuilkin's most extensive treatment of the work of the Holy Spirit is *Life in the Spirit*,[5] in which he proposes ten activities of the Spirit that are designed to transform our lives.[6]

He groups together seven of those activities as having an inward focus: creating, revealing, redeeming, indwelling, transforming, filling and overcoming. He presents the other three activities as having an outward focus: gifting, sending and glorifying. His discussion of those ten activities is intensely practical and is not intended as a detailed biblical-theological study. For that reason, the book suggests other avenues of study that could be pursued, including the exegetical underpinnings for McQuilkin's taxonomy.

The question for this brief study is: how do the uses of πνεῦμα, *pneuma* and its cognates in Paul's letters correlate with McQuilkin's list of the ten activities of the Spirit as presented in *Life in the Spirit*? In brief, when Paul's teaching on the work of the Holy Spirit is viewed through the lens of McQuilkin's ten activities of the Spirit, we find that nine of those activities are present in his letters. In addition, we find that Paul's letter to the Romans offers a comprehensive overview of the Spirit's work, with chapter 8 presenting a particularly rich discussion of the Spirit's provision as we seek to pursue lives of obedience that bring glory to God.[7]

Paul and the Holy Spirit

In the New Testament, Paul is the undisputed theologian of the Holy Spirit, with 129 references in his letters.[8] Luke-Acts (77) is the closest, with Matthew (10), Mark (6), John's writings (30), and the General Letters (14) lagging far behind. Not surprisingly, references to the Spirit in Paul's letters are not distributed evenly. A profile of Paul's uses of πνεῦμα, *pneuma* and its cognates shows that 146 of the 171 occurrences are in Romans, First and Second Corinthians, Galatians and Ephesians.

Romans (37)	Galatians (19)	Colossians and Philemon (5)
1 Corinthians (56)	Ephesians (17)	1 & 2 Thessalonians (8)
2 Corinthians (17)	Philippians (5)	1 & 2 Timothy and Titus (7)

When references to the human spirit[9] and to other spirits[10] are removed, the resulting distribution gives Romans and First Corinthians even greater prominence:

Romans (34)	Galatians (17)	Colossians and Philemon (2)
1 Corinthians (32)	Ephesians (12)	1 & 2 Thessalonians (5)
2 Corinthians (11)	Philippians (3)	1 & 2 Timothy and Titus (5)

Further, within First Corinthians, half of the occurrences are in chapters 12 to 14, and eleven focus on spiritual gifts:

Chapters	Holy Spirit	Human Spirit	Other
1-11	(15)	(6)	(7)
12-14	1(6)	(5)	(1)
15-18	(1)	(1)	(4)

As a result, it appears that Romans, with its thirty-four references to the Holy Spirit, provides fertile ground for exploring how Paul's teaching on the Spirit's work correlates with Mc-Quilkin's ten activities of the Spirit. Before looking at Romans in detail, however, it will be helpful to survey Paul's other twelve letters using the same grid.

The Spirit in First and Second Corinthians

Of the combined forty-three references to the Spirit in First and Second Corinthians, thirty-five may be grouped under four of McQuilkin's activities: revealing, redeeming, indwelling and gifting. The other eight occurrences relate to filling (see 1 Cor. 12:3, two occurrences), sending (see 1 Cor. 2:4 and 2 Cor. 6:6), transforming (2 Cor. 3:17–18, three occurrences)[11] and glorifying (see 2 Cor. 3:8).

All twelve references to the Spirit's revealing work occur in First Corinthians, with ten concentrated in 2:1–3:1.[12] God reveals the mysteries of what He has freely given to us through the Spirit (see 2:10, 12) because the Spirit searches and comprehends the thoughts of God (see 2:10, 11). The Spirit teaches spiritual things to spiritual people (see 2:13–15, four occurrences; 3:1), things the natural person is unable to understand (see 2:15). Paul is therefore able to claim the Spirit's authority for his own teaching (see 7:40; 14:37).

References to redeeming (3) and indwelling (9) are less concentrated. The Spirit justifies (see 6:11) and gives life (see 1 Cor. 15:45; 2 Cor. 3:6). Indwelling is described as the Spirit being written on believers' hearts (see 2 Cor. 3:2) and being in believers (see 1 Cor. 3:16; 6:19). As a result, believers have the guarantee of the Spirit (see 2 Cor. 1:22; 5:5), are baptized into the body of Christ (see 1 Cor. 12:13, two occurrences) and enjoy the fellowship produced by the Spirit (see 2 Cor. 13:14).

All eleven references to the Spirit's work of gifting occur in First Corinthians 12 and 14. In chapter 12, the focus is on spiritual gifts (see 12:1), particularly the fact that the Spirit gives different gifts (see 12:4; 12:8–9, three times) as He wills (see 12:11) for the common good of the church (see 12:7). Believers, then, should pursue spiritual gifts (see 14:1) because those gifts make it possible both to speak and understand the mysteries of God (see 1 Cor. 14:2) and to edify the church (see 14:12).

The Spirit in Galatians and Ephesians

After Romans and First and Second Corinthians, Galatians and Ephesians have the most extensive teaching on the Spirit with seventeen and twelve occurrences, respectively. Of those twenty-nine occurrences, Galatians 6:8 (glorifying) is the only verse that is outwardly focused. The remaining verses highlight the Spirit's inwardly focused activities.

As part of His revealing work, the Spirit made known to the New Testament apostles and prophets the mystery of the Gentiles' inclusion among God's people (see Eph. 3:5) and revealed God's special plans for believers (see 1:17–19). Three other verses touch on the Spirit's overcoming work of helping us wait patiently for our hope of righteousness (see Gal. 5:5), using God's Word as a sword in times of spiritual warfare (see Eph. 6:17) and praying for us (see 6:18; Rom. 8:26–27).[13]

Paul most frequently mentions the Spirit's work of redeeming and indwelling—often in ways that make it difficult to distinguish between the two. Paul describes the Spirit's redeeming work in us as being "born according to the Spirit" (Gal. 4:29) and "having begun by the Spirit" (3:3). It is by "hearing with faith" that a person receives the Spirit (3:2; see 3:14) whom God sends into our hearts (see 4:6; 3:5). The Spirit then seals us (see Eph. 1:13) and indwells us (see 4:30). As a result, we are incorporated into the body of Christ (see 4:3–6; 1 Cor. 12:13) where we all have access to the Father (see Eph. 2:18) and are built into a dwelling for God (see 2:22).

The Spirit's work of filling receives the fullest treatment, a focus on the character and actions He produces. Ephesians 3:6

and Galatians 6:1 each touch on the topic briefly. In its immediate context, Paul's prayer that his readers would be "strengthened with power through his Spirit in your inner being" (Eph. 3:16), may be seen as closely connected with the Spirit's filling.[14] Similarly, "you who are spiritual" (Gal. 6:1) suggests the recognizable result of the Spirit's filling in the individual's life.

Ephesians 5:15–21, of course, is the immediate context for the explicit command to "be filled with the Spirit" (5:18) and provides a more extensive discussion.[15] Three aspects of this command are worth noting. First, the filling is expected of all (plural), involves customary/habitual action (present tense), is accomplished by another (passive voice), and has the Spirit as its agent. Second, the contrast between being filled with the Spirit and being drunk with wine (see 5:18) highlights the idea of being under the influence of or being controlled by the Spirit. Third, the marks of being filled are: corporate edification (see 5:19), worship (see 5:19), thanksgiving (see 5:20) and mutual submission (see 5:21; developed in more detail in 5:22–6:9).

Galatians 5:16–26 is closely related, and McQuilkin includes it in his chapter on "What 'Full' Looks Like."[16] The repeated contrast in this paragraph between the flesh and the Spirit makes it clear that at any given time one or the other controls the believer.[17] Being under the Spirit's control means that person walks by the Spirit (see 5:16, 25; Rom. 8:12–13), is led by the Spirit (see 5:18; Rom. 8:14–15) and exhibits the fruit of the Spirit (see 5:22–23).[18]

The Spirit in Philippians through Philemon

The fifteen references to the Spirit in Philippians through Philemon are scattered across the eight letters and reflect the pattern seen elsewhere. Only one of McQuilkin's outwardly focused activities is mentioned, if First Timothy 3:16 ("was justified/vindicated in/by the Spirit") is understood as the Spirit's glorifying activity.[19] The inwardly focused activities are central, although creating is again omitted.

Paul mentions the Spirit's revealing work in Colossians 1:9 ("filled with . . . all spiritual wisdom and understanding") and First Timothy 4:1 ("the Spirit expressly says") as well as His redeeming work in First Thessalonians 1:5 ("our gospel came to you . . . in power and in the Holy Spirit") and Titus 3:5 ("he saved us . . . by the washing of regeneration and renewal of the Holy Spirit"). Second Thessalonians 2:13 explicitly notes the Spirit's transforming work in sanctification ("through sanctification by the Spirit"), and Philippians 1:19 highlights His overcoming work in Paul's life ("the help of the Spirit").[20]

The Spirit's indwelling (three times) and filling (five times) are most prominent in these letters. God gives the Spirit to believers (see 1 Thess. 4:8), whom He indwells (see 2 Tim. 1:14), and who are warned not to quench His work (see 1 Thess. 5:19). The Spirit's filling is evident in the fruit He produces: love (see Col. 1:8; 2 Tim. 1:7), joy (see 1 Thess. 1:6); sound judgment (see 2 Tim. 1:7),[21] fellowship with other believers (see Phil. 2:4) and worship (see Phil. 3:3).[22]

The Spirit in Romans

The Greek word πνεῦμα, *pneuma* and its cognates occur thirty-seven times in Romans, but only three of them refer to the human spirit (see Rom. 1:9; 8:16; 11:8). The remaining thirty-four refer to the Holy Spirit, with the heaviest concentration in Romans 8.

Chapters 1-7	(6)
Chapter 8	(20)
Chapters 9-16	(8)

Together, these thirty-four references cover nine of Mc-Quilkin's ten activities and provide a comprehensive overview of the Spirit's work.[23] Because of the heavy concentration of occurrences in Romans 8, that chapter will be examined separately.

Romans 1–7

The six references to the Spirit in Romans 1–7 highlight a range of activities. Paul's statement that Jesus "was declared to be the Son of God in power according to the Spirit of holiness by his resurrection from the dead" (1:4) is most naturally understood as referring to the Holy Spirit (see Ps. 51:13), specifically His glorifying work. Seven verses later, Paul writes that his desire in visiting Rome is to "impart . . . some spiritual gift" (Rom. 1:11), which previews the topic of gifting he discusses later in the letter (see 12:3–8). At the end of chapter 2, Paul concludes his discussion with the statement that true circumcision is "of the heart, by the Spirit" (2:29) and so identifies the Spirit as the agent who performs circumcision as part of His redeeming work.

Indwelling is clearly in mind when Paul refers to the Spirit as the One "who has been given to us" (5:5), which corresponds to the idea of the Spirit as a pledge of final redemption (see 8:23; 2 Cor. 1:22; 5:5; Eph. 1:13–14; Gal. 3:4; 1 Thess. 4:8). The statement in Romans 7:6 that "we serve in the new way of the Spirit and not in the old way of the written code" is best understood as parallel to the call to "walk by the Spirit" (Gal. 5:16) and also the result of His indwelling work.[24] Finally, when Paul writes that "the law is spiritual, but I am of flesh, sold under sin" (Rom. 7:14), he highlights the Spirit's revealing work as the authoritative source behind the law and the One whose help is essential to understand the law properly.[25]

Romans 9–16

The eight references to the Spirit in chapters 9–16 are somewhat more concentrated, with five occurring in chapter 15. The activities of the Spirit differ from those in chapters 1–7. When Paul writes, "I am speaking the truth in Christ—I am not lying; my conscience bears me witness in the Holy Spirit" (9:1), he describes the Spirit's testifying work. Although not one of McQuilkin's ten activities, this work is closely related to indwelling by the Spirit who has been given to us (see 5:5; 8:15–17).

The command to "be enthusiastic in spirit" (12:11, NET) is best understood as a reference to the Holy Spirit because the parallel command that follows ("serve the Lord") clearly involves another member of the Trinity.[26] That understanding suggests an outward expression of the Spirit's filling. The results of the Spirit's filling are also seen in 14:17 ("For the kingdom of God is not a matter of eating and drinking but of righteousness and peace and joy in the Holy Spirit"), 15:13 ("May the God of hope fill you with all joy and peace in believing, so that by the power of the Holy Spirit you may abound in hope") and 15:30 ("the love of the Spirit").[27]

The missionary context of 15:14–21 highlights the Spirit's sending work where Paul refers to the Gentiles who have come to Christ through his ministry as "sanctified by the Holy Spirit" (15:16) and where he writes that "the power of the Spirit" (15:19) has enabled him to preach the gospel from Jerusalem to Illyricum. The latter verse also highlights the Spirit as the One who not only gives spiritual gifts (gifting) but also makes them effective.[28] Finally, when Paul mentions the "spiritual things" for which the Gentiles are indebted to the saints in Jerusalem (see 15:27), he underscores the totality of the blessings the Spirit has bestowed on followers of Christ.

Romans 8 in the Context of Pauline Theology

Paul's letters are occasional documents and are not intended as textbooks on systematic theology. Romans, however, is the fullest exposition of Paul's gospel and brings together many of the major contours of his theology. Prominent among those contours are the contrasting spheres of existence in which human beings live and the role Jesus Christ plays in transferring us from one sphere to the other (see Col. 1:13).[29] These elements are clearly seen in Romans 5–8.

For Paul, every human being is either "in Adam" or "in Christ" (1 Cor. 15:21–22). Both Adam and Christ were free to choose whether they would obey God's commandments, and Paul makes clear the impact of their choices in Romans 5:12–21. Adam's act of disobedience led to a verdict of condemnation and a sinner status, with the ultimate result of sin reigning in death. In contrast, Christ's act of obedience led to a verdict of acquittal and a righteous status, with the ultimate result of grace reigning in life.

Romans 7 portrays life in Adam as characterized by the sinfulness of sin and the futility of the flesh. Sin takes advantage of the law to stimulate sinful thoughts and actions (see 7:8–9) and to deceive and produce death (see 7:10–11). Because we are totally unable to do good (see 7:14, 18), any desire to do good is doomed to failure (see 7:15, 19). As a result, we cry out "Wretched man that I am!" (7:24) and are desperate for deliverance.

God provides the way of escape from the prison of being in Adam when we are identified with Christ in His crucifixion (see 6:5–7), burial (see 6:3–4) and resurrection (see 6:8–10). Through faith in Christ we move from being dead to God and alive to sin to being dead to sin and alive to God (see 6:1–14), and we move from being free from righteousness and enslaved to sin to being free from sin and enslaved to righteousness (see 6:15–23).

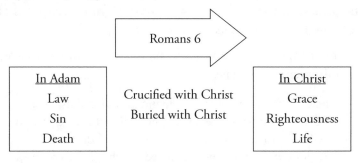

Throughout his presentation, Paul uses contrasting pairs: law vs. grace (see Rom. 6:14), sin vs. righteousness (see 6:20), death vs. life (see 6:23). The final contrast is flesh vs. Spirit (see 7:5–6). If Romans 7 portrays life in Adam as characterized by the futility of the flesh, Romans 8 portrays life in Christ as characterized by the victory of the Spirit. The "law of the Spirit of life" sets us free from the "law of sin and death" (8:1–2). As a result, we cry out "Abba! Father!" (8:15). Romans 8 and its discussion of the Spirit's work in the life of the believer, therefore, stands as a central Pauline text for understanding life in the Spirit.

The Spirit in Romans 8

Harold Burchett reminds us, "Always bear in mind that God deals with us according to grace, not law. Thus, his provisions enable us to fulfill our obligations. God first informs us, 'I have done thus and so for you'; then follows the command, 'You can and must therefore do thus and so.'"[30] As Romans 8 shows us, the Holy Spirit is God's provision *par excellence*. Paul sets out eight ways the Spirit provides resources that we need to pursue a walk of obedience that brings glory to God. Each of these provisions brings with it an implicit responsibility for us to fulfill. The first thirty verses divide nicely into eight units, and the chapter concludes with the assurance that "overwhelming victory is ours through Christ, who loved us" (Rom. 8:37, NLT).

1) Romans 8:1–4: The Spirit sets us free to fulfill the righteous requirement of the law.

> There is therefore now no condemnation for those who are in Christ Jesus. For the law of the Spirit of life has set you free in Christ Jesus from the law of sin and death. For God has done what the law, weakened by the flesh, could not do. By sending his own Son in the likeness of sinful flesh and for sin, he condemned sin in the flesh, in order that the righteous requirement of the law might be fulfilled in us, who walk not according to the flesh but according to the Spirit.

Paul states his thesis (see 8:1) and then sets out the reasons behind (see 8:2–17) and implications of (see 8:18–30) that thesis. The first reason there is no condemnation for those who are in Christ Jesus (see 8:33–34) resides in the Spirit's redeeming work (see 8:2),[31] which in turn rests on the Son's sacrifice as a sin offering (see 8:3). God's judicial act of condemning sin in Christ's flesh also leads to the Spirit's transforming work of enabling us to fulfill the righteous requirement of the law (see 8:4). In order to experience the latter provision, it is our responsibility to walk "according to the Spirit" by placing ourselves under His control and adopting His values.[32]

2) Romans 8:5–8: The Spirit guides our thinking toward life
and peace.

> For those who live according to the flesh set their minds
> on the things of the flesh, but those who live according to
> the Spirit set their minds on the things of the Spirit. For
> to set the mind on the flesh is death, but to set the mind
> on the Spirit is life and peace. For the mind that is set on
> the flesh is hostile to God, for it does not submit to God's
> law; indeed, it cannot. Those who are in the flesh cannot
> please God.

The second reason there is no condemnation for those who
are in Christ Jesus resides in the Spirit's transforming work as it
is reflected in the way we think (see Rom. 8:5–6). Those who are
in Adam are characterized by the mind-set of the flesh (see 8:5),
which guides their thinking toward death (see 8:6). That mind-
set is characterized by hostility toward God, rebellion against
God and an inability to please God (see 8:7–8). In contrast,
those who are in Christ are characterized by a mind-set that focuses on "the affairs of the Spirit"[33] and guides our thinking toward life and peace. As those who are now in the realm of the
Spirit, our responsibility is to adopt the orientation and attitude
of the Spirit.[34]

3) Romans 8:9–11: The Spirit indwells us and gives us life.

> You, however, are not in the flesh but in the Spirit, if in fact
> the Spirit of God dwells in you. Anyone who does not have
> the Spirit of Christ does not belong to him. But if Christ
> is in you, although the body is dead because of sin, the
> Spirit is life because of righteousness. If the Spirit of him
> who raised Jesus from the dead dwells in you, he who raised
> Christ Jesus from the dead will also give life to your mortal
> bodies through his Spirit who dwells in you.

The third reason there is no condemnation for those who are in Christ Jesus resides in the Spirit's indwelling work. The New Jerusalem Bible captures the idea as "the Spirit of God has made a home in you" (see Rom. 8:9). The Spirit's indwelling produces two results: because of Christ's imputed righteousness, the Spirit gives life to our spirits (see Rom. 8:10),[35] and because the Spirit dwells in us, God will give life to our bodies at the final resurrection (see 8:11; Eph. 1:13–14).[36] As those who are indwelt by the Spirit, our responsibility is to learn to live out the righteousness that is ours.

4) Romans 8:12–13: The Spirit enables us to put to death the deeds of the body.

> So then, brothers, we are debtors, not to the flesh, to live according to the flesh. For if you live according to the flesh you will die, but if by the Spirit you put to death the deeds of the body, you will live.

In 8:12, Paul moves to the implications of his thesis that there is no condemnation for those who are in Christ Jesus.[37] The first relates to the Spirit's overcoming work. The transfer from being in Adam to being in Christ is instantaneous and removes our obligation to live according to the flesh (see 8:12). Learning how to live in Christ, however, is a process that requires us to take advantage of the Spirit's provision. In order for us to overcome old patterns of thought and behavior, we must rely on the agency of the Spirit (see 8:13). As we submit to the Spirit, He makes it possible for us to put to death the practices of the body and establishes in us new patterns of thought and behavior that bring glory to God.[38]

5) Romans 8:14–15: The Spirit leads us.

> For all who are led by the Spirit of God are sons of God. For you did not receive the spirit of slavery to fall back into fear, but you have received the Spirit of adoption as sons, by whom we cry, "Abba! Father!"

The second implication of the freedom from condemnation that Christ brings relates to the Spirit's transforming work. Specifically, the Spirit's leading confirms our status as God's children (see Rom. 8:14). "Leading" is distinct from "guidance" and focuses on being obedient to the inner promptings of the Spirit as He helps us identify and implement the most effective means of living as God's sons and daughters.[39] As we respond to the Spirit's leading we are transformed "from one degree of glory to another" (2 Cor. 3:18).

6) Romans 8:16–17: The Spirit assures us that we are God's children.

> The Spirit himself bears witness with our spirit that we are children of God, and if children, then heirs—heirs of God and fellow heirs with Christ, provided we suffer with him in order that we may also be glorified with him.

The third implication relates to the Spirit's testifying work.[40] The Father predestines us to adoption (see Eph. 1:5), and the Father's act of adoption rests on Christ's completed work (see Gal. 4:4–5). The Spirit's role is to confirm our adoption and make us aware of it. As the Spirit bears witness with our spirit, He assures us of our acceptance by God (see Rom. 8:16).[41] That assurance gives us confidence to begin exercising our privileges as heirs of God and fellow heirs with Christ. Along with our privileges as co-heirs with Christ, we also share in His sufferings (see Col. 1:24). Our responsibility, therefore, is to share in the sufferings that lead to glory (see Rom. 8:17).

7) Romans 8:18–25: The Spirit guarantees our final redemption.

> For I consider that the sufferings of this present time are not worth comparing with the glory that is to be revealed to us. For the creation waits with eager longing for the revealing of the sons of God. For the creation was subjected to futility, not willingly, but because of him who subjected it, in hope that the creation itself will be set free from its bondage to corruption and obtain the freedom of the glory of the children of God. For we know that the whole creation has been groaning together in the pains of childbirth until now. And not only the creation, but we ourselves, who have the firstfruits of the Spirit, groan inwardly as we wait eagerly for adoption as sons, the redemption of our bodies. For in this hope we were saved. Now hope that is seen is not hope. For who hopes for what he sees? But if we hope for what we do not see, we wait for it with patience.

The concept of present suffering leading to future glory (see Rom. 8:17) prompts Paul to set our individual sufferings in the context of the cosmic suffering of creation (see 8:19–22). Like creation, we groan while we wait eagerly for the unseen hope of our resurrection bodies (see 8:24–25). In parallel with other New Testament uses of "firstfruits" (e.g., James 1:18; Rev. 14:4), the indwelling Spirit serves as a promise that God will follow through on His promise to consummate our adoption as His children by giving us glorified bodies (see Rom. 8:23; Eph. 1:13–14).[42] Our responsibility is to hope and wait expectantly for what we do not yet see.

8) Romans 8:26–30: The Spirit intercedes for us with the Father.

> Likewise the Spirit helps us in our weakness. For we do not know what to pray for as we ought, but the Spirit himself intercedes for us with groanings too deep for words. And he

who searches hearts knows what is the mind of the Spirit, because the Spirit intercedes for the saints according to the will of God. And we know that for those who love God all things work together for good, for those who are called according to his purpose. For those whom he foreknew he also predestined to be conformed to the image of his Son, in order that he might be the firstborn among many brothers. And those whom he predestined he also called, and those whom he called he also justified, and those whom he justified he also glorified.

In the same way that the Spirit gives us hope of future glory, the Spirit also gives us help for effective prayer. The Spirit comes to our aid when we pray (see Rom. 8:26) and intercedes for us with "unspoken groanings" (8:26) that are "according to the will of God" (8:27). Because of the Spirit's overcoming work in prayer, we can be confident that everything happens for our good (see 8:28). Our responsibility is to trust in the promise that God's sovereign working always accomplishes His purposes (see 8:29–30).

Summary

Paul's discussion of life in the Spirit in Romans 8 highlights five of McQuilkin's suggested ten activities of the Spirit: redeeming (see 8:1–4), indwelling (see 8:9–11), transforming—both in guiding our thinking (see 8:5–8) and leading us (see 8:14–15), overcoming—both in putting to death the deeds of the body (see 8:12–13) and interceding for us (see 8:26–30), and glorifying (see 8:18–25). To those five activities, Paul adds a sixth: testifying (see 8:16–17). As a blueprint for Christian living, Romans 8 also sets out eight ways the Spirit provides resources we need as we seek to pursue lives of obedience that bring glory to God.

Romans 8	The Spirit's Provision	Our Responsibility
8:1-4	The Spirit sets us free and enables us to fulfill the righteous requirement of the law.	We must live under the control of and according to the values of the Spirit.
8:5-8	The Spirit guides our thinking toward life and peace.	We must adopt the orientation and attitude of the Spirit.
8:9-11	The Spirit indwells us and gives us life.	We must learn to live out the righteousness that is ours in Christ.
8:12-13	The Spirit enables us to put to death the deeds of the body.	We must allow the Spirit to establish in us new patterns of thought and behavior.
8:14-15	The Spirit leads us.	We must be obedient to the Spirit's promptings on how to live as God's children.
8:16-17	The Spirit assures us that we are God's children.	We must share in the sufferings that lead to glory with Christ.
8:18-25	The Spirit guarantees our final redemption.	We must hope and wait expectantly for what we do not yet see.
8:26-30	The Spirit intercedes for us with the Father.	We must trust that God's sovereign working always accomplishes His purposes.

Each of those provisions carries with it a responsibility for us to fulfill. The following table summarizes those provisions and responsibilities.

Conclusion

In examining the question of how Paul's teaching on the work of the Holy Spirit correlates with McQuilkin's list of ten suggested activities, we have found that nine of those activities are present in Paul's letters. In addition, we have found that Paul's letter to the Romans offers a comprehensive overview of the Spirit's work, with chapter 8 presenting a particularly rich discussion of the Spirit's provision as we seek to pursue lives of obedience that bring glory to God. McQuilkin's taxonomy, therefore, is validated as a helpful lens through which to view the Spirit's work, and Paul's reputation as the New Testament theologian of the Spirit has been confirmed. Hopefully, this study reinforces the exegetical foundation on which McQuilkin's work is built, supports his desire to correct the general evangelical lack of teaching on the Spirit, and contributes to his practical objective of helping us experience the impact of the Spirit's work in our lives.

Part IV

World Missions

Chapter 7

Recalibrating Missionary-Sending Agencies for the Twenty-First Century

Steve Richardson

J Robertson McQuilkin's redeployment to the leadership of Columbia Bible College (now Columbia International University), after twelve years of church-planting ministry in Japan, proved to be a timely provision not only for the college but also for the broader North American mission community. Robertson and Muriel were convinced in prayer that their "demotion" from frontline ministry would serve in the long run to help unleash growing numbers of new workers for Japan and to the "regions beyond." It is no surprise that under McQuilkin's oversight CIU continued to build strong momentum as a leading incubator for cross-cultural workers and as a standard-bearer for the global mission of the church.

Robertson was not one to be satisfied with an indirect or tangential contribution to world evangelization. He applied himself rigorously to the art of institutional leadership, but also to reflecting, teaching, speaking, writing and mentoring young leaders for the specific purpose of strengthening the overall global mission effort. His passions for Scripture, prayer, victorious Christian living, world evangelization and evangelical collaboration seemed to be set like many diamonds in the ring of God's unfolding, global, redemptive plan. It was when engaging topics related to world missions that McQuilkin often appeared to be the most energized and animated. He had a profound awareness and foresight with regard to the theological and missiological issues most likely to influence the long-term trajectory and health of the global missionary enterprise.

Columbia's commitment to a set of clear core values, its emphasis on theologically integrating life and ministry, and the blending of these elements with a compelling focus on the Great Commission greatly attracted and impacted me as a student in the early 1980s. The educational experience seemed skillfully tailored to help new laborers establish an authentic walk with God and an enduring, disciplined foundation for fruitful service. The intellectually rigorous yet practically grounded ethos of the college was certainly a reflection of the school's collective leadership and institutional history—but it was more than that. I sensed that, to a significant degree, the global heartbeat that in many ways seemed to distinguish Columbia from many similar institutions was a reflection of Robertson McQuilkin himself and of God's unshakable missionary calling on his life. Robertson's personal interest and involvement in the prayer days, the mission chapels, the Student Missionary Fellowship, various national and international mission forums and in the lives of individual students who were preparing for a lifetime of cross-cultural engagement all testified to McQuilkin's determination that the name of Christ be made known among the nations.

It was against this backdrop, arguably during some of the most demanding seasons of McQuilkin's life, that he gave quiet encouragement and counsel to one particular emerging mission initiative. This embryonic new mission agency, encouraged along by McQuilkin's perceptive questions and persistent prayers, would someday help to recast the way that many next-generation missionaries would connect to the unfinished task. Eventually called Pioneers, this new initiative attracted a small but growing number of Columbia students. In time, it emulated many of the attributes and values championed by Columbia International University and by McQuilkin himself.

New Wineskins: A Case Study

Pioneers was launched in 1979 when God impressed on forty-four-year-old Korean War veteran and *Wall Street Journal* executive Ted Fletcher the needs of entire nations and cultures awaiting the gospel. Ted had found Christ in Korea during evangelist Billy Graham's brief visit to the front lines. Though enjoying a successful career in sales, Ted had a growing desire, rooted in Scripture, to become more directly involved in world missions. He and his wife, Peggy, applied for service with a number of mission boards. In each case the response was polite but firm—"too many children," "insufficient theological education," "too old."

Indeed, despite all its remarkable strengths and achievements, the mission era of the 1970s and 1980s was not particularly favorable to the formation of new agencies. When Ted finally decided to start his own small ministry with the blessing and help of their local church, he was greeted with a fresh wave of skepticism. "You've never been a missionary!" "Don't we have enough agencies?" "Shouldn't you at least change the name to 'Africa Evangelical Outreach' rather than 'World Evangelical Outreach' (Pioneers' original name)?"

"No, I believe God has given us a vision for the whole world," Ted replied, often reminding himself of the Father's promise to His Son in Psalm 2:8: "Ask of Me, and I will give You the nations for Your inheritance, and the ends of the earth for Your possession" (NKJV). Ted had a growing conviction that there ought to be ways for God's people to more easily connect with the global harvest.

The new agency, rebranded as Pioneers in 1984, began to grow. Columbia Bible College and Graduate School proved to be a source of particular encouragement. A faculty member joined the board; McQuilkin, among others, endorsed the vision; and more than a few visionary young leaders expressed desire to join this untested entity.

Over the next thirty-five years, Pioneers flourished into an international movement with twenty national offices, recruiting and fielding church-planting teams in more than one hundred countries. Since 2000, the US base, now representing only a portion of Pioneers, has continued its steady growth trajectory, tripling its membership from 500 to more than 1,600 long-term workers. The international roll now exceeds 3,000.

I was personally drawn to this embryonic vision in 1981, along with a few other Columbia students who were preparing for missionary service at the time. In the years since, I have watched Pioneers mature into a significant global movement. Its growth occurred against the backdrop of numerous challenges:

- The role and context of mission agencies had begun to shift dramatically.

- The need for Western missionaries was being questioned.

- Church, donor and fiduciary expectations were rising.

- The founder had never himself been a missionary.

- Many agencies were experiencing little or no growth.

- A younger generation of workers was less likely to think in terms of a long-term commitment, portending higher attrition rates.

- Most Pioneers workers were destined for hostile places where conventional mission activity was not an option.

- Threats to missionaries' physical safety were increasing.

- The challenges of screening, training and deploying missionaries were mounting.

The Pioneers story may provide some helpful guideposts for sending agencies that want to remain relevant in coming decades. What were the main factors that generated unusual momentum? What insights can benefit our mission endeavors in the rapidly changing global environment of the twenty-first century?

A Few Caveats

Reflecting on the early expansion of Pioneers, Ted Fletcher (who died in 2003) often observed that "there is a sovereignty" in such things. God knows and defies our tendency to favor formulas over faith. There is risk in prescribing specific models or offering simplistic answers to sweeping questions. Each agency is a unique response—involving a unique culture, group of people and time period—to a specific set of opportunities and challenges.

Enduring growth also requires a synergistic confluence of positive influences with significant and sustained interplay between key factors. No individual measure taken in isolation will assure a healthy organization, much less reverse a process of decline. Furthermore, sustained agency growth, while desirable in many cases, may not be the ideal scenario for every agency. In some cases, it may be better for an agency to serve its purpose for a season before gifting its remaining resources in a timely fashion to a new and vital movement that God has raised up.

Key Growth Factors

I believe we can identify five overarching factors that have contributed significantly to Pioneers' growth, resilience and fruitfulness during the past thirty-five years. These broad categories are: (1) effective mobilization, (2) clear and compelling values, (3) strong sense of community, (4) decentralized structure and (5) constant theological reflection.

Factor 1—Effective Mobilization in the Sending Culture

Pioneers was born in response to a missiological breakthrough in the latter half of the twentieth century. Wycliffe Bible Translators founder, Cameron Townsend, and visionary missiologist Ralph Winter had effectively reframed the unfinished task and the church's understanding of the Great Commission in terms of unreached ethnolinguistic people groups. Pioneers' mandate to plant churches among unreached people groups was clear from the beginning. The organization deliberately and strategically positioned itself at the center of a major stream of God's activity in missions over the past thirty years, riding the wave of renewed interest in missions in general and unreached peoples in particular. The presence and timing of a mission wave, however, does not fully account for the remarkable growth of Pioneers. Other agencies, including several agencies that were launched in the same era, rode the same wave without commensurate growth.

The church's refocused sense of mission occurred in tandem with a powerful cultural wave—the accelerating reorientation of the West toward a postmodern worldview. Recognizing the inherent challenges as well as opportunities, Pioneers set out to practice good missiology by contextualizing its mission and message to a postmodern missionary generation. Leadership is highly relational and nonhierarchical, for example. Loyalty is rooted not primarily in the organization but in a powerful identification with the vision for which the organization exists, the ways in which the organization pursues that vision and the sense of community experienced along the way. Ministry opportunities are customized. Transparency, authenticity and entrepreneurialism are valued. Believers are invited to merge their individual stories into the broader metanarrative of God's unfolding redemptive plan. The organization's vision and methodology are broad enough to accommodate the personal development and aspirations of a great diversity of players, within a flexible and empowering ministry environment.

Relating effectively to its "customers" (the least reached, sending churches, missionaries and new candidates) has always been a passion for Pioneers. In its early years, Pioneers benefited from a "fortuitous naiveté." Because Ted Fletcher had not been a missionary himself, his thinking was fresh. He asked straightforward questions about the goals and the processes of mission agencies. He surrounded himself with younger men and women who were passionate about reinventing missions for their generation. He took significant risks by entrusting leadership responsibility to these youthful leaders.

Mobilization came naturally to Ted Fletcher. He was trained and gifted in marketing and had helped to greatly expand the circulation of the *Wall Street Journal*. He did it primarily through new strategies in telephone marketing. In starting Pioneers, he discovered yet another opportunity to apply his love for marketing and communication—the recruitment of missionaries. His approach was highly relational. Each prospect quickly felt that he or she was a personal friend. Communication was prompt and personal. Key questions centered on what the Holy Spirit was doing in the individual's life. Follow-through was immediate.

Subsequent leaders and mobilizers modeled a similar concern and care for the individual, asking questions such as: "What has been your journey with the Lord?" "What are you and your sending church dreaming about as it relates to the unreached, and how might that contribute to a church-planting movement?" "Have you considered doing this in the context of a team?" Such questions clarified the vision that God had already given applicants and their sending churches. Pioneers leaders developed a default position of embracing and empowering individuals toward strategic fruitfulness in God's service. There was a confidence that, given the opportunity, most individuals would grow and mature on the job by God's grace.

Factor 2—Clear and Compelling Organizational Values

As with CIU's five core values and McQuilkin's "Five Smooth Stones," Pioneers early on discovered the power of a clear and compelling set of guiding concepts. When asked why they are drawn to Pioneers, new candidates most frequently cite two factors—the organization's core values and relationships with Pioneers missionaries they know and trust. One key mobilizer, when asked the main reason Pioneers continues to grow, responded without hesitation: "Values, values, values!"

To Pioneers members, the values are much more than a set of propositional statements in a document or on a website. The values are known and embraced. Any missionary in Pioneers can speak intelligently about them and their implications for ministry. They are the focus of leadership development. Much time is spent unpacking the core values and wrestling with inherent tensions. When new initiatives and policies are discussed, it is always against the backdrop of the core values.

Pioneers focuses on eight organizational core values. Succinctly stated, they are:

Passion for God—The first and most important core value underscores the spiritual foundations of the movement, highlighting the primacy and authority of God's Word, the role of the Holy Spirit, faith and prayer.

Unreached Peoples—What defines where we go and where we focus our energy? While specific definitions may vary, Pioneers focuses on people groups with the least opportunity to hear and understand the gospel.

Church-Planting Movements—What do we want to see happen among these groups? What goal will shape our strategies? Our desire is to see movements of healthy, multiplying churches.

Ethos of Grace—Understanding that each person bears the image of God, we endeavor to cultivate an atmosphere of mutual acceptance and respect, encouraging each member to grow in grace, and to reach his or her full potential in Christ.

The Local Church—On both the sending and receiving ends of the missionary spectrum, wherever possible, Pioneers seeks to serve and partner with committed local churches.

Team-Centered—Teams that are both task- and member-focused are the core functional unit of Pioneers.

Innovation and Flexibility—There is room for tremendous creativity in the specific strategies and approaches used to accomplish the task.

Participatory Servant Leadership—What will characterize the way in which leaders conduct themselves and make their decisions? Pioneers has a decentralized leadership structure that applies an interactive and principle-driven approach to decision making, rooted in high levels of trust.

No core value stands by itself. The power is in the package and in the extent to which these values bring organizational alignment as they are articulated, embraced and applied throughout the movement. The cumulative effect in Pioneers has been the creation of a common global language and a strong, positive organizational culture.

Factor 3—Authentic Community

While each core value has played an important role in Pioneers' development, the emphasis on teams merits special mention because of its far-reaching impact on the organization's growth and ministry trajectory. Pioneers has benefited from three decades of consistent, thoughtful application of the concept of apostolic teams. While the team concept is no longer a new idea in the mission world, Pioneers was one of the early adopters of this approach. Pioneers reduced many pages of "principles and practices" borrowed in its early days from an established agency—describing field conferences, executive committees and voting procedures (the predominant post-World War II democratic model)—to a one-page outline of how a team would function. This single structural and philosophical choice would prove to be transformational.

Pioneers' application of the team concept in the mission world may be likened to house churches in the church world. Why did the church grow rapidly in China in the latter half of the twentieth century, for example? The multiplication of smaller, low-profile, versatile house churches was an important factor. Why has Pioneers grown? One reason is the consistent, geographically unrestricted multiplication of apostolic teams.

Though widely accepted today, the team concept is not always consistently applied by mission organizations. There are many variations on the theme, involving delicate but important nuances in such areas as accountability, leadership philosophies, decision-making processes and communication protocols. Like a twelve-string guitar, slight variations in these themes produce significant, and sometimes discordant, differences in culture and tone. The way in which Pioneers members relate to each other, show respect, pray for one another, hold each other accountable and conduct themselves in leadership contributes to a strong and attractive organizational culture that goes well beyond a bare-bones concept of team.

Pioneers teams generally feature eight important characteristics reminiscent of the high-impact missionary teams of the first century:

- Teams have a **clear goal**. Most Pioneers teams focus on starting a church movement in a particular unreached ethnic group, though the specifics of each strategy will vary greatly from place to place.

- Teams are **cohesive**. Members are deeply committed not only to the work but to one another. They see the wisdom of experiencing the journey together rather than going it alone.

- Most teams are relatively **small**. A healthy team will often attract more and more workers and eventually multiply, but most Pioneers teams have six to ten members.

- Teams are **versatile**. Being small, committed and specialized, they can navigate more easily around ministry roadblocks. A resourceful team will find ways to share the gospel and plant churches whatever the situation.

- Team membership is **fluid**. Some members will be committed for the duration while others may serve for a season before taking new roles or launching a new work.

- Teams have capable **servant leaders**. Most teams tend to be nonhierarchical, relational and empowering. Effective teams and good leaders go together.

- Teams enjoy significant **autonomy** in the field, within a decentralized accountability framework. This framework includes experienced field leaders, sending churches, nearby teams and local partners. An area leader monitors the overall progress of the team, but the strategy and day-to-day decisions take place at the team level.

- Finally, teams are **diverse**. When people from different backgrounds and with different perspectives—often from different cultures or countries—blend together on a team with a common vision and mutual understanding, tremendous potential is unleashed.

Why is the team concept so important? First, from a mobilization perspective, a postmodern generation longs for authentic community. These smaller communities, when linked and networked with many similar communities (and periodic large-scale gatherings and celebrations), provide an ideal environment for deepening relationship, personal development and spiritual support. From a member care perspective, they help many new workers not only to survive in difficult environments but to thrive. The team becomes the primary locus for reciprocal care and accountability. From a ministry perspective, the team provides a context for multiplicity of perspectives, synergized gifts and longer-term presence. Apostolic teams, when properly understood and implemented, enhance both ministry productivity and individual development.

A global network of teams also is very helpful to the development of a globalized, multicultural movement. At last count, Pioneers had 280 teams in one hundred countries. With a great diversity of teams and ministry microcultures, there is room for various nationalities and personalities to find a place within the broader network, either by starting a new team or by joining an existing team that wants to embrace the joys and challenges of multicultural team life. Teams also are very helpful for the multiplication of partnerships. Most partnerships are initiated at the grassroots level. This makes possible far greater levels of cooperation (on the whole) than a centralized system. Pioneers teams partner with literally thousands of churches and ministries, with very little formal involvement from senior leadership.

In summary, Pioneers has found that the apostolic team can be a powerful vehicle to impact the world and to help carry the gospel to difficult places. The emphasis on biblical love and body life attracts and retains passionate workers. While far from immune to the costs of frontline ministry, Pioneers has experienced the rewards that healthy teams can yield in terms of morale, retention and ministry impact.

Factor 4—A Decentralized Global Structure

Hudson Taylor's China Inland Mission is a leading example of how mission agencies have long wrestled with very real and consequential tensions between office and field and between centralized and decentralized decision-making processes. The tensions are not so much personal—though strained relationships can easily result—as they are philosophical and practical. Who is best positioned to make decisions? What stakeholders need to be included in a particular decision and in what sequence? What authority structure better lends itself to growth and to the characteristics of a movement? Is the leadership prepared for the commensurate risks? Can sending churches be encouraged to communicate their concerns directly with field leadership rather than through the home office?

Pioneers has the feel of a franchised mission network in which dozens of leaders and teams carry out their part of the bigger picture, all within a common motivational, theological, missiological, educational and relational framework. I have described Pioneers as a hybrid between an organization and a movement. We try to ensure as much freedom as we can for field teams to carry on their work without undue burdens or interference. As the apostle James advised his brothers in a different context, "We should not make it difficult for the Gentiles who are turning to God" (Acts 15:19, NIV).

What does this look like in practical terms? First, leadership is decentralized. There is a multiplicity of sending bases, leaders and field entities—including teams, areas and regions. All leaders are on location in the field, relating directly with the people and situations they serve. Base leaders may speak into, but not make, decisions for the field. Field leaders may speak into, but not make, decisions for the sending bases. Each base reports to its own board of directors. All the bases cooperate with one another via a semiformal International Ministry Agreement that outlines the statement of faith, core values, base membership and international leadership structure and protocols. Considerable energy is spent on maintaining high levels of relational trust.

Second, strategy and methodology are decentralized. While field teams have the same overarching goal of facilitating a church planting movement, the methodology they use is largely up to them. What church-planting model do they prefer? Who do they want to partner with? Do they need to set higher or lower support levels? Do they want someone from Egypt or Mongolia to join them? Within the context of appropriate stakeholder dialogue (decisions are not made in a vacuum), these choices—and a thousand more—are made close to the action. Creativity is unleashed, and a richly entrepreneurial environment is developed. Over time, other teams emulate the more successful ministry models.

Ironically, the decentralized and freedom-giving environment in Pioneers, while allowing for a higher risk threshold in localized environments, actually creates a conservative environment for the organization as a whole. No one person or unit can create or implement a plan that "rolls the dice" and causes undue risk for the global movement. This approach also allows each member and each unit within Pioneers to focus on what they do best, increasing efficiency and productivity. Bases, for example, focus primarily on mobilizing workers. Field leaders focus on strategic issues and the training and nurture of the work force. Teams focus on their church-planting task.

One important byproduct of decentralization is the enhanced capacity to globalize organizationally. Because Pioneers International is facilitated but not controlled by individual sending bases, there is greater appeal for other sending countries to become part of the fellowship. A growing number of Pioneers teams are international and multicultural in nature. Another byproduct is the capacity and propensity to open new teams and ministries. Ministries are not geographically bound. New teams and ministries proliferate each year, providing new ministry opportunities and mobilization potential.

This type of highly decentralized global ministry structure requires intentionality in the selection and training of leaders. With 280 teams, Pioneers has become increasingly leadership-rich. Yet all these team leaders—as well as area, regional and base leaders—must be effectively equipped if they are to participate in a cohesive, reproducible global effort and if they are to speak with a common organizational language. Specialized training for multicultural teams has also become a growing need throughout the movement. Since the early 2000s, Pioneers has invested heavily in a formal, customized two-year leadership development process for all of its senior and mid-level management. Each region also complements this leadership training with various levels of basic skills training for team leaders and church planters.

Factor 5—Unending Reflection on the Spiritual Core

The final underlying factor in Pioneers' momentum involves the spiritual and theological "nuclear core" of the movement. This is a foundational and nonnegotiable aspect of the "software" needed for any healthy community of God's people. How does a group discover and sustain a truly dynamic spiritual environment that will animate all the other organizational and relational factors? How do we hear what God is saying as He, the Lord of the Harvest, leads us on mission into the uncharted waters of an increasingly chaotic and unpredictable global environment?

It is perhaps in this area that the impact of McQuilkin's life will be most widely and enduringly felt. A hallmark of his work has been the relentless integration of theology and practice: the irrefutable inspiration of *A Promise Kept*; the heart's cry to live worthy of God's calling in the powerful poem "Let Me Get

Home Before Dark"; the fundamental importance of *Life in the Spirit*; the overarching biblical priorities of the Bible, the church, the Spirit, the mission and the model of the Lord Jesus. This unending pursuit of life and ministry fully subservient to the authority of God's Word is surely the North Star for any disciple, church or ministry community.

My aim here, once again, is not to suggest that Pioneers has stumbled onto a long-buried secret that is unfamiliar to other groups. I simply suggest that, against the backdrop of today's fast-paced managerial mind-set, we sometimes forget or neglect the supernatural dimension of God's work. It doesn't take long for spiritual cholesterol to build up in the organizational bloodstream. A deliberate, reflective, sustained emphasis on biblical body life and theological discipline is a crucial factor in determining the long-term vitality of a mission movement.

Amid the many demands of organizational life and a complex global ministry, Pioneers devotes a significant amount of time to worship and prayer. *Soli Deo* (God alone) is not a program or event but a deliberately cultivated spiritual environment that permeates the movement. A global, virtual team known as *Soli Deo* leads the organization in prioritizing its first and most important core value—passion for God. Heartfelt worship and extended seasons of prayer and biblical reflection are prevalent at team events and leadership gatherings. Spiritual authenticity and reliance on God's Word must be hallmarks of community life.

Pioneers' first core value—passion for God—encapsulates this broader, vital dimension of organizational health: "We want to have faith in God. We want to be passionate about knowing Him, trusting and glorifying Him in everything we do. This will be reflected in our dependence on disciplined prayer and our enthusiastic obedience of His Word. We want to be a group of people who are genuinely led by God." Pioneers' desire is to see beyond their own team and organization to a great and sovereign God worthy to be worshiped and adored by all the nations of the world. From His throne room flows an endless supply of life-giving power, sourced in the Word of God. The organization and our own individual ministries are almost incidental to this perspective-giving larger reality.

This recurring cycle of prayerful theological reflection and celebration has had a profound impact on the history and development of Pioneers. Significant seasons of prayer have preceded major leadership appointments and structural changes. The core values took shape amid weeks of intermittent deliberation and prayer over a period of years. The decision in the mid-90s to globalize as a movement came in a season of concentrated theological reflection, prayer and worship. Worship and the teaching of God's Word are major emphases during annual regional gatherings, training events and periodic larger-scale global leadership gatherings. Abundant prayer for more laborers has played an undeniable role in drawing new workers to the movement.

A regular process of theological reflection also can point the way forward on vital strategic and missiological concerns: What are the theological, not just pragmatic, merits of various church-planting strategies? What is the biblical rationale for the challenging work of building multicultural teams or partnering with the local church? And to what degree do various streams of missiological and contextual thought square with the full counsel of God's Word?

Humble, God-seeking hearts and a constantly renewed posture of seeking to understand and obey God's Word are indispensable foundations for any enduring ministry. As

Moses spent regular time with God in the tent, so should God's servants. Nothing is a higher priority, especially for senior organizational leadership.

Conclusion

Today's rapidly changing global environment provides missionary-sending agencies with an important opportunity to recalibrate their ministry models and to review their assumptions and organizational cultures from a biblical as well as a contextual perspective. Robertson McQuilkin's personal example of integrated and reflective leadership—spanning both the missiological and theological arenas for several decades (How many seminary presidents have spent a decade planting churches cross-culturally? And how many missionaries have delved so deeply into matters of ethics, Christian living and biblical interpretation?)—serves as a compelling model for engaging in this kind of critical, regenerative process.

Pioneers is but one of a host of Christian institutions that have benefited from the influence of McQuilkin's life and ministry. Modeling an unusual level of resilience and relevance during a challenging era for most sending agencies, Pioneers has enjoyed a consistent 5 to 10 perecent annual growth rate since its beginning in 1979. Five overarching priorities within Pioneers appear to have created the conditions for this sustained growth: contextual mobilization in a postmodern environment, clear mission and values; meaningful community expressed primarily through apostolic teams, a flexible and decentralized organizational structure, and a constant renewal of the theological core.

Pioneers may be an effective model for how various missions, particularly missionary-sending agencies, can maintain relevance in coming years. Will Pioneers continue to thrive, or is the organization simply experiencing the rise and fall of a typical organizational life cycle? I suspect the future will remain bright as long as the movement remains:

- *Vision-driven*, rather than history-driven

- *Values-based*, not policy- or personality-based

- *Decentralized*, with an expanding network of teams and "niche ministries"

- "*Amateurized*," with a flexible, positive and open system that attracts spiritual entrepreneurs and tomorrow's leaders

- *Reflective*, often asking as a community, "What is God saying to us through His Word?"

- *Global* and multicultural, serving to unleash the whole church into the whole world

How can various organizations learn from the Pioneers experience and from one another? A process of reflection and discussion on each of the five key areas may serve as a springboard for fruitful discussion. How has each topic been approached in the history, development and present practice of a particular agency? Can steps be taken to further cultivate the spiritual core of their ministry through seasons of openhanded prayer, worship and theological reflection? These periods of waiting on God can carry an organization into uncharted—perhaps even risky— but fruitful ministry territory.

Chapter 8

The Case for Prioritism

Christopher R. Little

O ne of the most important debates, perhaps the most important, among those committed to God's mission is the relationship between word and deed, proclamation and demonstration of the gospel, and world evangelization versus world reparation. At once it goes to the very core of one's mission theology, which directly affects mission practice. In conventional terms, it deals with the difference between prioritism and holism. On this subject, J. Robertson McQuilkin couldn't have been clearer:

> There is a theological reason for giving priority to the evangelistic mandate so far as the mission of the Church toward the world is concerned. It has to do with the character of God as Father (rather than King), with the nature of salvation and eternal destiny, with the purpose of God toward humankind. If all people on earth could prosper and be given a college education, full employment prevailed, all injustice and warfare ceased, and perfect health prevailed, but people remained alienated from God, his father-heart would still be broken. His *first* priority for alienated human

beings is reconciliation to himself. The reason is not hard to find. Continued alienation in time means alienation for eternity. If utopia could be created for time but human beings were lost for eternity, the Father's heart could never be satisfied. So God's first priority is to bring lost sheep into the fold.[1]

McQuilkin subsequently stated, "Without apology, we may love others in many ways: seeking their health, promoting justice, advancing education. But above all, we should love them into eternal life, away from eternal death."[2] In doing so, he acknowledged a secondary role in mission for addressing the temporal, physical needs of humanity, but only relative to the primary one of evangelism.[3]

An Old Debate Still Necessary

McQuilkin's perspective is now the minority view among evangelicals, as a consequence of recent very successful steps toward promoting a more holistic or integral framework for mission, as expressed in the Iguassu Affirmation (1999), the Micah Declaration (2001) and the Cape Town Commitment (2010).[4] For some, the issue is settled, with no need to rehash old ground. Others, like A. Scott Moreau, surmise that "the next generation of evangelical missionaries—and perhaps missiologists—will *assume* holism as the appropriate biblical picture rather than explore the text to discover whether it is" and are "convinced that the question of the scope of the ministry of the church among evangelicals is not fully settled."[5]

In fact, the debate has been going on for a long time. So why not just agree to disagree and move forward? The stakes are too high to overlook, set aside and not contest. These include, first and foremost, the eternal destiny of the unevangelized. Since they are the ones who have the most to lose, their concerns should be front and center. Second, generous Christians in the West, in revealing their priorities, are now giving more to humanitarian causes than to what traditionally has been known as missions. Recent statistics show that evangelicals are donating more than $1.9 billion to relief and development but only $1.3 billion to foreign missions.[6] Third, the way in which such terms as gospel, kingdom and mission are being redefined is unprecedented and calls for redress. Fourth, those who think the matter is settled are premature in their estimation. In reality, the tenets undergirding holism have yet to be proven biblically. Last, given the largely unchallenged shifts transpiring in mission today, it is essential to equip the church, both locally and globally, to reflect, communicate and act in a more missiologically informed manner.

Contrasting Prioritism and Holism

The most classic statement on prioritism in print comes from Donald McGavran:

> A multitude of excellent enterprises lie around us. So great is the number and so urgent the calls, that Christians can easily lose their way among them, seeing them all equally as mission. But in doing the good, they can fail of the best. In winning the preliminaries, they can lose the main game. They can be treating a troublesome itch, while the patient dies of cholera. The question of priorities cannot be avoided. . . .
>
> Among other desires of God-in-Christ, He beyond question wills that persons be found—that is, be reconciled to Himself. Most cordially admitting that God has other purposes, we should remember that we serve a God Who Finds Persons. He has an overriding concern that men

should be redeemed. However we understand the word, biblical witness is clear that men are "lost." The Finding God wants them found—that is, brought into a redemptive relationship to Jesus Christ.[7]

There is no lack of definitions for holism. It is entirely appropriate, however, to quote the one provided by C. René Padilla who, more than anyone else, should be credited with convincing evangelicals in the late twentieth century of the need to embrace a holistic approach to mission:

> Holistic mission is mission oriented towards the meeting of basic human needs, including the need of God, but also the need of food, love, housing, clothes, physical and mental health, and a sense of human dignity. Furthermore, this approach takes into account that people are spiritual, social and bodily beings, made to live in relationship with God, with their neighbours, and with God's creation. Consequently, it presupposes that it is not enough to take care of the spiritual well-being of an individual without any regard for his or her personal relationships and position in society and in the world. As Jesus saw it, love for God is inseparable from love for neighbor (Matt. 22:40).[8]

A careful review of the literature on both sides of the debate uncovers further contrasts between the two views, as depicted in the following chart:[9]

PRIORITISM	HOLISM
Evangelism/disciple making/church planting are more important than other ancillary activities	Evangelism/disciple making/church planting are equally as important as other ancillary activities
Apostles and the early church as models for mission (Representationalism)	Jesus as model for mission (Incarnationalism)
Kingdom of God in the church through conversion	Kingdom of God in church and society through socioeconomic, political action
Social activity as means to the end of conversion	Social activity as means to the end of improving society
Focuses on what Christ has done for the church	Focuses on what the church can do for society
Gospel is what Christ has done for the church	Gospel is what the church does for others
Gospel communicated only through word	Gospel communicated and demonstrated through word and deed
Theological hierarchy of proclamation over ancillary activities	Theological equality between proclamation and ancillary activities
Mission as specific task	Mission as everything the church does
Committed more to the lost than to the poor	Committed more to the poor than to the lost or equally committed to both

To clarify further, prioritism is not fundamentalist in the sense that it rejects social action, and holism is not universalistic in the sense that it repudiates gospel proclamation. What contrasts prioritism with holism is not a dichotomy between word and deed but a hierarchy of word over deed. Thus, if there is one criterion which describes the essential disparity between the two views, it would be that prioritism affirms evangelism as primary, paramount, central—at the core, hub, or heart of mission—and thereby deserving of the pride of place in relation to all other missional activities, whereas holism does not.

The Road to Evangelical Holism

Evangelicalism historically has exhibited a genuine commitment to social action and evangelism, but it would be a mischaracterization to claim that it has been equally committed to both.[10] This is because the three post-Reformational movements which provide the foundational roots for evangelicalism—German Pietism, English Puritanism and the American Great Awakenings[11]—stressed, based upon scriptural authority, personal conversion and the recruitment of those converted into the process of converting others.[12] This posture toward the world has been labeled "the evangelical impulse,"[13] and without it, evangelicalism betrays itself.[14]

This impulse materialized very clearly at a conference organized by Dwight L. Moody in Northfield, Massachusetts in 1886, when A.T. Pierson challenged the university students present with the watchword "the evangelization of the world in this generation."[15] This slogan was later adopted by the World Missionary Conference in Edinburgh in 1910, demonstrating the overall direction of the Protestant missionary force at the beginning of the twentieth century.[16] As an outgrowth of the conference in Edinburgh, the International Missionary Council

(IMC) was formed in 1921 "to encourage and assist churches and mission societies in their missionary task, understood as sharing with people everywhere the transforming power of the gospel of Jesus Christ." The IMC was subsequently incorporated into the World Council of Churches (WCC) in 1961 and renamed the Commission on World Mission and Evangelism (CWME), with the stated purpose "to further the proclamation to the whole world of the gospel of Jesus Christ to the end that all men may believe and be saved."[17]

The same year this merger took place, the WCC's assembly in New Delhi redefined evangelism as the "commission given to the whole Church to take the whole Gospel to the whole world," where "whole Gospel" was interpreted as "witness to all realms of life—physical, social, economic, and spiritual." Moreover, it was understood that "witness to the Gospel must . . . be prepared to engage in the struggle for social justice and for peace; it will have to take the form of humble service and of a practical ministry of reconciliation amidst the actual conflict of our times."[18] Thereafter, the WCC's Nairobi assembly (in 1975) "distinctly and without hesitation [brought] together evangelism and social action as integral parts of the 'whole Gospel.'" Yet it was also voiced at this meeting "that in broadening evangelism to avoid a narrowness, almost anything can be classified as evangelism."[19] These developments had a suffocating effect on the IMC's, and later the CWME's, initial vision for world evangelization.

Evangelicals eventually lost confidence in the WCC and organized the Lausanne Congress for World Evangelization in 1974, under the leadership of Billy Graham. The well-known Lausanne Covenant, penned by John Stott, included the phrase, "World evangelization requires the whole Church to take the whole gospel to the whole world,"[20] showing that Lausanne did not operate in a historical vacuum. This inclusion at once paved the theological path for Lausanne over the next several decades; it appears both in the Manila Manifesto in conjunction with Lausanne II (1989)[21] and in the Cape Town Commitment in relation to Lausanne III (2010).[22]

The original Lausanne charter did declare that in "the Church's mission of sacrificial service evangelism is primary," but also that "socio-political involvement [is] part of our Christian duty."[23] This dual affirmation of evangelism and social action reveals the internal tensions present within the Lausanne Movement from its inception. Those who held to a restrictive view of evangelism "accused Lausanne's stated social vision as being the old Social Gospel in evangelical clothing," while those who held a broader view believed that "the affirmation of socio-political involvement . . . did not go far enough" since to them "social concern still felt like an appendage to the 'real work' of the gospel." This latter group felt led to form an *ad hoc* committee of about two hundred participants at the Congress. This committee drafted a document entitled "Theology [and] Implications of Radical Discipleship," which described the gospel as the "Good News of liberation, of restoration, or wholeness, and of salvation that is personal, social, global and cosmic" and which "repudiated the dichotomy between evangelism and social concern, challenged the language of the primacy of evangelism, and broadened the scope of God's salvific work in the world."[24]

In evaluating the Lausanne Movement, Arthur Johnston asserted that the Congress "made unnecessary concessions to the pressure of the incarnational theology fadism current with the nonevangelical institutionalized churches" to such an extent that "evangelism was blunted . . . and lost some of its historical 'cutting edge' by introducing issues related to the duties of the church." In essence, for him and many others, the issue was not just that evangelism should be primary in the church's mission, but that its unique status in mission, as related to various other responsibilities of the church, was not upheld. Moreover, Johnston feared that making room for social action in the church's mission would eventually lead "to a this-worldly or horizontal preoccupation."[25] He was not alone in his concern. Harold Lindsell believed that the same fate suffered by American mainline denominations as a result of capitulating to theological liberalism awaited evangelicals who likewise opened the door to "social and economic or political action" in mission.[26]

The call for Lausanne to accept a holistic posture in mission finally won out at the 2004 Forum for World Evangelization, when Padilla delineated the parameters of evangelical mission in this way:

> Mission is faithful to scripture . . . when it crosses frontiers (not just geographic but also cultural, racial, economic, social, political, etc.) with the intention of transforming human life in all its dimensions, according to God's purpose, and of enabling human beings to enjoy the abundant life that God wants to give to them and that Jesus Christ came to share with them. The mission of the church is multifaceted because it depends on the mission of God, which includes the whole of creation and the totality of human life.[27]

That mission as holistic has now become a mainstay within the Lausanne Movement is evident in the Cape Town Commitment (2010), which, while setting aside priority-centric language about evangelism, articulates mission in this way: "This is true of mission in all its dimensions: evangelism, bearing witness to the truth, discipling, peace-making, social engagement, ethical transformation, caring for creation, overcoming evil powers, casting out demonic spirits, healing the sick, suffering and enduring under persecution."[28]

The direct outcome of evangelicals embracing a holistic vision for mission is that, confirming the fears of Johnston and Lindsell, the essential task of evangelism is having to be defended against a wider notion of mission. As J. Andrew Kirk points out, "Mission, which in some circles used to be almost identified with evangelism, is now almost completely disassociated from it. It is now aligned, more or less, with service to the community and ethical pronouncements and action in the political sphere, referred to as its prophetic ministry."[29]

Furthermore, Chris Wright reminds evangelicals (in regard to a historical reversal in which holism originally made space for social action in relation to evangelism) that without "declaring the Word and the name of Christ," mission is "defective [and not] holistic."[30] What this indicates is that "over the past thirty years, many evangelicals have moved toward positions closer to conciliar thinking than earlier evangelicals would have dreamed."[31] Indeed, it is striking to contemplate how evangelicals have not only paralleled the trajectory of the WCC in the twentieth century but have even gone beyond it in the twenty-first.

Why Not Holism?

There is no question that holists are some of the most respected, intelligent, self-sacrificing and Christ-honoring people involved in God's mission among the nations today. But holism, as presently conceived, cannot bear the weight of expectations placed upon it as a viable paradigm for the mission of the church. Besides the hermeneutical problems involved,[32] it falls short in other significant areas as well.

1. Kerygmatic Issues. The gospel from a holistic perspective is now being characterized as something the church is,[33] lives,[34] embodies and[35] demonstrates,[36] and evangelism is being characterized as "all actions"[37] which the church performs in inviting people "through word, deed, and example . . . to follow Christ."[38] Apparently, the terms "gospel" and "evangelism" have no limits; but if that is so, they also have no meaning, and mission easily becomes doing what is right in one's own eyes. Yet the fact is that the "gospel is not infinitely malleable, and cannot without fatal loss be reduced to whatever constitutes good news in a given culture"[39] and "evangelism needs to be defined carefully so that its special task is not lost within the wider demands of mission."[40] Toward this end, Scott McKnight suggests the contemporary church must return to "the earliest days of the church" and consider the "apostolic gospel tradition" as revealed in First Corinthians 15:1–8: that Christ died, that Christ was buried, that Christ was raised and that Christ appeared. This framework points to "something at the grassroots level: the word *gospel* was used in the world of Jews at the time of the apostles to announce something, to declare something as good news—the word *euangelion* always means good news. 'To gospel' is to herald, to proclaim, and to declare something about something." Thus, McKnight rightly deduces, "the gospel is to announce good news about key events in the life of Jesus Christ."[41] Hence, "the gospel itself is always an external word that comes to me announcing that someone else in history has accomplished my salvation for me,"[42] which thereby implies, "we are not the Good News, but its recipients and heralds; not the newsmakers, just the reporters."[43] As such, "the biblical gospel is inherently a verbal thing [which] cannot be preached by our deeds,"[44] "social action and caring for the poor is not . . . the gospel [but] implications" of it,[45] and "evangelism is the act of giving verbal witness to the good news, confident that its power does not fluctuate with the strengths or weaknesses of the messenger."[46]

If, in relation to the mission of the church, "we want to be New Testament Christians," then "this gospel must once again become our gospel."[47]

2. Kingdom Issues. The kingdom of God, at the beginning of the twenty-first century, was heralded by evangelicals as the means to "break the impasse between evangelism and social action."[48] But unfortunately, instead of clarifying the mission of God, this emphasis confounded it. For example, "Kingdom Missiology" is now being advanced to challenge the church to "faithfully [perform] the whole work of the kingdom of God to the whole world,"[49] which necessarily involves "more than simply winning men and women to Christ [but] working toward shalom and the redemption of structures, individuals, families, and relationships."[50] From this perspective, kingdom work strives "for the redemption of people, their social systems, and the environment that sustains their life,"[51] using "the current trends toward capitalism and economic development to [raise] the standard of living . . . for all,"[52] and surprisingly results in "something permanent, something that will not be displaced in the world to come. . . . When a well is dug, a school is built or an orphanage opens its gates, the dream of God [i.e., the kingdom] becomes actualized in our time."[53]

In challenging such views, George Eldon Ladd states that "the church cannot build the Kingdom or become the Kingdom, but the church witnesses to God's Kingdom—to God's redeeming acts in Christ both past and future";[54] Arthur Glasser observes, "to preach [the kingdom] is to issue a call to conversion" for "apart from the new birth one cannot see, much less enter, the Kingdom of God";[55] and I. Howard Marshall notes, "the kingdom consists of those who respond to the message in repentance and faith and thereby enter into the sphere of God's salvation and life."[56] Accordingly, Christians should "be wary of making over-ambitious claims for particular manifestations of the [kingdom's] presence,"[57] "not call social change the coming of the kingdom,"[58] realize that "efforts to make the world a better place do not inherently qualify as kingdom work" since non-Christians can "work to make the world a better place, but they are not, in doing so, building *Christ's* kingdom,"[59] and accept that "the phrase 'kingdom work' is confusing and nonbiblical and . . . should be jettisoned."[60]

3. Missiological Issues. Without question, the most disturbing trend within evangelical missiology today, one which confirms that the greatest challenges facing this academic field are not "methodological [but] theological,"[61] is the wholesale attempt to renegotiate the boundaries within which mission occurs. Among self-declared evangelicals, mission now includes: "caring for the environment,"[62] "creating jobs and wealth,"[63] "giving to fellow believers in need,"[64] "political action, in fighting social injustice,"[65] and "anti-trafficking work, care for AIDS and malaria patients, food for the hungry, clothing for the naked, release for the prisoners."[66] This expansive definition of mission justifies Carl Braaten's concern that "holistic mission has contributed to such a great inflation in the meaning of mission, including everything the church is doing, that there is the danger that evangelism, which is the heart of mission, will become buried in an avalanche of church activism."[67]

In the middle of the last century, Stephen Neill faced the same state of affairs with the WCC, as it began to label every praiseworthy work of the church as mission. As a corrective, he set forth his now famous dictum: "If mission is everything, mission is nothing. If everything that the Church does is to be classed as 'mission', we shall have to find another term for the

Church's particular responsibility for 'the heathen', those who have never yet heard the Name of Christ."[68] He later expounded upon this statement by defining mission as "the intentional crossing of barriers from Church to non-church in word and deed for the sake of the proclamation of the Gospel."[69] However, David Bosch interjected a contravening viewpoint when he stated, "Whoever we are, we are tempted to incarcerate the *missio Dei* in the narrow confines of our own predilections, thereby of necessity reverting to one-sidedness and reductionism. We should beware of any attempt at delineating mission too sharply."[70] In this vein, Wright, working within the framework of a biblical theology of the redemption of the entire cosmos, believes, in contradiction to Neill's statement, that "it would seem more biblical to say, 'If everything is mission . . . everything is mission.'. . . Everything a Christian and a Christian church is, says and does should be missional in its conscious participation in the mission of God in God's world."[71] As such, the evangelical church is now faced with a situation where, according to Timothy Tennent, "the word [mission] has been [so] broadened . . . to mean 'everything the church should be doing,'" that it has lost "any distinctive emphasis or character."[72]

In light of this predicament, missiology needs to reconsider the question: what is and what is not mission? In other words, is the church responsible for both world evangelization and world reparation? McQuilkin points in the right direction when he deems "the question of final destiny [to be] *the* theological issue for missions." Consequently, if the church has to choose among competing agendas, if it has to accept its limitations, if it has to grope for the narrow way, then it should chart its missional course in reference to those who have the most to lose (and gain) in the debate—the not-yet evangelized. Hence, Neill's viewpoint should trump Bosch's, and the church should embrace "lostness" as the only nonnegotiable boundary for mission and "final destiny" as the leading theological impetus for all its interactions with the world.[73]

Why Prioritism?

Prioritists would do well to continue to listen to and learn from holists, as all "see in a mirror dimly" and "know [only] in part" (1 Cor. 13:12, NASB). However, more persuasive arguments will need to be articulated by holists for prioritists to compromise any of the following convictions.

Almost two millennia ago, Augustine of Hippo referenced the Great Commandment as he shed light on the nature of mission, commenting that the "divine Master inculcates two precepts—the love of God and the love of our neighbor—and as in these precepts a man finds three things he has to love—God, himself, and his neighbor—and that he who loves God loves himself thereby, it follows that he must endeavour to get his neighbour to love God, since he is ordered to love his neighbour as himself."[74] Augustine says two things here which must not go unnoticed: (1) the way to loving oneself is to love God, and (2) the way to loving one's neighbor is to encourage him to love God as well. Thus, although there are many ways to express the Great Commandment, its purest manifestation comes when God's people persuade others to love God. This is the highest display of love a person can ever show because, as John Piper notes, "our greatest satisfaction" and "our greatest good, comes to us *in* God."[75] Therefore, "the primary deed of love that one can do for a fallen world is to share the gospel with that world."[76] Indeed, when it comes to the lost, the best way to obey the Great Commandment is to live by the Great Commission.

This point leads to the next. In the face of horrendous injustices in the economic, social, political and environmental spheres of present-day human existence, there is one injustice which far surpasses the rest—lack of access to the Word of God. The most recent statistics indicate that those subjected to this type of in-equity amount to over 2.1 billion unevangelized people.[77] Surely this is the most currently pervasive and eternally consequential injustice confronting the mission of the church. This is not to excuse or minimize human suffering in any way, since "Chris-tians are rightly concerned about the grievous imbalances of wealth and food and freedom in the world." But Christians must go beyond the horizontal dimension to the vertical one and press the question, "What about the most devastating imbalance of all: the unequal distribution of the light of the knowledge of God in Jesus Christ?"[78] This is what the early church, as well as the church during the modern missionary era, focused on—and which the contemporary church must focus on again.

In addition, Jesus and Paul have much to interject into this discussion on mission. It is not necessary to paint a contrast-ing picture between these two, which prioritism has sometimes inadvertently done as a result of allowing holism to define the terms.[79] There is clear continuity between the Son of God and His Apostle to the Gentiles regarding mission. Luke 4:18–19 has been described by holists as the mission statement for Jesus' life, which combines "faith with action to overcome injustice and oppression."[80] But a closer look at the passage reveals "of the four infinitives from Isaiah that show the purpose of the Spirit's anointing and sending of Jesus, three involve preaching. . . . Luke, then, regards the primary activity of Jesus' ministry as preaching."[81] Moreover, at the end of Luke 4, one encounters the statement "I must preach the good news of the kingdom of God to the other towns as well; for I was sent for this purpose" (4:43; see also Mark 1:38). Hence, a careful reading of this chapter shows that the "mission statement" of the Messiah centers on proclamation (see Matt. 20:28; Mark 10:45; Luke 19:10; John 3:17). In conformity to Jesus' mission, Paul testifies, "For Christ did not send me to baptize, but to preach the gospel, not in cleverness of speech, so that the cross of Christ would not be made void" (1 Cor. 1:17; see also Acts 26:16–18). If such an orientation marked out the two greatest missionary exemplars of the New Testament, one needs to come up with a legitimate reason to say that it does not hold true for all those involved in mission today.

Another vital subject which is rarely if ever considered in this discussion is the ministry of the Spirit of God in the witness of the church. According to Harry Boer, "there is a surprising and unanimous testimony in the New Testament to the relationship between the Spirit poured out at Pentecost and the witness of the Church." The evidence he presents in support of this thesis is at least twofold: (1) the terms associated with the activity of the promised Paraclete as described in John 14 to 16 include "teach, remind, guide, show, convict, witness" and thereby indicate that the Spirit is "Christ's witness in and through men to the Church and to the world"; and (2) both the apostles being "filled with the Holy Spirit and [speaking] in other tongues as the Spirit gave them utterance" (Acts 2:4) and Peter in particular proclaiming the truth about the life, death and resurrection of Jesus, "establish that the central task of the Church is to witness to the great works of God in the power of the Spirit." In light of this, Boer concludes: "If the Holy Spirit given at Pentecost is so centrally the origin and the undergirding, informing and empowering principle of the missionary witness of the Church, it would seem reasonable to expect that He should also have the greatest significance for the concrete manner in which the actual missionary work of the Church is performed."[82]

Word Over Deed

If there is one remaining question for prioritism to clarify, it is: In what sense can evangelism be considered the priority in relation to all other ancillary activities in the mission of the church?

There is, first of all, a *theological priority*. It is disappointing that in some of the major contemporary works on holistic/integral mission the reality of hell is either given scant recognition or ignored altogether.[83] The explanation for this may be that there is a need to address the physical aspects of humankind over against the spiritual in an effort to overcome the supposed dualistic tendencies of prioritism, in which the spirit takes precedence over the flesh.[84] But what prioritism asserts is not that the spirit is more important than the flesh but that eternal realities always outweigh temporal ones. Indeed, "Placing that which is temporal and unsatisfying alongside that which is eternal and teleologically final as special components of a life of service presents a mystifying incongruity. 'Labor not for the bread that perishes but for that which endures to eternal life' [John 6:27]."[85] One can only hope that those who affirm "the nonultimacy of death" will eventually come around to advocating the primacy of evangelism.[86]

Second, there is an *abiding priority*. Stott believed the "distinction between evangelism and social action is often artificial. Although some individual Christians are called to specialist ministries (some as evangelists, others as social workers, and so forth), the Christian community as a whole should not have to choose, any more than Jesus did. In many missionary situations such a choice would be inconceivable. The evangelist could not with integrity proclaim the good news to the victims of flood or famine while ignoring their physical plight."[87] What is implied here is that the existential context should be allowed to set the agenda for mission. However, neither context nor the world nor anything other than divine revelation can be allowed to establish the direction of the church in mission. The reason why this is the case is because "If . . . social advance is put first in time . . . it is obvious that faith in Christ is not the foundation but the coping stone of social and moral progress [and consequently] we have, by deeds which speak louder than words, taught men to seek 'all these things' first [rather than] the Kingdom of God and His righteousness."[88] Jesus was able to avoid this pitfall throughout His missional activities, in direct contradiction to the holistic mandate. In John 6, when the hungry multitudes sought the blessings of the kingdom apart from submission to the King, Jesus redirected their attention to this truth: "I am the bread of life; whoever comes to me shall not hunger, and whoever believes in me shall never thirst" (John 6:35). By implication, this shows that: (1) there can be mission without social action, but the same cannot be said for proclamation; and (2) the personal aspirations of God's servants are not what determine the mission of the church, but rather the eternal needs of the lost.

Third, there is a *practical priority* to word over deed. Lesslie Newbigin is well-known for saying that "to set word and deed, preaching and action, against each other is absurd. . . . The words explain the deeds, and the deeds validate the words."[89] But such an assertion does not reflect mission realities on the ground. Besides the fact that philanthropic efforts by non-Christians make those of Christians redundant, a rarely acknowledged truth on the part of holistic practitioners is that compassion ministries are "a bane as well as a blessing" since they tend to produce rice Christians.[90] Furthermore, the high aspirations of holism make "the church *alone* responsible for the disintegration of society [and thereby links] the church with a cause that cannot succeed in the present age."[91] In reality, the church "never can *promise* the

solution of economic, social and political problems . . . for the
simple reason that the Church cannot pretend to govern the economic and political factors that determine the outward course of
the world at large."[92] This truth should be a source of encouragement to those in mission, because in the history of the church,
"the gospel has been spread . . . without [holistic ministries], and
we need to be reminded that they are not indispensable. If we
forget it we make social progress our gospel and become more
concerned about social progress than spiritual regeneration."[93]
As such, a hierarchy of word over deed, not a dichotomy between them, is the wisest way forward in mission.

Finally, there is a *financial priority*. There is historical evidence showing that efforts to improve the socioeconomic conditions of people have, both in time and in treasure, taken away
from evangelistic ministries.[94] While this may seem justifiable
in the eyes of holistic advocates, one church in Ethiopia was
taken aback "by the fact that there were more financial resources
[made] available for relief and development work than for evangelism."[95] Of course, one wishes there were an endless amount of
funds to accomplish the church's mission, but this is simply not
the case, and therefore the church must face reality. Although it
is possible to "make a good case that the church has a responsibility to see that everyone in their local church community is
cared for, . . . you cannot make a very good case that the church
must be the social custodian for everyone in their society." As
such, the "church should tend toward doing those activities and
spending its resources on those projects that *more directly*, rather
than *less directly*, further its central mission. . . . That doesn't
mean that the church will only ever do activities that are a direct
fulfillment of its mission. . . . The point is simply that there is in
fact a mission given to the church by its Lord that is narrower
than 'everything we could do'."[96]

In conclusion, it is not as difficult as it first may seem to discern between prioritism and holism. If anyone is able to answer the following questions in the affirmative, then that person leans toward prioritism:

1) Are the eternal needs of human beings more important than temporal ones?

2) Is what Jesus did for humanity on the cross infinitely more significant than anything the church can do for others?

3) Does the gospel involve what Jesus has done for others, not what the church can do for them?

4) Is the greatest injustice in the world today not social, economic, political or environmental in nature, but the unequal distribution of the Word of God whereby the lost may be reconciled with their Creator?

5) Is it acceptable to move on to unevangelized areas to introduce the gospel rather than remain behind to address the perennial humanitarian problems Christians face?

6) Is it appropriate to spend the majority of the church's resources on evangelistic rather than social ministries?

Ultimately, the prioritist will passionately defend and act upon the view that although the good news of salvation through Jesus Christ may not be the only thing the church in mission has to offer the world, it is without question the greatest thing it has to offer.

Part V

Christian Ethics

Chapter 9

Culture and the Missional Engagement with Good and Evil:
What We Learned About Contextualization from J. Robertson McQuilkin

Robert J. Priest and Ron Barber Jr.

Deeply felt ideas of good and evil are nearly always acquired from culture, and yet these ideas only partly correspond with what is taught in Scripture. Thus culture poses difficult challenges for missionaries and local pastors everywhere, challenges usually discussed in missiology under the language of contextualization.

As a career missionary and missiologist (Ron Barber) and a seminary professor of missiology (Robert J. Priest), we look back on our studies under J. Robertson McQuilkin in the late 1970s and 1980s as seminal. Although our courses with McQuilkin were not in missiology, and although he never formally wrote a systematic treatise on contextualization, we nonetheless learned from him many of our most basic convictions about how to contextualize biblical messages related to good and evil. In this paper we attempt to articulate principles for how to minister in a way that is contextually wise, whether in Japan, Malawi or the United States. Even where we sometimes propose principles not fully attributable to McQuilkin, it is the fruitfulness of our own engagement with what he taught us that has helped us develop and refine these ideas.[1]

The Education, Controlling Assumptions and Commitments of Would-Be Contextualizers

McQuilkin spent much of his life leading and strengthening Columbia International University, an educational institution intended to prepare people as missionaries. He clearly believed that wise engagement with contextual realities does not begin at the moment of missiological encounter but is dependent on first acquiring appropriate educational foundations and controlling assumptions. That is, before any individual is in a position to provide leadership on difficult matters of contextualization, and before one should discuss formal steps in how to do contextualization, the appropriate educational foundations and controlling assumptions need to be in place. These include the following:

The Bible

Through God's revelation in Scripture we have knowledge about God and His standards, purposes and plans for us. Evangelists, missionaries and pastors have a message and mandate provided in Scripture. This requires that such ministers of the gospel have a deep and profound knowledge of the Bible, a knowledge that is hermeneutically responsible and that is combined with a deep trust in Scripture and commitment to its message and functional authority. Anyone wishing to provide leadership in contextualization needs formal biblical training and a pattern of ministry engagement that continuously brings the Scriptures functionally and with authority into every part of life and ministry.[2]

Culture

McQuilkin reports that as a young missionary he was prepared to exegete the biblical text but was "clueless" about "exegeting" his audience—and thus turned to anthropology for help.[3] Indeed he was at the forefront of a new breed of missionaries that stressed the importance of understanding culture.[4] Earlier missionaries had talked about the value of indigeneity, defined as a concern that new churches be self-supporting, self-governing, and self-propagating. But all three of these emphases were exclusively sociological, asking *who* is in charge, *who* pays the bills and *who* does the evangelism. The *who* question is not the same as the culture question—the matter of how to engage cultural values and rituals, linguistic categories, music or architecture, for example. The later shift by missiologists from a vocabulary of "indigeneity" to a vocabulary of "contextualization" was a shift reflecting a concern with culture and not just sociology. And long before this new word came into use McQuilkin was writing articles on Japanese culture and the importance of missionaries understanding culture.[5] He was committed to CIU having faculty and coursework related to the understanding of culture. He actively recruited those with strengths in understanding cultures and religions, believing this was needed in the education of missionaries. Those wishing to provide leadership in contextualization need formal training related to culture, and a pattern of ministry engagement that continuously works to ensure that appropriate cultural realities are being understood at every step of the process.

Missions

For McQuilkin, the impulse to contextualization is grounded in the missionary task itself. Paul aligned with Jewish culture to reach Jews. He adjusted to Gentile culture to reach Gentiles.

Missionaries today, like the first great Christian missionary Paul, are called to "become all things to all people, that by all means [we] might save some." (1 Cor. 9:22). The missionary task involves communicating and commending the gospel to those not yet Christian (especially those with least exposure to the gospel) with the goal of bringing people into relationship with God and into relationship with other believers in church plants where converts are discipled to become faithful Christians in all areas of life.

McQuilkin stressed that believers should live out commitments to justice and social action, but he treated this under discipleship and sanctification rather than under missions, and he expressed concern that "holistic mission" too easily allowed social agendas to displace the gospel focus. Yet he also believed that the church's credibility and its witness are enhanced when deed and word accompany each other.[7]

Whenever Christians focus on witness to unbelievers, lovingly desiring to commend the gospel to unbelievers through word and deed, then issues of contextualization are central. This is true whether in Nepal or America. That is, contextualization is a concern specifically in the context of churches' and individuals' efforts to position themselves for faithful gospel presence and witness. Those who can best provide leadership in contextualization are those whose passion, life commitment and ministry involve a simultaneous concern for authentic Christian lives wisely lived out in context and for commending the gospel to those not already in the church.

Whose Is the Task of Contextualization?

Discussions of contextualization often feature "contextualization of theology," which might naturally lead to the inference that seminary-based theologians are the best agents of contextual reflection. McQuilkin, however, exemplified an approach that placed the missionary at the center of the contextualization task. Missionaries, unlike most theologians, do not primarily spend their lives talking with, reading and teaching Christians. Rather the missionary impulse and normal pattern of ministry brings them into continuous relationship with those who are not Christian, and in very practical terms presses home the importance of a wise engagement with those not already a part of the church. That is, the social location of the missionary is far better than that of the theologian for considering practical matters of contextualization. And unlike those who engage non-Christians from within a "culture war" mentality, trying to win political battles in society, the missionary is moved by a love that desires to woo and win others to the faith. It is missionaries who, like the apostle Paul, are centrally preoccupied with how to commend the Christian message to those who are not believers that are in the best position to consider matters of contextualization.

Of course McQuilkin was also quite aware that missionaries are often cultural foreigners and thus bring their own cultural baggage and ethnocentrism with them. While missionaries ought to be centrally focused on contextual concerns, their understandings and insights about realities in the host culture are likely to be flawed and limited. Consequently, indigenous believers and church leaders must themselves become the real center of efforts at contextual responsiveness.[8] But, like missionaries, only those Christian leaders with prior biblical and cultural/missiological training and with deep commitment to commend this gospel to an unbelieving world will be ideally positioned to provide leadership in contextualized ministry.

Finally, McQuilkin did affirm the value of specialized missiological training, not only when he pushed to make this a core part of the CIU curriculum but also when he encouraged each of us to pursue the PhDs that we did—Ron Barber in missiology and Robert Priest in cultural anthropology. In McQuilkin's mind, only individuals with some degree of dual competence, who combined both biblical/theological foundations and cultural foundations, would be in a wise position to integrate such understandings and provide leadership in contextual missional engagement.[9] This integration, of course, is what missiology aims for.

Missionaries, church leaders and missiologists all play central and unique roles in grappling with contextualization. But of course any Christian who combines both biblical and cultural knowledge and who is burdened with a deep concern to commend the gospel to a wider world should be involved in this task.

Formal Steps on How to Do Contextualization

Individuals who have acquired the appropriate education and the controlling assumptions and commitments outlined above are ready to follow the steps needed in contextualization.

Step One: The Starting Point

Content of Our Message: The content of the biblical message provides the most natural starting point for contextualization. If one wishes to speak about God, then it is important not only to examine what Scripture says about God but also systematically to explore discourses about God within the culture, wherever those discourses appear. Attention to vocabulary, metaphors, songs, stories, the socialization of children, etc. are all part of this. Our own messages about God enter an arena of prior cultural discourses about God and they need to be knowledgeably articulated with awareness of the prior discourses that have shaped our audience. If we wish to speak of sin, then again it becomes important that we acquire deep understandings of the moral vocabulary and moral discourses of everyday life.[10] If we wish to speak of suffering or of death, contextualization requires that we not only focus on biblical passages related to suffering and death but also explore the narratives about suffering and death that are common in everyday life. Our own sermons and evangelistic Bible studies should emerge out of deep engagements with both sides of the issue.[11]

In practical terms the best way to commence this process of contextualization is to make it part of the weekly rhythm of ministry preparation. If preaching a sermon that focuses on God's ideals for sex and marriage, then one should not only devote sermon-preparation hours to biblical study but also to acquiring deeper understandings of sexuality and marriage as idealized and practiced in culture. If teaching about love, then one should explore vocabulary and teachings about love from Scripture. But one should also study the vocabulary and discourses about love in the wider culture as they appear in music, poetry, story or interactions of other sorts.

Alternatively, if you are doing Bible translation, then every important word not only in the Greek or Hebrew text but also in the target language must be studied carefully to understand its normal range of use and meaning in everyday life. The Bible translator strives to acquire not only better and deeper understandings of the biblical vocabulary but better and deeper understandings of the vocabulary useful for conveying truth into the receptor community. Good Bible translation and good preaching or Bible teaching require systematic and sustained efforts to contextualize the message and to engage and understand the language, lives and cultures of those to whom one wishes to communicate.

Christian Practices: While the content of the biblical message and the effort to convey and exposit that content provides one natural starting point for contextualization, distinctive Christian practices provide another starting point. Consider, for example, worship music. Christians around the world sing and play musical instruments in worship. The musical forms and instruments are cultural in nature, bearing no intrinsic relationship to special revelation. People everywhere are shaped by musical cultures, ones that may be rather distant from the musical culture of a foreign missionary. This means that the Christian practice of singing and playing instruments should from the very beginning be conceptualized as requiring contextual considerations. Missionary motivations press for the use of musical forms such that people outside the church do not encounter a musical distance that they find difficult or impossible to cross or a musical aesthetic they find distasteful; rather, people outside the church must find the music aesthetically attractive and meaningful and encounter a musical language in which they already have fluency. When new believers with musical gifts can immediately use those gifts to help produce beautiful and meaningful worship, the worshiping community will itself become missionally attractive to other members of the community.

Furthermore, Christians around the world mark marriages, births and deaths with special Christian rites, but missionaries never enter a vacuum with reference to such rites and practices. Rather, weddings, birth rituals and funerals exist prior to and beyond the walls of church. These rites involve a ritual grammar and semiotics, and they position participants within a world of positive values, which Christians should not be ignorant of or ignore. Thus, the instantiation of Christian practices in new social settings ought ideally to be informed by a consideration of contextual dynamics.

Cultural Practices: Sometimes the need for contextual engagement emerges not out of the effort to wisely commend biblical truth nor the effort to wisely inculcate some distinctive Christian practice but rather out of awareness of some normative cultural practice that might possibly contradict or pose unique challenges for Christian faithfulness. Around the world missionaries and local Christians have struggled with how to address such practices as traditional rites mandating ancestral respect and veneration, puberty rites involving such things as male and female circumcision and healing rites performed by traditional healers (herbalists, shamans, acupuncturists). A wide variety of traditional marital practices around the world have also posed difficult questions of contextual response, ranging from arranged marriage and bride price to polygamy, as well as newer practices like gay marriage. Additionally there may be cultural practices that people enjoy and find meaningful that may not be intrinsically antithetical to Christian faith but that may be distant from the practice of missionaries (such as the use of drums, dance or tattoos). There is no reason that an awareness of such valued cultural practices might not be a good starting point for thinking about contextualization—that is, about the possible usage of such cultural patterns within explicitly Christian settings or in service of Christian mission.

Cultural Beliefs: Prior to the presence of Christian belief, there are already culturally accredited beliefs that may compete with or be difficult to reconcile with Christian beliefs. Secular American audiences, for example, may hold deep beliefs about homosexuality or evolution, raising difficult challenges for unprepared Christians wishing to speak with credibility about God's creation or God's ideals for marriage. It is sometimes the encounter with a pervasive belief within a community that poses interesting challenges for the missionary—challenges of how to relate biblical teaching credibly and wisely to an audience's assumptions and convictions. Beliefs about the ongoing activity of deceased ancestors pose further challenges. The belief, common in much of the world, that every death or misfortune is supernaturally caused by neighbors, relatives or colleagues acting through witchcraft poses difficult issues for churches to address.

Problems or Failures in Contextualization: In the modern world missionaries are seldom if ever the first to establish a church within a community. Rather, there is usually a long history of contextual decisions made by believers long ago on such questions as how to deal with polygamy, witchcraft, homosexuality or ancestors. Sometimes earlier decisions should be revisited since at times they have been made with defective linguistic and/or cultural understandings. For example, is it wise in a Hindu context to encourage converts to eat beef as proof of their faith? Is the requirement good that converts adopt "Christian names" (like Paul or Helen or Charles) that are simultaneously a repudiation of the parents who named them and an expression of allegiance to the culture of the missionary? Is it acceptable when through Bible translations Chinese Christians are encouraged to view the Chinese *long* (dragon), which historically was associated with positive values and with Chinese ethnic identity, as Satan (see Rev. 12:9; 20:2), contributing to the perception that Chinese must choose between being Chinese and being Christian?[12] If the musical instruments and aesthetics sacralized by missionaries of a bygone era are truly distant from the musical culture of most contemporary non-Christians, should there not be a reconsideration of contextualization in the area of music? That is, the very points at which earlier versions of Christian faith create problems for contemporary Christian life and witness are themselves good places to start grappling with matters of contextualization.

In short, there is no one starting point for triggering a contextualization process but rather a variety of points at which the need for contextualization might emerge. The above are some of the most common and appropriate such starting points, but doubtless readers can think of others.

Step Two: Acquiring More Focused Knowledge and Understanding

Once any of the above has become a trigger for contextual reflection, then a more focused effort at acquiring in-depth knowledge and understanding related to the particular realities at hand is needed. Each of the following sorts of knowledge need to be acquired—preferably pursued simultaneously and dialectically rather than individually with any one necessarily coming as the initial, exclusive focus.

Biblical and Theological Understandings: Whatever the focus of interest, one should seek to identify all relevant biblical texts and theological doctrines and should spend sustained time focused on these while simultaneously focusing on the other arenas listed below.[13] If worship music is the topic, then one would review what Scripture does and does not say on this topic. If polygamy is the topic, then one should systematically consider every biblical passage in which polygamy is referenced and every biblical passage spelling out God's plan for marriage. The same would be true for the topic of homosexuality and gay marriage today. Prior treatment of the designated topic by biblical scholars and theologians should be carefully reviewed.

Cultural Meanings and Practices: Whatever one's topic, one should systematically explore discourses within the society or social group that focus on or make reference to the topic (from gossip to proverbs to songs to myths to stories to political discourse to childhood socialization) in order to acquire a composite understanding of the vocabulary, symbols, metaphors, beliefs, moral judgments and themes most closely linked to the topic. What are the cultural practices related to the topic? How do these cultural elements form a meaningful system? What social functions do they serve?

If, for example, one wishes to understand how suffering is understood and culturally experienced in Korea, one will find it helpful to study discourses related to *han* and will want to understand the role of the *moodang* (shamans) in helping people "unravel *han*." Acquiring requisite cultural understandings should also be done by immersing oneself in relevant research literature by anthropologists and other scholars who have focused on the culture and related themes.

Prior Christian Approaches and Resulting Outcomes: Almost invariably, local missionaries and other Christians have already created older patterns of Christian response in relation to whatever one's topic might be. Such prior patterns are often indebted to inappropriate foreign cultural forms and may have been developed out of poor understandings of everything at stake. But by virtue of coming first, such patterns may have become deeply embraced as "Christian." Insofar as such patterns are overly indebted to foreign (or outdated) cultural elements— whether from church architecture to music to the requirement that a Javanese convert named Ajisaka adopt a "Christian name" like 'Hendrik'—the patterns often have serious and adverse results for Christian life and positive local witness. Just as patterns developed by Judaizers in biblical times needed to be critiqued and rethought, so it is important to reconsider older ways of contextualizing. When nineteenth century Scottish Presbyterians in Malawi taught converts that traditional marriage was illegitimate "self-marriage" and that the only true marriage was through an expensive Christian wedding in a church with such requirements as a white dress, the legacy today in the Church of Central Africa Presbyterian (CCAP), the largest Presbyterian church in Africa, is that few Presbyterians can afford a Christian marriage. Most CCAP young adults resort to a traditional marriage that requires they subsequently undergo church discipline. Older missionary ways of addressing marriage in Malawi have contributed to unhealthy marital patterns up to the present day.[14]

Comparison Across Space and Time: Whatever one's focus, it is possible to explore the ways other Christians in other times and places have addressed this area. Problems surrounding extortion, bribery and church discipline have been faced by Christians through history and around the world; thus there is likely to be a rich legacy of prior historiographic and missiological treatments of such topics. Witch accusations—that is, accusations that some old woman or orphan child is really a supernaturally empowered evil person who has caused the misfortune of others—has played a role in European church history and does so across Africa and New Guinea today. Such accusations result in serious adverse consequences for those being accused, and pose difficult issues. Not only is it helpful to explore such patterns within a culture and against the backdrop of what Scripture and theology do or do not say on a topic, it is critical to draw from and interact with the issues as they've been experienced and reflected on elsewhere. And since we exist in a globally connected world, it makes sense to foster a global conversation about the patterns involved, making sure that African and New Guinean Christian leaders are central to the conversation, as well as church historians and Christian missiologists and anthropologists.

Step Three: Making Actual Decisions on Contextualization

There are many possible Christian responses to any particular cultural reality. Cultural patterns force Christians to make assessments and responses. Consider Halloween in America. How do Christians understand it? How do we respond? Even if we do not wish to participate, children knock on our doors and ask us to give them candy. Some Christians lock their doors, turn off the lights and post a sign demanding not to be disturbed. Some children's Sunday school classes stress that Halloween is satanic and to be avoided. Others ignore it, and yet others do crafts with Halloween motifs. Some churches discourage participation in neighborhood trick-or-treating by creating a functional substitute for Halloween, encouraging Christians to instead participate at church in a "fall festival" or "Reformation party," where children dress up and get candy in a spiritual setting in which they carefully observe rules on appropriate costumes, avoiding such things as witches or vampires or monsters. Some churches attempt to transform the occasion for Christian ends—such as by creating a special "hell house" featuring the evils of abortion, the consequences of sin and the torments of hell. Or the children's sermon might feature a "gospel pumpkin" that has been selected, washed, had the "yucky" stuff inside cleaned out, given a new smiling face and had a light placed inside—illustrating what God can do in our lives. Should Christians participate along with neighbors in carving and displaying jack-o'-lanterns on their porches? If they have their own small children, should they use this distinctive American celebration as a way to get to know their neighbors on the one night of the year when neighbors are likely to welcome them at the door, building relations through the nonthreatening means of doting over each other's children and their costumes? Do Christians themselves welcome the neighborhood children (and their parents) with open arms, oohing and aahing at the beautiful princesses, the scary ghosts and so on? My [Priest's] own neighbors, a seminary president and his wife, their own kids long gone, open their garage with hot drinks and doughnuts and chairs and music, creating a popular stopping point for parents of all the trick-or-treaters passing through. This, for them, is a contextualized form of relational evangelism.

Clearly, even with a single topic such as Halloween, a brief paper cannot consider all possible contextual responses and the varying possible outcomes of each. And contextualization concerns a much wider diversity of realities than are exemplified in the Halloween topic.

In this article we do not conceptualize contextualization as carried out through the articulation of an abstract template that can be imposed in a top-down fashion. Rather we view contextualization as a bottom-up process beginning with a wide variety of possible starting points but grounded in the right knowledge foundations and undergirded by the right controlling assumptions. In actual practice, healthy contextualization involves an improvisational process governed by the following practical commitments.

1) *A commitment to believing and obeying Scripture.* No cultural adjustment by Christian contextualizers should have the effect of endorsing beliefs contradicted by Scripture or behaviors banned by Scripture; none of the following principles should be carried out in a way that violates this one.[15]

2) *A commitment to being rightly understood.* Christian messengers must communicate the Christian message using the

language and cultural symbols of the people being spoken to rather than through a foreign language and culture they do not understand. A constant preoccupation of missional contextualizers should be, "How are we being understood?" Moreover, "How can a better understanding and use of language and culture enhance the effectiveness of our communication of the gospel?"

3) *A commitment to celebrating the goodness and beauty present in culture.* While some missionaries only see evil in other cultures, McQuilkin often praised the values, insights and beauties of Japanese culture. He writes, "God loves beauty and so do the Japanese. American missionaries often do not. While the [Japanese] temples and their grounds are places of exquisite beauty, we erect Quonset huts with no gardens at all and call them churches."[16] Christians who recognize, celebrate and make use of the artistry, values and strengths of a given society will position themselves in a way that both gives and wins respect.

4) *A commitment to engaging the consciences of those to whom we speak.* The biblical message requires that we speak of sin, repentance and forgiveness. This is best done by engaging the consciences of those to whom one speaks. Even those without the written law of God operate with a prior understanding of good and evil "written on their hearts" (Rom. 2:12–15)—a conscience that is shaped by culture yet overlaps with scriptural teaching. The more effectively our ministry connects with and is ratified by the conscience of listeners, the more subjectively compelling the biblical message will be for people in that cultural context.[17]

5) *A commitment to a Christian testimony seen in context as exemplary.* People judge each other by their own culturally shaped moral and ethical values. When a given community, based on its own deepest moral convictions and values, perceives Christians consistently as immoral, unethical, immodest, disrespectful or

rude, healthy contextualization has not occurred. A contextualized church will work hard to exemplify virtue both as required by Scripture and as perceived by the surrounding community. A good reputation requires attentiveness to culturally shaped moral and ethical values.[18]

6) *A commitment to reducing cultural distance.* Every Christian and Christian institution is shaped by faithfulness to Scripture and by culture. Words, music, artistry and interactional patterns (such as whether to call a pastor by his first name) are fully cultural. When Christians from one culture attempt to spread the faith elsewhere, there is naturally a significant cultural distance to be crossed. Rather than attempting to incarnate a faith that requires potential converts to align with and laboriously become resocialized to what are for them foreign cultural patterns, a contextualized church will attempt to use cultural patterns that allow potential and new converts to bring the language they already speak, the musical abilities they already skillfully use, the cultural competencies they have already acquired and the aesthetic standards they already recognize into play naturally within the body of the church and its ministry and witness.

7) *A commitment to social presence.* As much as possible, Christians in every culture should be present in the widest variety of social arenas possible, faithfully living out a Christian social presence in all arenas of life.

8) *A commitment to indigenous Christian leaders being the final arbiters of contextualization.* Those Christians who are both spiritual and widely respected cultural insiders and who have a deep passion for reaching others in their own community must be respected and empowered to provide leadership in efforts at contextualization.[19]

Conclusion

At the end of the day, we see through a glass darkly (see 1 Cor. 13:12). Every effort to wisely engage cultural contexts for kingdom purposes should become simply the new starting point for further consideration and refinement. Careful follow-up research to discover how any particular contextualized effort is playing out in the life and witness of the church is needed. We will make mistakes and need to have the processes in place that allow for correction. But we will also experience successes that need to be documented through research and shared in conference presentations and publications in order to help the wider community of Christians to better "become all things, to all people," that we may "by all means . . . save some" (1 Cor. 9:22).

Chapter 10

Biblical Perspectives on Ethics in the Twenty-First Century

Paul Copan

J Robertson McQuilkin has been a friend for over thirty years. I first met him in the late 1970s when I was attending Ben Lippen School—a private Christian high school which was in Asheville, North Carolina at the time. I came to know him as a friend in the early 1980s when I studied at Columbia International University, where he was president. He taught two of my classes—Biblical Hermeneutics my freshman year and Biblical Ethics my senior year. McQuilkin's unpublished manuscript on biblical ethics, which I used while at Columbia, became a Tyndale House publication, *An Introduction to Biblical Ethics*, in 1989. Under Tyndale, the book went through two editions and various translations.

Ever since my college days, McQuilkin and I have remained in contact, writing to or visiting with each other over the years and praying for each other as well. In June 2009, McQuilkin contacted me about possibly securing an ethicist as coauthor for a revised third edition of the book. I wrote to him, expressing how much his book influenced me while in college, and, as we had the same vision and basic approach to ethics, I expressed a willingness to join him on this project.

He immediately replied, "If you do ethics, too, I can think of no one I'd rather bequeath this project to! I think the book has had a unique niche and, from what you say, still could. Maybe my query to you was a 'God-thing'!"[1] The happy ending to this story is that the biblical ethics book does indeed have new life in a third coauthored edition with IVP Academic![2]

In light of this, I am privileged to contribute to this volume honoring the life and work of McQuilkin. In my essay, I would first like to review important features of McQuilkin's own ethical reflections that have guided and shaped the thinking of many evangelicals over the years. Then I would like to draw on those reflections to explore further important considerations for ethics in the twenty-first century.

Notable Features of McQuilkin's Ethical Reflections

In this section, I want to address noteworthy features of McQuilkin's ethical thought expressed in the second edition of his ethics book (1995). I will highlight love, commitment to biblical authority, humility, comprehensiveness and nuance.

Love—But Not Without Law

McQuilkin's book uses the framework of the Ten Commandments to discuss classic and contemporary ethical issues. Rather than beginning with law, he begins with love, highlighting the proper ordering of love—first for God and then for others. Contrary to some ethicists who stress a duty to love self, he does not view love of self as a command to be obeyed—"love your neighbor *and* yourself"—but rather as a fact to be acknowledged—"love your neighbor as yourself" (Matt. 22:39, NASB). It is fitting that a book on biblical ethics emphasizes committed, self-giving relationship rather than rules. That said, McQuilkin takes the challenge of situation ethics, a view that has emphasized "love" at the expense of "law" and "commands," seriously. It is "love" without backbone, love without truth. Divine law, however, offers a needed corrective to the situation ethicist's misrepresentation of love in all its fuzziness and malleability. Indeed, love summarizes the two tables of the Ten Commandments—love toward God and love toward others. And McQuilkin points out how the psalmist delights in and loves God's law (see Ps. 119:97, 113); his book expresses this delight as well.[3]

Commitment to Biblical Authority

On the first page of his ethics book, McQuilkin lays out his approach: "Though we may utilize other sources for assistance in understanding and applying biblical truth, we shall treat the Bible as our final authority. And we will seek to apply biblical principles as well as direct mandates, but we will attempt to go only as far as Scripture itself goes and maintain the emphases of the Bible itself."[4] While working together on this project, he constantly emphasized how he did not want to impose philosophical/ethical systems on the biblical text. In his aforementioned query to me about a third edition to his book, he asked:

> Has anyone produced a BIBLICAL ethics textbook? By that I don't mean true to Scripture, but actually starting from Scripture and dealing with all ethical issues of Scripture and contemporary issues in the light of Scripture. When I was working on the original [book], organizing out from the Ten Commandments, it was the only ethics text that did so. The rest were philosophical ethics, though "biblical" in that they were true to Scripture.[5]

This indicates that as much as possible, he wanted to let the biblical text speak with full clarity. As we were writing the ethics book together, I offered certain ethical extrapolations and inferences, but he graciously replied in response to a few of them, "Almost thou persuadest me!" He preferred not to go beyond what Scripture directly mandated or the clear principles it expressed. And so I pulled back on what I intended to say.

Humility

At points in our coauthored work, we had disagreements on the topics of alcohol, the Sabbath/Lord's Day, complementarianism/egalitarianism and the capitalism/socialism question. I asked him how we should approach these matters. McQuilkin replied in an e-mail: "When we differ I feel it won't hurt to say so up front. [This approach] may lend greater authenticity."[6] And so we proceeded accordingly. In our book, we have represented "McQuilkin's view" and "Copan's view" on these points. I can't express how appreciative I am of McQuilkin's graciousness—a demeanor one does not always encounter in scholars who have developed firm views over the years!

At other points, when I might leave a statement unqualified—such as the permissibility of deception under certain conditions—he graciously questioned me. In one e-mail about a statement I made in the introduction, he asked, "Do we need to add, at least parenthetically, something to the effect that 'these issues are controversial and will be examined extensively [later in the book]'?"[7] Such was the nature of his e-mails in this process—ever humble, full of wise suggestions and willing to defer to my best judgment.

Comprehensiveness

The problem with standard ethical theories in textbooks is this: their proponents take a legitimate truth or insight about ethics and they reduce all ethical thinking to that particular insight. Some ethical theories center on duties (e.g., Kantianism/deontology) and others on consequences (e.g., utilitarianism), character (virtue ethics), circumstances (e.g., relativism and situation ethics), choice (existentialism), self-interest (egoism) and the like. But ethics in the kingdom of God can't be reduced to any of these.

Even though McQuilkin follows the structure of the Ten Commandments, he does not just emphasize duties or obligations. These are not the sum total of the moral vision of Christ's kingdom. Rather, McQuilkin has a place for discussing "virtues and vices" as well as a discussion of "root sins" such as pride—very relevant to virtue ethics. The very beginning of his book focuses on the relational virtue of love. Even when he criticizes Joseph Fletcher's relativistic "situation ethics," he reminds us that love is not so elastic a virtue as to do away with all law and duty. To love Christ is more than keeping His commandments, but it is not less.

In my biblical ethics course at Palm Beach Atlantic University, I review a number of ethical theories and their particular contributions to the moral discussion, yet I also point out how the strength of each of them proves to be a weakness. That is, ethical discussion is typically wedded to its signature feature, which results in forsaking all other aspects and thereby leads to its own logical demise. The following chart spells out various ethical theories with their particular emphases and insights, although by themselves, they are deficient.

Ethical Theory	Emphasis	Insight	Deficiency
Relativism	The rightness of acts depends on culture or circumstances. ("True for you, but not for me.")	Moral decisions or actions include concern for context; context can and should shape certain ethical judgments: "And Samuel said, 'How can I go? If Saul hears it, he will kill me.' And the LORD said, 'Take a heifer with you and say, "I have come to sacrifice to the LORD"'" (1 Sam. 16:2).	a. Makes circumstances the sole ethical consideration; b. Denies humans have fundamental dignity and rights; c. Undermines the possibility of genuine moral reforms since no objective standards exist; d. Repudiates the objectivity of evils such as the Holocaust or Soviet labor camps; e. Still appeals to moral standards such as "tolerance."
Egoism	One must do what is in one's own self-interest (e.g., giving to the poor so that I won't feel guilty).	One's own well-being is not disconnected from living rightly. "That you may live, and that it may go well with you" (Deut. 5:33).	a. Makes self-interest the sole ethical consideration—as opposed to say, communal life; b. Fails to see that personal fulfillment must be a by-product rather than a goal: "whoever loses his life for my sake will find it" (Matt. 16:25).
Existentialism	One is morally obligated to make passionate personal choices regardless of what one chooses.	One must go beyond avoidance or even mental acceptance of alternatives to taking personal responsibilities for one's actions. "I have set before you life and death.... Choose life, that you and your offspring may live" (Deut. 30:19).	a. Makes personal choice the sole ethical consideration; b. Fails to acknowledge that some acts (e.g., rape, baby torture) are intrinsically wrong.

Ethical Theory	Emphasis	Insight	Deficiency
Utilitarianism	The rightness of ethical acts or principles is determined by their consequences. ("The greatest good for the greatest number." "The end justifies the means.")	Moral acts will have varying consequences to consider, which will impact the moral nature of the act itself (cf. relativism). "Remember those who led you… and considering the result of their conduct, imitate their faith" (Heb. 13:7, NASB).	a. Makes consequences the sole ethical consideration; b. Ignores the fact that good consequences can come from bad actions or bad motives; c. Fails to recognize the intrinsic value of humans; d. Undermines natural family obligations for the sake of society.
Social Contract View	What people in society agree to makes something right. (The legal is identical to the moral.)	In a democratic society, agreement, political compromise and engagement in persuasion are important. "In abundance of counselors there is victory" (Prov. 11:14, NASB). "It seemed good to the Holy Spirit and to us" (Acts 15:28).	a. Makes agreement the sole ethical criterion; b. Confuses the legal and the moral (e.g., adultery can be legal but not moral); c. Fails to recognize metaphysical foundations for human value/rights (i.e., the image of God), which are not the result of social consensus.

Ethical Theory	Emphasis	Insight	Deficiency
Deontology (Kantianism)	One ought to obey moral rules regardless of consequences (e.g., you should tell the truth to an ex-murderer chasing after a friend; he would be guilty for killing, not you for telling the truth).	Some duties are inescapable and intrinsically right to do (e.g., worshiping and loving God). "Fear God and keep his commandments" (Eccles. 12:13).	a. Makes moral duty the sole ethical consideration; b. Fails to consider virtuous character from which right moral choices spring; and it neglects the consequences of actions, which also have moral weight; c. Makes obedience too joyless. "His commandments are not burdensome" (1 John 5:3); d. Takes for granted the existence of human dignity and moral autonomy without offering a metaphysical basis for this.
Virtue Ethics	Virtuous character and its formation (in the context of community / friendship) are central to the good life.	Moral acts and habits do not take place in a vacuum but must be cultivated in the context of community (friendship). "The fruit of the Spirit is love, joy, peace, patience, kindness, goodness, faithfulness, gentleness, self-control" (Gal. 5:22–23).	a. Makes character the sole ethical consideration; b. Overlooks the place of duties, which must be attended to in the ongoing cultivation of character; c. Fails to see that what is "natural" isn't always good; d. Does not account for deep human sinfulness.

So we see, none of these moral theories is sufficiently robust to properly sustain the moral life—particularly when they have no room for God as the basis for objective moral values and human dignity. What's more, any of these ethical theories is a pale shadow and a sterile system compared to the robust ethical outlook of God's end-time kingdom. This kingdom has come crashing into human history through God's agent, Jesus of Nazareth. In this inbreaking kingdom and the new Jesus community as subjects within it, King Jesus has a dual role as the second Adam and the true Israel.

First, He comes as the new (second) Adam to restore a fallen humanity (see Rom. 5; 1 Cor. 15). As *the* true human and *the* image of God (see Col. 1:15; 3:10; Heb. 1:3), He comes to make us, God's damaged image bearers, truly human as we become conformed to His image. Part of this restoration of humanity is that the second Adam brings about a new creation through His resurrection as a foretaste of our own.

Second, He is the new Israel—the true Son that ancient Israel was not. He faithfully lives out Israel's story. How does He do this? By coming out of Egypt, passing through the waters of baptism as the leader of a new exodus (see 1 Cor. 10:1–4), being tested in the wilderness for forty days, calling twelve apostles to Himself, eventually experiencing the curse and exile of disobedient Israel and all humanity, dying naked on a cross, but rising from the dead as the beginning of the restoration of God's people (see Hos. 6:1–2; 2 Cor. 5:17; Gal. 6:15). This grand and robust gospel story involves the creation of a new humanity and a new covenant community. As the image of God, Christ comes to restore the vocation of God's image bearers as priest-kings (see 1 Pet. 2:9; Rev. 1:6; 5:10; 20:6): to worship God and to rule creation with Him.

This grand story is one that can't be reduced to the tepid and bland gruel of this or that textbook ethical theory!

Nuance

The noted lexicographer Samuel Johnson once said that the existence of twilight is not a good argument against the distinction between day and night. I likewise remind my students that simply because ethical murkiness exists, this does not negate clear black-and-white moral distinctions. Furthermore, when we engage in ethical decision making, we should start from the clear and move to the unclear. For example, we don't begin with difficult end-of-life issues or when a woman has a life-threatening pregnancy but rather with the clear: torturing babies for fun is wrong; kindness is a virtue and not a vice; Mother Teresa was morally superior to Adolf Hitler.

McQuilkin is adept at pointing out the clear, but his work is marked by subtlety and nuance. At important points, he takes care not to overstate his case. Here I offer the examples of capital punishment and deception.

When McQuilkin talks about capital punishment, he accepts it as a morally appropriate expression of justice (see Gen. 9:6). However, he does not advocate it in sweeping terms with a one-size-fits-all approach. He writes:

> My personal conclusion is a mediating one. Capital punishment cannot be inherently immoral because God commanded it. On the other hand, God himself did not insist on it, either for the first murderer, Cain, or for the most prominent, David. Therefore, it cannot be wrong to show mercy. . . . In summary, if capital punishment is part of a reasonably just system and is used only in cases of premeditated murder with no mitigating factors and certain proof, it would probably enhance the value of life and the fabric

of justice in a society. But if it is invoked capriciously or in unjust ways, it would be better to set aside this God-given prerogative of human government.[8]

Another area of nuanced discussion is that of deception and truth telling. McQuilkin recognizes that while deception is generally wrong and that we ought to give the truth "to whom it is due" (Prov. 3:27), there are exceptions that Scripture highlights and which, we should note, a wide range of philosophers/ethicists also recognize as justifiable.

McQuilkin argues that deception is permissible in three specific areas:[9]

1. Inconsequential social arrangements: Light social deception includes jokes, games or sporting endeavors. This also includes replying "fine" to the question/greeting "How are you?"—even when one is not doing all that well.

2. Warfare: Not only does God tell Joshua to set an ambush (see Josh. 8:2), but He Himself sets an ambush on one occasion (see 2 Chron. 20:22). And Rahab engages in deception and is commended for it (see Heb. 11:31). McQuilkin observes: "If war is legitimate [McQuilkin does take a just-war view], then ambushes, camouflage, spying, deceptive strategy, communicating in code, as integral parts of war, are also legitimate."[10]

3. Opposing criminal activity: The Hebrew midwives deceived the Egyptian authorities and God blessed them (see Exod. 1:15–21). God Himself encourages deception in light of king Saul's potential threat to the prophet Samuel's life in going to anoint a new king in Bethlehem: "And Samuel said, 'How can I go? If Saul hears it, he will kill me.' And the LORD said, 'Take a heifer with you and say, "I have come to sacrifice to the LORD"'" (1 Sam. 16:2).

These, then, are a few examples showing how McQuilkin's ethical approach is biblically informed, supple, nuanced, relevant and engaging. His work offers much rich moral guidance for present and future generations.

Doing Ethics in a Post-Christian Society

In January 2014, over one hundred Wheaton College students protested the coming of Rosaria Butterfield—a former lesbian and literature professor who became a follower of Christ and, later, the wife of a pastor and the mother of several children. These particular students at Wheaton, which has been an evangelical bastion for many decades, claimed that Dr. Butterfield's story was not the only valid one and that Christians could follow Christ while still engaging in same-sex behavior. In a statement issued by college president Philip Ryken, he reminded the college community of the covenant each member must sign in order to belong to it: "Scripture condemns . . . sexual immorality, such as the use of pornography (Matt. 5:27–28), premarital sex, adultery, homosexual behavior and all other sexual relations outside the bounds of marriage between a man and woman (Rom. 1:21–27; 1 Cor. 6:9–10; Gen. 2:24; Eph. 5:31)."[11]

While Wheaton is committed to this historical understanding of sexuality as presented in Scripture, Ryken went on to affirm that the school does not shrink from evenhanded discussion and debate over these topics. Indeed, Dr. Butterfield herself met with the protesters for discussion—even though the students themselves had not been honoring the covenant statement they had signed.

This event illustrates a certain fading of the Christian "received view" on homosexual activity. The traditional view of marriage throughout history (which includes the biblical position) has been replaced by "the new normal," so we can expect more Wheaton-like scenarios.

How should we as believers respond to "the new normal"? I believe that McQuilkin's work on biblical ethics serves as a model for ethical engagement in the present and into the future. At this point, I would like to extend and apply some of McQuilkin's lines of reasoning on the topic of homosexuality and gay marriage.

Acknowledge the Minority Position

In light of the dramatic change of public attitudes toward homosexuality and gay marriage, particularly in the last few years, Christians—though rightly dismayed at this indicator of social and moral decline—should acknowledge this shift. They should first recognize their increasingly minority status, but Christians should also declare and defend a biblical ideal in speech and way of life.

The temptation for Christians, when holding to less-accepted positions, is to overreach by imposing laws with which the majority in society disagrees. Sociologist James Davison Hunter has contrasted "traditionalist" or "orthodox" groups with the "progressive" in our nation.[12] He notes that they operate from two different and competing sources of moral authority. The orthodox believe in an external, transcendent moral authority, whereas the progressive tend toward subjectivism ("Whatever makes you feel good," or "I have my rights"). The progressive side is more reticent to speak of social or moral limits and boundaries concerning what is acceptable and tends to ignore the positive influence of the biblical faith in society; the orthodox have a tendency to over-legislate, which can backfire if people's hearts and minds have not been persuaded to appreciate and accept the point of that legislation.

McQuilkin rightly reminds us of this danger when writing in the context of the homosexuality question:

> My contention is that most civil law seeks to legislate morals, and that Christian people should without apology work for laws that enforce the biblical ideal. Nevertheless, in a democratic society, legislation that is not acceptable to the majority of the people, or even to a large minority, may do a disservice to morality in general, adding impetus to lawlessness.[13]

So we must acknowledge our increasingly minority position. We should not deny reality by attempting to cling to a long-lost (or nearly so) societal ideal—though I do not deny the importance of preserving important moral, democratic and social goods by available political and social means.

Recognize the Church's Central Role in Societal Transformation

Although we are living in the post-Christian West, kingdom opportunities abound. After all, the church must be the church, regardless of the kind of society in which it finds itself. And as more and more Americans willingly identify themselves as "nones" (not having any religious affiliation) rather than "Christians," this has an upside. The West has been plagued by a cultural Christianity in which being a "Christian" has served as a protective religious cover for all manner of relativistic thinking, theological syncretism and deviant behavior—not to mention a socially acceptable country-club mentality. There is nothing like serious cultural housecleaning to bring clarity to the church's identity and calling as the salt of the earth and the light of the world.

When the church is truly the church in society, remarkable things happen! Historians have documented the dramatic societal changes wrought by the Christian faith throughout history and various societies. These began not with new laws or a political regime change, but with transformed individual hearts and families, then communities and finally societies. Faithful Christian living has resulted in moral reforms, promotion of human rights (including women's and civil rights), the emergence of modern science, widespread literacy and advancements in bioethics, arts, literature and education.[14]

Recent groundbreaking work by political scientist Robert Woodberry of the National University of Singapore has documented how "conversionary Protestant" Christians in particular have been responsible for remarkable gains in the West and elsewhere.[15] These include:

> The development and spread of religious liberty, mass education, mass printing, volunteer organizations, most major colonial reforms [abolishing slavery, widow-burning, foot binding, female circumcision, pre-pubescent marriage of girls, etc.], and the codification of legal protections for non-whites in the nineteenth and early twentieth centuries.[16]

Wherever Protestant missionaries would go, the following phenomena would invariably accompany them: literacy and education (to promote the reading of God's Word—the Bible), mass printing and print technology (in order to spread God's Word) and democracy/civil society (the result of educating all, rather than merely social elites). Woodberry's research also shows that countries with more Protestants are more democratic and have more stable democratic transitions. This is not surprising given the democratizing roots of the Reformation, which emphasized the priesthood of every believer before God, the right of every believer to study the Bible for himself in his own language and the appropriateness of pursuing any honest vocation to the glory of God.

During colonial rule, European Protestant missionaries often sought to protect indigenous peoples from abusive colonial power. Without Protestant missionaries and ministers, mobilizing mass protests to promote reform would have been difficult. These missionaries helped create a kind of "cocoon in which non-violent, indigenous political movements could develop" to press for democracy and decolonialization.[17] Woodberry urges us to look at any map where Protestant missionaries have been; there we will find more printed books and more schools per capita. Moreover, in Africa, the Middle East and parts of Asia, "most of the early nationalists who led their countries to independence graduated from Protestant mission schools."[18]

As we think about life in a post-Christian society, we must keep political involvement and cultural engagement as part of our calling in proper perspective. Scripture, with its mustard seed and leavened dough parables, reminds us—and history clearly teaches—that ultimate societal change is a ripple effect that begins with transformed human hearts through the gospel. Yes, we should be concerned about legislation promoting gay marriage and adoption into gay families and about pop culture that normalizes and even celebrates homosexual behavior. But we must remember that this lifestyle flows from a background of broken homes and lives that are in need of God's transforming power and a Christian community that welcomes homosexuals as Christ would, though without affirming their behavior.

Utilize Broadly Recognized Authorities

While McQuilkin's approach to ethics rightly emphasizes Scripture as the final authority on such matters, he also recognizes that one cannot simply quote Scripture to establish a point concerning morality. Consequently, he appeals to statistics and clinical/scientific studies to support biblical truth. This is important for Christians in a post-Christian culture. As faithful and wise witnesses in our society, quoting Scripture (special revelation) will have increasingly less impact in persuasion. We must not only establish personal trust with unbelievers through friendship and by living exemplary, transformed, vibrant and joyful lives. We must also appeal to general revelation—the revelation available to us in nature, conscience, reason and human experience. Not only does Scripture make publicly available, historically verifiable claims (e.g., 1 Cor. 15:3–8), its truths are actually borne out in the realities of human living.

Scripture itself gives us clues about strategy in a minority-Christian culture. Consider how Peter's speeches in Acts 2 and 3 and Paul's in Acts 13 are addressed to Jews. Such speeches are full of Old Testament Scripture quotations such as Joel 2 and Psalm 110. However, when Peter gives another speech to Gentiles in Acts 10:34–43, he does not directly quote Scripture. And in Paul's speech to the Athenians in Acts 17, he not only does not quote the Old Testament, he quotes pagan authorities of his day—Epimenides and Aratus. This speech and his earlier one to pagans in Lystra (see Acts 14), while not quoting the Old Testament, have thoroughly biblical themes—God is the Creator and Sustainer of all, and every human is accountable to Him and therefore should repent.

In similar fashion, First Corinthians and Paul's letter to the Romans are written to house churches with both Jewish and Gentile Christians and are full of biblical quotations. Yet letters to house churches with few or no Jewish Christians do not explicitly quote Scripture, as we see in Philippians or Colossians. As with Paul's speeches in Acts 14 and 17, Paul does not ignore the Old Testament and its themes. He simply does not cite Scripture since his audience did not have a background in Scripture as Jewish Christians did.[19] We must do likewise, engaging with unbelievers in a wise, context-sensitive manner. Gone are the days in which we could establish our point in society with "but the Bible says . . ." Of course, our goal, by God's grace, is to open people's eyes to the convicting and life-changing power of the Scriptures (see Heb. 4:12)—as was certainly Paul's goal at Athens.

Let's move from the book of Acts to the present. Dr. Butterfield, who was mentioned above and who authored, *The Secret Thoughts of an Unlikely Convert*,[20] wrote a *Christianity Today* article about her pre-Christian experience with believers who quoted the Bible to establish their point. It turned out to be a turnoff. She writes: "As a university professor, I tired of students who seemed to believe that 'knowing Jesus' meant knowing little else. Christians in particular were bad readers, always seizing opportunities to insert a Bible verse into a conversation with the same point as a punctuation mark—to end it rather than deepen it."[21]

We can learn a lesson here: we can invite post-Christian conversation partners into a respectful Mars Hill dialogue to talk about delicate, sometimes emotion-laden issues. In addition to establishing personal trust and friendship, we can engage on difficult social questions such as homosexuality or gay marriage and even abortion, and we should be wise about whether or how to appeal to Scripture.

Like Paul's appeals to the presumed-authoritative pagan thinkers Epimenides and Aratus, we can appropriate widely respected authorities—scientific research, sociological studies—to reinforce a biblical understanding of social ethics. This includes making a case for, say, traditional marriage and sex within the confines of marriage, showing the harm that comes when this is ignored. And Christians should seek to persuade hearts and minds, making clear how their argument and policies would promote the public good—not merely traditional Christian interests.

In pressing their case in the public sphere, Christians call for fair representation and principled debate. Often, those who challenge gay marriage or the "scientific basis" for same-sex attraction are politically bullied, shouted down or misrepresented. Consider the case of Robert Spitzer, a giant in the American Psychiatric Association. He was instrumental in helping remove homosexuality from the 1973 *Diagnostic Statistical Manual of Mental Disorders*—the result of political pressure, not scientific research. Yet in 2003, he investigated the claims of same-sex attracted persons undergoing sexual orientation change efforts (SOCE). He concluded, "The majority of participants gave reports of change from predominantly or exclusively homosexual orientation before therapy to a predominantly or exclusive heterosexual orientation in the past year."[22] Yet he was denounced by ideological opponents and forced to back down to the point of admitting that people could misread the data by assuming that same-sex attraction is a choice or that SOCE always leads to a "cure."[23] Though initially finding these reports "believable,"[24] he was "adamant" that he would not continue this research after the "terrible personal attacks from militant gays."[25]

Such hostile bullying makes fair-minded investigation much more difficult. (Tellingly, Spitzer's fellow researcher remained anonymous and was not named in the article.) Ironically, the gay community is often appealing to science, referring to a "gay gene" to account for same-sex attraction, though no such thing has been found. Yet ad hominem attacks follow when scientific research conflicts with or challenges the gay community's narrative. What are some of these challenges to this narrative? Here are a few:[26] (a) there is no discovered genetic component that

makes same-sex attraction inevitable; (b) various same-sex attracted persons can experience diminished same-sex attraction
or even become opposite-sex attracted; (c) the most relevant side
of the debate—the *nurture* component—is routinely ignored by
the gay community;[27] (d) same-sex attracted persons desiring to
change are not evidently harmed in this pursuit;[28] (e) children
with gay/lesbian parents—contrary to an official 2005 American
Psychological Association (APA) report—do *not* fare as well as
they do in homes with heterosexual parents;[29] and (f) catego-
rizing "fixed" homosexual identity in youth is more fluid than
proponents in the gay community will admit.[30]

What is the way forward? Dr. Elizabeth Moberly, a theologian long involved in ministry to homosexuals as director of Psy-
chosexual Education and Therapy for Bible Centered Ministries
International, rightly calls for fair representation on both sides
of the homosexuality debate:

> Neither side should make inflated claims or distort data.
> Both sides need to be frank about their own shortcom-
> ings. Truth-seeking also implies an essential concern not to
> misrepresent others and not to withhold research grants or
> publication from persons who hold other views. Genuine
> and principled disagreement needs to be respected, not dis-
> missed as homophobia or bigotry. This debate is not an easy
> one. But if we all seek to act with integrity—if we promote
> truth-seeking and show real respect for those with whom we
> disagree—then we may realistically hope for the future.[31]

Such an approach of integrity, truth seeking, respect and
graciousness exemplifies McQuilkin's work in biblical ethics and
furthermore sets a standard for present and future generations
of Christians as they grapple with difficult ethical matters in a
post-Christian context.

Part VI

Christian Leadership

Chapter 11

Encouraging the Twenty-First-Century Church:
A Letter to My Son

Roy M. King

When I entered seminary in 1977, one of my first teachers was the president of Columbia International University, J. Robertson McQuilkin. A few weeks into the course, I was granted a meeting with him in his office. I approached him with an idea for a prayer chapel on campus. Patterned after one I had used at the Campus Crusade for Christ (now CRU) headquarters in California, I encouraged him to be present to reflect the priority of prayer he spoke of in his class. He received instruction from me, a brash first-term student, with grace and openness, and the seed was sown to develop a lifelong friendship.

Robertson prays for me and my family each day. What a treasured gift from a mentor and sponsor who has opened doors for me with the school, networking relationships and publishers! My two adult children consider Robertson an adopted grandfather and spiritual leader in their lives. I have written my chapter as a letter to my son, recalling many conversations and prayer times I have shared with Robertson in his living room.

Mark,

As a father I enjoy giving you gifts. Remember your first backpack and sleeping bag? Today I have a gift for you as a young leader in your twenties who has served on staff in an established church and is now launching to work bivocationally planting a church. As God works through you to establish this missional community, I am so proud of you. I am always learning from you. Thanks for sharing new music and technology and for keeping me up to date on Spiderman!

Before you open my gift, let me remind you of a vision of the church that you gave me on one of our "guy nights," Sunday, November 13, 2011. This is a paraphrase of what you said:

> Dad, what we call the "evangelical church" often reminds me of a planned community like the Summit. There are lots of rules, including no boats or RVs in the driveway. Everything is groomed and orderly. Most of the landscaping and the houses are uniform and predictable. A Sunday service with the band, the lighting and the screens feels like going into a Disney World attraction. It is a perfectly crafted, plastic-like world.

> To me it comes off as too perfect, too groomed, too planned and orchestrated. It lacks authenticity. It subtly encourages me to sit back and let myself be entertained. It is church to be consumed. It feels tame, like visiting animals in the zoo.

> The Spirit is described as "wind," "fire," and "streams of living water," and as I read the book of Acts, I see a Spirit-birthed church that is alive and uncontrollable. I am sure

you recall those tall sea oats on the dunes we saw when we went backpacking on Cumberland Island. The ocean breeze catches the seeds and blows them in all directions to many destinations. And where the seeds land, more oats sprout. Church is an alive wildness, and it cannot be tamed, controlled, predicted or manufactured. That is the church I want to join. I am not sure what leadership looks like in this Spirit-blown church. But I see the church as clusters of Christ followers in deep community with each other, knowing they are being planted by God among people God loves. These clusters provide tastes of the life God gives.

Mark, I have been haunted with your vision ever since that late night when it poured out of your heart. So here is my gift to you: First I want to respond to your vision of the church. Then, I would like to describe the contribution of leaders in the wild, sea-oat-spreading church that Christ is building.

Responding to Your Vision of the Spirit-Blown, Wild Church

Let me assure you—you are not alone. The dream of the church God has placed in your heart echoes in the hearts of other Christ followers. There are seminary students who are seeking to retool for the second half of their adult lives who want more than to just get their ticket punched to ride at the ministry amusement park. The younger adults preparing for a life of ministry are in school to accumulate the biblical understanding, church history and theology they're missing. But I see the spark in their eyes when they see, often for the first time, what God is doing around the world. So I think your vision is an excellent biblical vision of what Christ is building that dismantles the strongholds of Satan. When the wind of the Spirit blows, the enemy of God yields to His force and falls.

Disappointment with the church as it is and longing for it to be more is not new to your generation. For example,

> Alfred Loisy, the nineteenth century historian, was right in saying that Jesus came proclaiming the Kingdom of God but what appeared was the Church. The disappointment was, and continues to be, severe. But the great irony is that today we alleviate our disappointment with the contemporary Church by pointing back to the New Testament Church which was the great disappointment to begin with! Our restless discontent should not be over the distance between ourselves and the first-century Church but over the distance between ourselves and the Kingdom of God, to which the Church, then and now, is the witness.[1]

I believe every generation of Christ followers should be aspiring to see the church serve as a better apologetic for the kingdom. Elements of your dream reflect some of the values Neil Cole sees as the changing of price tags in what is longed for by those leading twenty-first-century churches. He sees it as a shift from a "modern" to "postmodern" worldview. I am not so confident in breaking worldviews into historical chapters. I think people are always shaping and being shaped by their environment. But I do believe these contrasts show up in your longing for the "wild church." They are: "Relationship over Mission," "Authenticity over Excellence," "Experience over Proposition," "Mystery over Solution," "Diversity over Uniformity" and "Journey over Destination."[2]

Perhaps in your desire for the church there is a correcting of assumptions about how to be the church. Margaret Wheatley is talking about businesses but her critique fits many congregations of the twentieth century:

We believe that people, organizations and the world are machines, and we can organize massive systems to run like clockwork in a steady-state world. The leader's job is to create stability and control, because without human intervention, there is no hope for order. It is assumed that most people are dull, not creative, that people need to be bossed around, that new skills only develop through training. People are motivated using fear and rewards; internal motivators such as compassion and generosity are discounted.

This is not the real world. The *real* real world demands that we learn to cope with chaos, that we understand what motivates humans, that we adopt strategies and behaviors that lead to order, not more chaos. . . .

Everywhere, life self-organizes as networks of relationships. When individuals discover a common interest or passion, they organize themselves and figure out how to make things happen. Self-organizing evokes creativity and leads to results, creating strong, adaptive systems. Surprising new strengths and capacities emerge.

In this world, the "basic building blocks" of life are relationships, not individuals.[3]

The twenty-first-century church will continue to wrestle with how to live in a tension of chaos and order that encourages life without imploding. Alan Hirsch borrows from former Visa Credit Card President Dee Hock: "Hock calls this the "chaordic" principle: enough order at the center to give common identity and purpose, enough chaos to give permission to creativity and innovation. When you think of it, that is exactly how the first-century Jesus movement was organized."[4]

I wonder if church history is God's wild working, coupled with a thirst for Him in the heart of some people, exploding on the scene. Over a period of time a trap is built to contain the church. But the God who cannot be tamed keeps stirring up the dream in a fresh generation of people, and the church escapes its nice containment. As Reggie McNeal observes,

> The movement founded by Jesus was largely a marketplace phenomenon, an organic connection among people who were experiencing life together. The early days of the movement focused on simple teachings of Jesus, with particular attention to living lives of sacrifice and service to one another and to one's neighbor. Even though the movement spread very rapidly among the slave populations and common people, its appeal transcended all cultural lines. The spiritual expression of Jesus followers was not characterized by a set of religious activities layered on top of other interests. Jesus invaded all areas of life. Church was not an event or a place; it was a way of life.[5]

There is great diversity in our culture and the attractional church is being used by the Spirit to reach some people. The Sunday morning "show" does attract hurting and hunting people. I hear the stories of their journeys, and I am encouraged that God is transforming lives. I am sure that in your lifetime there will be a greater diversity of models of how churches spread the gospel. I am also confident that the missional model of putting the majority of energy and resources into "going to" will touch people not attracted to the polished energy of the modern attractional churches. And even when you look beneath the corporate services of the attractional church effective in making disciples, you will unearth the biblical elements I present in my gift to you.

So let's focus on the gift and not the wrapping paper of the church Jesus is building and has been building for two thousand years. I would say that when the hearts of leaders contain a commitment to the following three realities I will describe in this gift, the wildness of God is often just below the surface. Leaders can be filled with joy as they contribute to "chaordic" churches!

First Reality: The Wild Spirit of God!

Frame your acts of leading every day with the reality, by faith, that the Spirit is growing and spreading the church. He was the creative Agent in the physical creation of this world, and He is the Agent of this new creation that is the foundation for the coming kingdom arriving with the new heavens and the new earth.

Contribute by being in a creative collaboration with the Spirit. He gives assignments and provides resources. He unsettles hearts in conviction and then quenches the thirsty heart and fills it with peace. He grows faith, hope and love in Christ followers, taking step after step of trusting obedience.

The Spirit of God is the only One capable of taking people of all ethnicities on the planet—all levels of education and economic resources, all ages, all interests and all sorts of physical and mental capacities—and weaving them into one family. He is the God of reconciliation across theological lines and historical, racial and gender barriers.

Those blown by Him bend to His activity. They humbly offer grace mixed with truth as seen in Jesus' redeeming embrace. These wild seeds, God's people, are always learning and are always willing to hold their inadequate resources and incomplete agendas up in open hands, catching the Spirit's wind and being directed by Him.

Since the Spirit has been at work for over two thousand years, do not be surprised that the very new is often colored and mixed in with the rich heritage of the past. The hearts of God's people will always shed tears and celebrate like the songs of the Psalms. The prophets will still warn, the evangelist cannot be silent from proclaiming, the teacher will unpack that old truth, the shepherd will respond in compassion and the apostle will always sacrifice the known to go to the unknown.

There will always be music when Christ followers gather (see Eph. 5:19). Disciples will always wrestle and be the first ones to see the flaws and failures of family members. The church will always need correction, comfort and celebration. The church will be like a fire about to go out and will require a fresh Spirit breath of reviving. But know, really know, "he who is in you is greater than he who is in the world" (1 John 4:4).

The Spirit raised Christ from the dead. He is up to the task of using imperfect vessels and filling them with the lightening of God.[6]

Second Reality: Prayer as Intimate Wild Conversation

The primary way church leaders contribute to the Spirit's building of the church is through prayer in the Spirit. In relation to this, McNeal says, "Biblical teaching on the church sees the church as the ongoing incarnation of Jesus in the world, an organic life form vitally connected to Him, even married to Him."[7] Seeing the church as people living out a marriage with Christ is a life-giving image. Presently we are longing for the end of a physical separation; this makes our conversation even more of a lifeline.

As you are learning in your marriage, there is talking and then there is intimate conversation. There is comparing calendars or choosing a restaurant, and there is a becoming one through opening and receiving in the heart (see 2 Cor. 6:11–13).

In prayer we begin to see as God sees. Perspective in leadership is everything. What and how one sees determines the destination you pursue and how you spend your time and money to make the journey. Prayer is listening, brooding over Scripture, fasting and uncertainty—and also unquenchable joy, gratitude and praise. Prayer as intimate conversation is the anchor and also the sail of a leader's navigation.

Prayer sustains a rhythm of life for the long journey. An adult in his/her twenties today may well have over sixty-five years of fruitful seed-sowing service. In 1900 the adult lifespan was only about twenty-five years. How will you determine where and when to invest what the Spirit entrusts to you over the equivalent of what used to be two adult lives? The answers become clear as you live each moment receiving from God, thanking Him and then turning and offering to give what has been given to you to another. Each day offers hundreds of moments of receiving God's gifts of grace and truth and then freely giving them away. And both are orchestrated in prayerfulness. McQuilkin once said: "At age twenty I discovered the motto of Frederic Franson, the pioneer who founded five Scandinavian mission agencies at the close of the nineteenth century. Franson's life theme was CCCC: Constant Conscious Communion with Christ. The moment I heard it my heart leaped. 'That's what I want, Lord!'"[8]

God's wild seeds also break the rules of a 24/7 working world by faithfully working six days and resting one. If Solomon was writing Ecclesiastes today he would include, "There is a time to be online and a time to be offline." There are rare, appropriate times for multitasking, but live most of life by monotasking—being fully present in each moment and wisely engaging in productive labor or renewing Sabbath. All of the spiritual disciplines in which you are investing are the means to living well, and they revolve around connecting with God in the time He gives you. To the world, even the twenty-first-century church world, you will look wild in your work and your Sabbath time will be perceived as wasted. Wheatley has some good advice on this:

> The only antidote to this culture of interruption technologies is for us to take back control of ourselves. We cannot stop the proliferation of seductive technologies or the capacity-destroying dynamics of distraction or the techno-speed of life. But we can change our own behavior. In the eighth century, the Buddhist teacher Shantideva admonished, "The affairs of the world are endless. They only end when we stop them." Goodness knows what was so distracting in the eighth century, but he speaks well for our time. To restore good human capacities—thinking, meaning-making, discerning—we need to develop discipline. We need to be mindful of distraction, and disciplined enough to shut off the computer, put the phone down, make time for casual conversations, sit patiently, and listen—all without getting anxious that we're wasting time, that we won't get through our to-do list, that we're missing out on something.[9]

Remember that prayer is always the primary means of grace for aligning your leadership contribution with God's wild leading.

Third Reality: Transformation as God's Wildness in the Human Heart

Two "hot" words among Western Christians are *missional* and *radical*. Both offer a correcting balance to the church. They call for clarity on God's goal and recalibrating to the reason the Spirit is building the church. Worship is not an end in itself. Community (what my generation called "fellowship") is not the goal. Teaching for understanding instead of for active obedience does not accomplish the purpose. Those are all good components, or the means, but none are the end. Christ's goal has never changed. He did not come to be served but to serve. His service was to provide a home with the Father for the lost. He brings light to the darkness. He brings life out of death. God comes with good news for all people because the world is choking on bad news (see Luke 2:10). Christ offers *transformation*. Notice I did not write "formation." Every person is spiritually forming. Some are forming into the likeness of the devil, an idol or some vision of the perfect self. But Christ followers are being transformed into His likeness. God-defined transformation can be found in Second Corinthians 3:18, which happens to be Mc-Quilkin's life verse: "And we all, with unveiled face, beholding the glory of the Lord, are being *transformed* into the same image from one degree of glory to another. For this comes from the Lord who is the Spirit."

Make no mistake—this transforming work of the heart is surely a wild wind work of the Spirit as much as the seeds of sea oats blown by the wind. Francis Chan writes, "I don't have a four-step guide to connecting with the Holy Spirit. I would, however, like to suggest two potential obstacles for you to consider: comfort and volume."[10] He then goes on to describe how the Spirit frequently invites us into situations where His calling is to go from a place of comfort to where we would be afraid without His hand. Chan then reminds us that Jesus' wildness will push against a lifestyle of constant noise and multitasking. Noise hinders us hearing the Spirit's navigation. For a committed lover, however, the Beloved gets full attention from the moment they come in contact.[11]

When the Spirit transforms, the heart is set free from bondage. The Spirit creates a heart motivated to pay a sacrificial price to love deeply. The Spirit knows that living out of fragmented commitments leaves one starving and thirsty. The Spirit is big enough to even use life's losses, which bring us to grieving, to transform our hearts.

Most deep-level transformation occurs within three feet of another person. Surely God does do surgery one-on-one. Times of being alone with God are essential. But just as essential is how the New Testament envisions the role of community.[12] Read John 10:1–18 often, and meditate on the shepherd side of leading. Those who know and trust the shepherd have a different reaction than those not in the flock. His sheep may not fully understand the shepherd's mission, but they place high trust in the heart of the shepherd. Openness to being influenced by those leading during change is much like choosing to open a locked door to someone on the outside. When the leader knocks, the person inside inquires, "Who is there?" If they do not recognize the voice, they may only open the door a few inches and carefully inspect the visitor before opening further. But if they see a longtime friend or a loved family member, they throw the door wide open or just shout out, "It is open! Come on in."

Leaders become known and trusted through their listening and caring investments over time. There is no way to shortcut this costly investment in growing trust. Simply flashing a badge of authority and crashing in will seldom produce a welcoming response. For leaders to simply say, "You should trust me!" does not work. Trusting is not a switch we simply flip off or on. Just ask a parent who has a rebellious teenager shouting a demand to be trusted. Trust is a safe place between two people, built one brick of loving faithfulness at a time. Trust is an essential ingredient in the wild transformation of individuals' hearts.

So when someone asks, "How's it going?" the great temptation is to put on a mask with a fabricated smile and answer with a counterfeit confidence: "Fine, just fine. Everything's under control." While beneath the mask may lay unrelenting hurt and need. Don't get me wrong. I support your right to wear a mask. Masks have real social value in that they allow you privacy and space in an often brutal world. But there is a price you pay for wearing a mask. Masks cause little deaths—little soul deaths. When you wear a mask nobody (not even you) gets to find out who you really are. When you wear a mask, nobody (not even you) gets to find out what you really need. And when you wear a mask, nobody (not even you) gets to find out what you really have to offer.[13]

God's transformation begins with Jesus showing us unconditional trust and love, which moves us toward a safe place where we can remove our masks (see Rom. 5:8). It is okay that transformation—which is radical change—will generate the heat of friction and resistance. Conflict and resistance are necessary occurrences when we walk with the Spirit in change. People responded to Jesus by moving through seasons of resisting, questioning and challenging before finally embracing the transformation He was calling them to taste as new life. Effective leaders honestly communicate that wild changes will produce some level of conflict. Count on it. All change is movement. All movement produces friction, and this generates dangerous heat.

Transformational change will always include what the Bible calls repentance. Repentance often feels like going from sixty miles per hour to a sliding, grinding halt. Brakes lock up, wheels slide, and just like a special effect in the movies, the driver spins the sliding car 180 degrees and goes in the opposite direction. Repentance begins with humbly admitting God's way is best.

Pride stiff-arms the challenge of a wild God. Remember the young man who chose not to follow the way of Jesus (see Matt. 19:16–22)? Repentance gives life but only after one dies to the way one was going in life.

Conclusion: Playing Your Contribution to Honor the Master

Mark, you are a pianist and you understand jazz. Jazz is freeflowing creative expression woven into the melody of the piece. Every performance of the song is unique. Musicians are given freedom within the song to depart from the melody and extemporaneously create a solo insert. A jazz-educated audience not only claps at the conclusion but during the piece when the musician returns to the melody line following the creative insert. When jazz musicians play together, they sense when a player is feeling the music carry him or her away from and then back to the basic melody. It is beautiful to sit in the audience as creation takes place in your hearing.

In the middle of a very challenging day of ministry leadership you shared with me what Aletha, your former jazz teacher, taught you. Let me summarize your lesson:

> Aletha Jacobs taught me that a solo should say something beautiful or dark or exciting. It is a conversation between the musician and the melody. I was often told by her, "Mark, you are playing a lot of notes but not saying a whole lot." The tendency with jazz musicians is to use the solo as a way to showcase one's technical ability, prove they are a star or blow people away with quickness. No one listens or remembers those musicians. The great jazz solo pays homage to the master who crafted the piece. It reminds listeners of something they already know and love but shows it to them from a different perspective. I think today I forgot the

melody I was supposed to be playing around. It was good to get back in the right jam again.[14]

I am convinced jazz was the sound track for God's creation of the heavens and the earth. What I love about leading people in the church is God composing the jazz. Right in the middle of the challenging interaction of questions and answers, God will give an idea that brings understanding and makes it possible to move forward with change. This is relevant to your life in at least three ways.

First, you may need to pull away from a contentious change process for a long walk with God, asking His Spirit to give you creative ways to move through change constructively instead of destructively.

Second, when you are coming into an awareness of God's presence, picture entering a room where three people are already engaged in conversation about you and are eager to include you in the discussion when you show up. In Romans 8 we see all three Persons of the Trinity involved in prayer:

8:27: The Father searches the heart and knows the mind of the Spirit.

8:28: The Spirit helps us in our weakness and intercedes for us.

8:34: The Son dies for us and now is at the throne interceding for us.

They are a jazz trio inviting you to make it a quartet and join the tune.

And third, often as a group wrestles (hopefully not physically) with change, the change might itself *be being changed*. The wild One may prompt the person who introduced a change to let it be reshaped by the contribution of others. What is ultimately accomplished looks very different from the initial thinking, but the final edition actually fulfills the mission better and lets creative glory shine. The modified change may even capitalize on resources not seen when the journey toward change began.

When a group of Jesus followers is clear on the purpose of the Spirit they are seeking to accomplish, relates with high trust and love for one another, and enjoys a freedom to learn from experiments and even failures, I am sometimes stunned by what the Holy Spirit can inspire in weak human flesh.

Earlier I compared change to movement and conflict to the heat of friction. Oil helps reduce the damage of friction to moving parts, and oil is also an image of the Holy Spirit. I often pray for the Spirit to help me and all those involved in change to not be damaged by the heat being produced. The section on the fruit of the Spirit in Galatians 5 ends with the idea that none of these things are against the law. There is always room for joy, kindness, gentleness and all the rest as relationships are stressed from different positions regarding change. The fruit of the Spirit is essential in reducing the heat we create in change.

Mark, you are a leader. But do not expect to be God's provision for all of the leadership capacity needed in your ministry assignment. Instead look expectantly for the wild One to call out leadership contributions from many people, including those not serving in official leadership positions. It is just another example of the wild Spirit playing jazz. As McQuilkin says, "An essential element of demonstrating that Christ is indeed Lord in a congregation is a heart attitude of humility and love. . . . Whatever the structure, if the New Testament model is to be followed, the authority and responsibilities of leadership will be dispersed among several, not reserved for a single leader." Diffusing the leadership contribution among several people spreads the joy tasted through exercising the three realities of my gift to you. Think of my gift to you as a large gift basket to unwrap and set on the table for many to enjoy.

Dance with the Spirit, and let Him lead. Enjoy intimacy throughout your day and in special moments alone with Him in prayer. He will whisper to you! Expect His work to be major heart surgery—transforming every aspect of thought, word and deed for the individual and the community of Christ followers. God is into personal and group change, so ride the wave.[16]

Chapter 12

Helping Young Leaders Become What God Intended

Hans Finzel

Leaders make things happen. Certainly J. Robertson Mc-Quilkin fits that description well. My reflections will not dive into his writings but into his personal impact on countless students like myself, who went on to many roles of leadership in the cause of the Great Commission around the world. Yes, his writings were significant, but in my opinion, more impactful is his real-life mentoring of countless future leaders. Robertson launched a whole generation of leaders from CIU during his years as president. But more than that, he continued to launch them long after he stepped down from formal leadership as the president of the school. Robertson's impact on so many crucial leaders in the kingdom of our Lord is a great demonstration of the power of influence in later years, long after vacating formal positions.

I'll never forget the day I arrived as a brand-new, wide-eyed student at Columbia Bible College (now CIU) for fall classes in 1971. Robertson had been recently appointed as the new president. He took the reins of leadership, arriving from Japan with his wife Muriel and family. They came to Columbia having left their first love and passion, the call of God to be missionaries to Japan. The Lord led the McQuilkins away from that call into a broader influence at CIU.

At that time, I had no inkling that the life of Columbia's new leader and president, Robertson, would intersect my own life in a mentoring relationship that would weather four decades! That year marked the beginning of a lifelong friendship.

Now, as I look into the rearview mirror of my own life as a ministry leader, pausing to reflect on the intervening forty years, I see clearly just how great an impact Robertson had on me in those formative years at CIU.

Yes, I was once young, and Robertson did indeed have a profound impact on my own life and direction into Christian leadership. It all began at that early stage of my journey. But, as we'll see the story unfold, Robertson not only helped launch me when I was a young student at CIU, he intentionally stayed in touch with me. All along my journey, he continued to encourage me, investing of his time and wisdom; and, as only Robertson can do, he always challenged my thinking and choices as I stepped into each of the roles I've served in through the years. Again, we're talking about four decades of ongoing impact on me since my graduation from CIU! Who does that in this generation? As you know, very few would care enough to stay connected at that level.

What makes this story even more stunning is that this was the pattern Robertson chose to follow with many, many of the graduates of his beloved CIU. This choice made by Robertson speaks so highly of his life of integrity, commitment and submission to his Lord Jesus, lived out day by day, month by month and year by year for these many decades. He has been laser-focused, as a mentor, on each of us.

In my case, I knew that Robertson was standing with me as our Lord Jesus' instrument to assure, as best he could, that I would maximize my own potential to become all God intended for me to be.

When I landed in Columbia, I had just recently become a follower of Christ while studying at the University of Alabama. Well, to be honest, I wasn't doing much studying. That era in America was the end of the turbulent 1960s, and I was very much in the middle of the hippie and antiwar movement. To say the least, I was a rebel without a cause until I found Christ. Actually, I realized later that Jesus was the one who found me and arrested my downward spiral into total lostness. Thanks to God's amazing grace and mercy, I was radically converted as a freshman student at the University of Alabama. Almost instantaneously I felt the call into ministry. It became obvious to me pretty quickly that I no longer had any interest in studying at the university but wanted to find a place where I could prepare for ministry. Looking back these many years later, I realize that God got me to Tuscaloosa, Alabama as a lost eighteen-year-old kid not to study but to find Christ through an active student movement there.

Soon after my conversion, I moved in with the four students who had led me to Christ. I was a sponge, soaking up everything I could put my hands on about my newfound hope and faith. These guys gave me a box of great books to read to feed my hunger, and, buried in the bottom of the box, under lots of other stuff, was a simple catalog. On the cover of that catalog was the slogan of CBC, "*To know Him and to make Him known.*" I could not believe there was a school that had that purpose statement, which totally aligned with my newfound passion to learn about and share Christ. Those words on the cover of that catalog leapt off the paper and grabbed my heart. Somehow these guys at the University of Alabama had some sort of connection with a small independent Bible college in South Carolina. So there it was, in the box with other books, obviously ordained by God to start me on my path of growth in Christ. As soon as I saw the motto, I told my friends, "I'm going to school there!"

A year later, I transferred out of the University of Alabama and began my new life at CIU, sight unseen. I did not need to visit the campus before deciding to go there; it was a clear call of God on my life.

It wasn't long after my arrival at CIU that I was introduced to Robertson. Well, not really introduced, but I began to see him in front of the student body in Shortess Chapel, as he would speak to the students during daily required chapel sessions. He was the president, and I was in awe of his leadership. It was my first exposure to a prominent Christian leader, and I immediately began to see that there was a difference in what the world thinks of as great leadership and leadership in God's economy. Eventually I had the chance to meet him personally, and a lifelong friendship began.

Robertson was not the easiest person to talk to, but I did sense that he genuinely cared about my fellow students and me. After all, we were lowly students and he had big issues to deal with as president. I guess that I was honestly intimidated by his presence. I was so new to the world of Christians and how we were supposed to behave and what we were to say.

As a side note, years later Robertson told me that at the time, he had doubted I would make it through CBC and graduate. Not because I was not smart or gifted enough but because I was a free-spirited ex-hippie thrust into a confining culture of rules and regulations. It is true that my arrival at Columbia was a huge culture shock for me as I'd grown up in the nominal-Christian world. But I soon discovered that the godly teaching and culture was exactly what I needed as I embarked on my new life in Christ. I am thankful that Robertson saw something of great promise in me despite those vast cultural differences.

I will always be thankful for the education I received at CBC. I did graduate with a bachelor's degree in 1974, but what happened to me during my time there was so much more than an education. I transferred into the school to learn about knowing Christ and making Him known, and on every level of my journey, that was embodied to me by student leaders, faculty and, of course, Robertson. I got to know my Master Jesus Christ, and as a huge bonus I met my future life mate, Donna Bubeck! I also received my call to missions while a student at Columbia. My life direction was set, and I was off to seminary, marriage and then full-time ministry.

It is amazing to me, looking back on those early years, that I was eventually invited to join the Board of Trustees of CIU, where I have now served, as of this writing, for twenty years. In that role, it is an honor to have been asked to reflect on the leadership legacy of Robertson. Specifically, I want to address how he launched future Christian leaders to "be all that God wanted them to be."

For me personally, having now spent forty years in leadership myself, it's a blessing to be able to share specific ways that Robertson influenced me and so many other young developing leaders. Although I had a lot of God-given, raw leadership strengths and ambitions as a young student at Columbia, a bird's-eye view back across the years has brought into focus the strong part that Robertson had in launching me. I'm so grateful for the lessons I learned from Robertson during those years at CIU; those lessons began to shape me into who I am today. But it was after I'd graduated and he had retired from the presidency that I learned the most from Robertson.

From the outset, Robertson was not what I envisioned as a strong leader; his personality was different. A lot of that had to do with my learning about Christian leadership in juxtaposition to the world's opinion, which is all I had ever known. He was rough around the edges—sometimes seeming almost gloomy or caustic in the way he communicated. He was hard to read and tough to get to know. He was always friendly, but smiles seemed to be somewhat forced. Why did he return from Japan, I wondered? Does he really fit this role? Was it just for the sake of carrying on the family business that he came back? The board must have seen a lot more in him.

As I will unpack in the following reflections, I came to see that Robertson came back for us. He came to serve me and the countless thousands of other students who would be highly impacted under his leadership. The world's view of effective leadership is often right out of Wall Street brashness and the corporate boardrooms of America. But I soon began to realize that Christian leadership is modeled after Christ and what is known as gentle, quiet servant leadership. Reluctant leaders make the best leaders, and Robertson became exhibit A.

As I pondered Robertson's mentoring role, I decided to highlight six characteristics of his life. He displayed all of these in his leadership, and each of these characteristics impacted generations of students at CIU. Even more notably, these characteristics endured after he left the leadership of the school, and continue to this day. I did not include obvious foundational factors seen in his great writings, godly character, spirituality and strong biblical foundations. These topics and characteristics, which are so evident in Robertson, are well covered in the other chapters of this book. Building on those foundation stones, I chose instead to focus on leadership characteristics that specifically helped launch a generation of Christian leaders into the harvest fields of the world.

Imperfection

When we are young, many of us tend to be full of ourselves. We think we know all the answers. We overestimate our gifting and underestimate the challenges of Christian leadership. That certainly was the case for me. It took God a number of years to help me realize how truly imperfect I really am. My first impression of Robertson was that he was not polished but rough around the edges. He seemed to know how far from perfect he was. It's hard to put my finger on, but he seemed to have a strength that came out of a place of weakness—much like what the apostle Paul meant when he said, "That is why, for Christ's sake, I delight in weaknesses, in insults, in hardships, in persecutions, in difficulties. For when I am weak, then I am strong" (2 Cor. 12:10, NIV).

Robertson seemed almost uncomfortable in his role of leadership, serving reluctantly because of the call of God, a sense of duty and obedience. As I already said, his first love was being a missionary in Japan. My hunch is he never aspired to the role of president at CIU. I've never asked about that, it just seemed obvious that he would have felt more comfortable, personally, staying in Japan and serving his Lord alongside his beloved wife, Muriel. But God had very different plans for this couple, to use them on a larger stage of leadership.

The first great lesson I learned about leadership from Robertson is that you don't have to be perfect to be used by God for leadership. You don't have to be eloquent or tall or strikingly handsome. The world's view of leadership is far from biblical. When we are weak, then God is strong through us. I am not at all saying that Robertson was not a strong, effective leader, because I think he was. It's just that he emanated a broken, imperfect, very human spirit through his persona. That humble spirit, I came to learn, is a huge requirement for effective leadership in God's economy. His example made room for all of us imperfect young students who were also aspiring to leadership for the cause of Christ.

Humility

There's no question in my mind that Robertson is a humble man. If you know him at all, you know that he is anything but proud about who he is and what he has accomplished. It reminds me of another leader God set apart for a special role, Moses. What does Robertson have in common with Moses? They both possess that critical trait of humility. When God chose Moses at the burning bush, there were a host of reasons Moses gave God for why it was not a good idea. I'm quite sure that Robertson gave the Lord a similar list of reasons when he left Japan to take over the presidency of CIU. What was the fundamental reason that God wanted to recruit Moses when He could have chosen so many other possible leaders? It was the trait of humility. Referring to Moses, Numbers 12:3 says he was "more humble than anyone else on the face of the earth" (NIV). Pride always comes before a fall, so humble leaders tend not to fall. That's certainly been true of Robertson. He finished his formal leadership roles so well. In these "afterglow years" of his life, Robertson's leadership legacy remains strong and unwavering. The last great act of any leader is to finish well, and we who were influenced by

Robertson are so thankful that he gave us that example to round out all that we learned from him.

Some young leaders already have the humility piece in place from the start of their ministry. It could be any number of thorns in the flesh that keep them from being proud. But others like myself need to be broken and humbled along the way to prepare us for better leadership. We can't get very far without humility, and we can't learn it in a seminary class or buy it on Amazon. It comes from a place of brokenness in life experience. Robertson helped us become the leaders God wanted us to be by living out that most important leadership quality of all—humility.

Accessibility

Today the millennial generation loves leaders who are vulnerable, transparent and accessible. I just think it's great that Robertson demonstrated those three characteristics long before they were popular. Though he was so very busy in his presidency and even though I was an "insignificant" student, he knew me by name. I guess it just proves that he was not in it for the power, prestige or position that comes with such a job. He was in it for us, the students. I always felt that no matter how busy he was with "more important stuff," we had access to him. Here is the lesson to be learned from him: we the students *were* the important stuff. It is so easy in ministry to get wrapped up in a position that we forget whom we serve. We serve the students, the congregation, the missionaries or whomever else it is that we say we serve.

I remember one occasion as a student at CBC in 1972 when a number of us were unhappy about the rules in the student handbook. If you compare the handbook then to the one today at CIU, you would think that there are no rules at all nowadays.

Speaking as a trustee of the school today, I like relaxing senseless rules but keeping enough to build character and discipline. Back then we had some crazy rules. For example, I was from Alabama and loved to go barefoot outside. One of the rules of the school was that we could not leave our dormitory without shoes on. I remember wanting to ask the administration, "Where do you find that in the Bible?" I was assuming that all the rules in the handbook would have a chapter and verse to legitimize them. Dumb assumption! Eventually Robertson agreed to meet with a number of us unhappy students to talk about the rules. And the thing that sticks out in my mind is that we did not meet in his office. In fact we did not meet in any building. We met outdoors under some trees in the nearby forest that surrounds the campus. I don't remember what was said that day. What I do remember is the accessibility of our president. He was willing to sit on the ground and talk to us face-to-face about our concerns. That was huge. In fact he did more listening than talking. I felt heard! What a model of great leadership he provided for all of us, all very young and aspiring leaders. I don't think many rules changed because of that conversation, but he did help us understand the discipline of having to follow rules to help shape character, and I certainly agree with that.

What is the lesson here? Vulnerability, transparency and accessibility are key leadership qualities that Robertson modeled for the up-and-coming young generation of leaders. He was way ahead of his time, doing what came naturally to him.

Not too long ago I experienced a major conflict with some of my international staff in our organization. I remembered that lesson from Robertson. Instead of having them all come to my office in my building on my turf, I flew to their country of ministry in Africa and met with them face-to-face in their living rooms. We resolved the conflict, and I think a lot of it had to do with that face-time lesson I learned so long ago. Robertson believed in FaceTime® accessibility in leadership long before Apple Computer registered that app as a trademark.

Reluctance as a Servant Leader

Reluctant leaders make the best leaders. This really goes back to that humility piece. When you aspire to leadership in the church or in ministry, you aspire to a good thing (see 1 Tim. 3:1), but you have to be very careful about your motives. There are many wrong motives for leadership, which include things like power, prominence, position, prestige and even a big paycheck. As I already mentioned, Robertson and Muriel really wanted to stay in Japan and serve as missionaries with The Evangelical Alliance Mission. But the Board of Trustees of CBC came calling, and they accepted the assignment. Just like when God approached Moses at the burning bush, He had another plan for the McQuilkins.

It was obvious to all the students that Robertson had a heart for missions. He often spoke of their work in Japan. I am sure he agreed to come and serve only on the condition that he would be able to send more workers into the harvest and influence a generation of future missionaries. And that is just what he was able to do.

I define servant leadership as simply caring more about the good of the team than your own career. Robertson became a great model of a servant leader—he did what he had to do. Whom did he serve? He served me. He served all the students who studied at CIU and graduated to go into their life's callings. He served the board of trustees and the faculty. Finally, he served the entire constituency of CIU. He taught the future leaders launched out of CIU that God often calls on us to walk into roles we don't really aspire to for the good of the cause. We often have to lay down what we desire for our lives and instead embrace what He needs us to do. That is the heart of servant leadership.

Living the Vow

Everyone was stunned when Robertson prematurely stepped down from the presidency to serve his ailing wife. He was not even close to retirement age. Many would say he was in the prime of his leadership. He reflected, after his many years of marriage to Muriel who sacrificed so much to take care of him, "I don't have to take care of her now; I get to." By the time he made that decision to step down, I was long gone from Columbia, so I was not as close to him or the school. I only know the story from the outside looking in. He laid aside his leadership to care for his beloved, Muriel, who was battling Alzheimer's. Both publicly and privately he said with great joy, "She served me all these years, and now it's my time to serve her." He did it with great joy. He cared for her full-time for thirteen years until her death in 2003.

I remember going to the little house on Monticello Road and visiting with him and Muriel. She was bedbound, and he would carefully wash, clothe, feed and read to her. In doing so, he lovingly cared for her every need. I don't think he ever anticipated that one of the greatest teachings from his life would come from this example to all of us husbands to love our wives in sickness and in health. Robertson is a man who lives by vows.

What a refreshing example Robertson is to us in today's society that has pretty well lost the concept of living by vows. People talk about being in starter marriages. It seems like spouses are traded in like used cars that have lost their appeal. Thank you, Robertson, for showing a generation what marriage is all about.

Lifelong Mentor and Encourager

Recently I completed a podcast and a chapter in a new book on the mentors of my life and what they taught me. I am so proud that Robertson was on that short list of the ten people who mentored me along my journey of growing as a leader for God's cause. Twenty years after I left CIU and had spent decades in ministry already, he continued to stay in touch with me and believe in me. When he left CIU to care for Muriel, he felt I was the kind of person who could come and lead CIU, and he voiced that belief to me! Robertson's belief in me was an enormous boost and encouragement to me.

Some of the most powerful mentors in my life were what I call organic, informal mentors. They never declared to me, "Hans, I would like to mentor you." No, they just came alongside me and believed in me, trusted me and encouraged me along my own leadership journey. I am one of many—probably hundreds—of young leaders that Robertson helped become what God intended. For that I will always be grateful.

I am grateful that I know Robertson McQuilkin. He enriched my life and modeled servant leadership for me from the first time we met. He helped me in my journey in countless ways. Through the years Robertson has always invited me to his home for lunch whenever I'm in Columbia for board meetings. I'm sure he extends the same invitation to a host of others, all of whom he has also impacted. I've taken him up on the invitation as often as I am able. I've enjoyed getting to know his wife, Deb, who is such a delight. I've always enjoyed the times with him personally at his home more than those in the formal settings around CIU. We've had some of the deepest talks about my own leadership journey in his living room, kitchen and backyard. He has always offered me great advice though the years. He cares about me, wants to keep up with what I'm doing and has helped me process some big life decisions along the way.

Donna and I are deeply grateful for the legacy we received from Robertson. CIU continues to train up effective servants of our Lord Jesus, built upon the cornerstone of Jesus Himself, its principles lived out in the life of leaders like Robertson. Today it's our joy to be able to pass along the same powerful lessons we learned from Robertson and CIU to our own family and to all those we've been called to lead in this generation.

Conclusion

Five Core Values for the Twenty-First Century

George W. Murray

Anyone reading this book will have realized by now that there is an intimate connection between J. Robertson McQuilkin and Columbia International University. Not only was Robertson's father the first president of the school, but Robertson himself is a graduate of CIU, taught theology at CIU for two years (after seminary), was the headmaster of CIU's boarding high school for six years and later served as CIU's president for twenty-two years.

Every family, organization and school has core values, whether those values are stated or not. These are the deeply held beliefs that drive the behavior of any given group. When Robertson left Japan with his family to return to the United States to become CIU's third president, one of the first things he did was to ferret out the core values of the university. He is quick to say that he is not the original formulator of these core values, but he took the pains to probe the organization, uncover CIU's core values and then articulate them succinctly. There are five: the authority of Scripture, victorious Christian living, world evangelization, prayer and faith, and evangelical unity. Now, almost twenty-five years after Robertson's presidential tenure at CIU ended, the university's leadership and family remain firmly committed to those five core values.

Let me give a brief description of CIU's five core values, show you how those values were exemplified in the life of Robertson, and then, let's briefly ask and answer this question: Are these five core values still relevant as we move into the rapidly changing world culture of the twenty-first century?

CIU's Five Core Values

First, *the authority of Scripture*. While CIU's five core values are not necessarily listed in order of priority, this first one is, because it is the foundation and basis of the other four. The CIU family (Board, administration, faculty and staff, students and alumni) believe that the sixty-six canonical books of the Bible are the God-inspired, inerrant, reliable Word of God and should have functional authority over every area of Christian living and service.

Next, *victorious Christian living*. Over the years at CIU, this core value has been given different names, the two most prominent being "authentic Christian living" and "the Spirit-filled life." No one quibbles about the terminology because everyone agrees on the essence, namely that personal victory over self and sin and all-sufficient power for Christian living and service are gloriously possible for every child of God through faith and obedience to Christ, God the Son, who dwells in us by His Spirit.

Then, *world evangelization*—that is, the imperative of reaching the entire world with the message of the gospel of Jesus Christ. At CIU we believe that when Jesus told us to go into all the world and preach the gospel to everyone, everywhere, that is exactly what He meant. He wants every man, woman, boy or girl living anywhere on planet Earth to have the opportunity to hear, understand and respond to the gospel. This will not happen unless those of us who have the gospel message deliberately take it to those who don't. And our understanding of "world evangelization" includes gathering those who respond positively to the gospel into local reproducing congregations for fellowship, accountability and mutual service.

Prayer and faith is another CIU core value. While two things are listed (prayer *and* faith), they are really one core value since they are inseparable. This is our way of stating that all our living and serving must be done in utter, helpless dependence upon the Lord. Jesus said that without Him we can do nothing (see John 15:5). Unfortunately, our human experience reveals that there are many things we can and do accomplish without Him (often with accolades from others), but none of those purely human accomplishments bring Him glory or last forever. Individually and corporately, those in the CIU family are believing, praying people. Or at least we should be. This is a core value that can only be validated by comparing stated belief in the importance of prayer with the actual practice of prayer since prayer is so contrary to self-sufficient human nature.

Last but not least, the CIU family believes in the importance of *evangelical unity*. We readily and intentionally join hands with all those who hold to the evangelical fundamentals of the faith, even though we may disagree on secondary (though not unimportant) biblical/doctrinal issues. Since unity itself is a strong biblical teaching, we look for all those areas of truth where we can agree in order to unite with others, rather than seeking areas of secondary disagreement as grounds for separation. Evangelical unity is not just something we tolerate; it is something we celebrate. We seek to practice the truth of the oft-quoted dictum of the early church father Augustine: "In essentials, unity. In non-essentials, liberty. In all things, charity."

McQuilkin and CIU's Five Core Values

Robertson, when he became CIU's third president in 1968, not only articulated (with the agreement of the CIU Board, administration and faculty) these five core values; he embodied them in his life and teaching. Both Brad Mullen and Ralph Enlow have already done a superb job earlier in this book giving us two accurate and insightful overviews of McQuilkin's writings and life. I would like to share some additional anecdotes from his life, especially as they relate to CIU's five core values.

I also had the privilege of working with Robertson and observing him close-up. When the McQuilkins came back from Japan in 1968, I had just finished my undergrad program at CIU and had also completed all the class work for a CIU master's degree in Bible. My fiancée needed to complete one more year of studies for her undergrad degree at CIU, and since we were committed to postponing marriage until after her graduation, I filled out a work application to join the school's staff, hoping to work in the music department. To my surprise, McQuilkin hired me as his personal administrative assistant, and my desk was in an office right next to his. He asked me to call him "Robertson" and treated me like a true ministry peer (though it took me many years before I felt the liberty to call him by his first name). What an amazing year we had together! The university had somewhat lost momentum during a presidential search that had lasted over two years, so there was lots of catch-up work to do. We regularly worked more than twelve hours a day, often including Saturdays. At the end of that year, he asked me to continue working with him but was quick to release me when I told him of the call of God on my life for missionary service in Italy.

Twice during our thirteen years of missionary service in Italy, Robertson asked me to come back to CIU for a quarter (ten weeks) while on furlough to teach as an adjunct professor of Bible and missions, which I gladly did. Twice he came to Europe to visit us and see our missionary work firsthand.

In 1980 I was writing my master's thesis while still living and serving in Italy. Knowing that I was under a lot of pressure to complete my thesis, the McQuilkins invited me to come back for six weeks to CIU, where I would have much better access to CIU's well-stocked library. Additionally, they invited me to live in their home during that time, which I did. Talk about a close-up view of their personal and family life! (More about that later.)

Then in 1985, after I had moved back to the United States with my family and had become the director of the Bible Christian Union, Robertson invited me to join the CIU Board of Trustees. I had the privilege of serving in that role for fifteen years. Always the teacher/mentor, Robertson during those years deliberately and periodically shifted me from one board committee to another in order for me to have exposure to all aspects of the university. He also asked me to chair various board committees, which meant even more intimate contact with him, as the president works closely with each board committee chairperson. Finally, he asked me to join the CIU Board executive committee where, among other things, thorny and challenging board issues were often debated and discussed before being brought to the full board. Again I saw the man close-up, often under high-pressure circumstances.

I was at the board table on the day that Robertson surprised us all with his resignation from the CIU presidency in order to return home and care for his wife, Muriel. In the years following that decision, I visited their home more than once and watched Robertson selflessly and lovingly tend to all of Muriel's needs. And, in the years since I have become CIU's fifth president and now chancellor, Robertson has been my chief confidant, advisor, prayer partner and cheerleader, second only to my wife. Through all of these close-up associations over many years, I have seen CIU's five core values embodied in Robertson.

Before I give some individual examples related specifically to each of the five core values, two big overall examples involving all five of CIU's core values stand out.

First is the way in which Robertson recruited and hired CIU faculty members. He rightly delegated the pursuit of new faculty to his academic deans and faculty search committees but wisely reserved the right to have final veto power over any recommended faculty candidate. President McQuilkin was committed to having faculty who were highly qualified academically, and did everything in his power to: (a) recruit candidates who already had an earned doctorate or (b) require existing faculty who did not have an earned doctorate to pursue doctoral studies.

However, during the school year of 1968-1969, when I was his administrative assistant, and in subsequent years when I served on the Academic Affairs Committee of the CIU Board of Trustees, more than once I watched him turn down faculty applicants who were highly qualified academically. And more than once I was dismayed at his rejection of these excellent candidates—that is until I realized the underlying fundamental reason for his 'no' verdict: those candidates did not understand and espouse CIU's core values!

Second is the manner in which Robertson mentored and trained all new faculty members and high-level administrators in the early years of their employment at CIU. Each year, all new faculty members and high-level administrators were required to attend a monthly extended orientation training session, during which time CIU's core values were carefully explained scripturally and illustrated practically. Although Robertson recruited veteran faculty members and administrators to help him teach these extended orientation sessions, he was always the lead instructor and was personally present for most of those sessions.

I am convinced that these two practices are what have enabled in a remarkable way the CIU family to consistently operate in unified conformity with its stated core values over these many years. But how did Robertson personally embody CIU's core values? Here are just a few of many more examples I could give.

The Authority of Scripture

Because this core value affirms the inerrancy and reliability of the Bible, it logically concludes that Scripture has functional authority over every area of life.

One day Robertson and I were participating in an off-campus funeral, and for unavoidable reasons, we left campus in our car later than we should have. Robertson was driving, and knowing how important it was for us to be at our destination on time, I fully expected him to fudge on the speed limit. He didn't (to my consternation), yet we still arrived on time (barely). It was a great lesson to me on living under the authority of Scripture, which clearly teaches us to submit to all governing authorities because those authorities have been established by God (see Rom. 13:1–7).

I also remember telling Robertson once that I would have a hard time working together with another Christian who did not believe in eternal security, a truth I held (and hold) to strongly. While commending me for my conviction, he chided me for my inability to work with those who did not hold to the same conviction, pointing out to that there is more than one clear warning in Scripture not to take one's salvation for granted. In doing so, Robertson, when it came to interpreting and applying Scripture, not only lived, but taught others to live by the principle "It seems easier to go to a consistent extreme than to stay at the center of biblical tension."[1]

Victorious Christian Living

A victorious Christian is one who is filled, or controlled, by the Holy Spirit. Moreover, since one of the Holy Spirit's main roles is to glorify the Lord Jesus, the fruits of the Spirit are those qualities of Christlikeness that become evident in the life of a trusting/obeying Christian. I personally saw Robertson manifest those fruits over and over again.

In my first year of employment at CIU, to my great disappointment, I discovered that the staff and faculty were not perfect people (something I had wrongly assumed during my CIU student days). More than once I would express my righteous indignation to Robertson about some of my fellow employees who were passive-aggressive, divisive or even deliberately lazy. While not excusing any of those wrong behaviors, Robertson would calm me down, urging me to love and pray for my fellow workers, reminding me that we need to work with people "as and where they are," just as our Lord patiently does the same with us. This was an invaluable lesson for me in the leadership roles I would fill in subsequent years.

For another case in point, I remember one local evangelical church where I had gone twice with a CIU student team to minister. In both instances, when we had poured ourselves out in service to that congregation, the pastor asked his people to generously contribute financially to a love offering for the CIU ministry team, which they did. And after both occasions, CIU never received a cent from that church, not even for travel expenses. I was quite upset with this injustice and asked Robertson what he thought I should do, to which he responded, "Nothing." He then pointed out to me that justice was ultimately God's responsibility (see Rom. 12:19), and that, with Christ, we need to delight in being taken advantage of (see 2 Cor. 12:10), knowing that the Lord will supply all our needs (see Phil. 4:19).

World Evangelization

In conformity to the biblical focus on the primary thrust of the apostle Paul's ministry, Robertson has always stressed the importance of preaching the Christian gospel to those who have never heard it. He has demonstrated this by actually going to one of the least-reached nations in the world (Japan), by always wishing he could go back (even after fruitful years of service at CIU) and by emphasizing in his writings the priority of reaching the "dark" (unreached) part of the world. More than one of his most-needed faculty and staff felt the call of God to leave CIU and go to an unreached part of the world, no doubt due to the influence of his speaking and writing, and he never stood in their way.

When I lived in the McQuilkin home, I observed Robertson early every morning praying earnestly over the individual pages of thick, three-ringed notebooks that contained the prayer letters of hundreds of CIU grads working among the world's least-reached peoples.

Prayer and Faith

When I joined the CIU Board of Trustees, one of the first things that amazed me was Robertson's insistence that the beginning of every board meeting be spent in an extended, unhurried time of worship and intercession. This wasn't just a nice preliminary to the board's business; it *was* the board's business. And at the end of every board meeting (which is often when CEOs are the most worn out), Robertson always stayed behind to gladly meet with board members who wanted to continue the extended time of corporate prayer.

Robertson's practice of periodically taking a whole day or several days for personal prayer and reflection set an example for me that I have imperfectly implemented in my own life. I can also verify that I have rarely had a personal conversation with Robertson about anything that has not, at his insistence, included prayer, either before or after and often both.

In CIU's historical archives, there are true stories of God's amazing financial provision for the school in response to prayer and faith. In some of the early years, large financial goals were set, and, often at the last minute, God would provide. In the fifteen years that I served on the CIU Board, I saw time and again how the Lord provided financially for CIU in response to the faith and prayer of the school's leadership. In more recent years, people have wondered if CIU continues to move forward by prayer and faith and if God has continued to provide as in the past. Permit me this one wonderful example of God's provision during my 2000–2007 tenure as the school's leader in order to show that this core value is still very current in the life of CIU.

From its beginning, CIU has had the unique system (deliberately designed by the school's leadership) of relying on monthly gift income in order to fully pay all faculty and staff. Many times through the years, if there has been a financial shortfall in a given month, the administration, faculty and staff have all taken a reduction in pay. If in subsequent months more than enough gift income is received, past reductions are restored. The only time this "payback" cannot occur is if there is still a shortfall at the end of

CIU's fiscal year (June 30). Therefore, every CIU president (myself included) has always prayed earnestly for strong gift income in June so that any monthly pay reductions within that fiscal year could be fully restored.

Since our giving constituency knows that June 30 is the end of CIU's fiscal year, the amount of gift income received in June is usually (and needs to be) quite high. For many years, we had a foundation that faithfully gave us an unrestricted gift of $100,000 every June. Though I always "prayed harder" in June for the Lord to provide for CIU's financial needs, I also had the comfort of knowing that, regardless of what others gave, at least our foundation friends would be sending us $100,000. One particular year, our need in June was unusually high; the end of the month was approaching, and the expected gift had not yet come from the foundation. I asked one of our staff to call the foundation to make sure the gift was still coming on schedule only to find out that, for whatever reason, our annual CIU grant request had not been included on the foundation's agenda of grant requests for that year. They regretfully informed us that all of their grant money for that year had already been allocated and that no gift would be coming to CIU in June! What to do? *We prayed!* And God answered in an amazing way.

Just days before the end of June, I received a phone call from an alumnus of CIU in Arkansas informing me that his older sister, also a CIU graduate, had just died. His sister had remained single all her life and had faithfully taught Bible for over fifty years in the public schools of rural Arkansas at a minimum wage salary. I immediately knew who he was talking about because his sister, by maintaining a very simple and frugal lifestyle, managed to be a faithful donor to CIU. Her brother informed me that he was executor of his sister's estate and that, frankly, he was sure his job would be very simple since she had almost nothing of this world's goods. To his surprise, he discovered that his sister had a lockbox at the local bank, and when the box was opened, in it was a gift for CIU—a gift that she had been faithfully accumulating for over fifty years. The amount? $100,000! That gift, along with many others, enabled us to pay our faculty and staff in full for the year.

Evangelical Unity

CIU's core value of evangelical unity does not mean unity at the *expense* of biblical truth, but unity as a *part* of biblical truth. This is not theological passivism (unity at any cost), but theological respect for equally Spirit-filled believers who sincerely differ with us on secondary issues.

Robertson has a core of essential doctrines that is consistent with biblical, historical Christian orthodoxy, but outside of that he not only permitted theological diversity, he promoted it. He taught us not only to respect those who differed with us theologically, but to seek and celebrate the unity that we could and should experience with others in spite of those differences.

I was teaching as adjunct faculty at CIU when the Vineyard church movement was birthed in California under the leadership of the late John Wimber. The movement was very controversial because of its strong and at times bizarre emphasis on "signs and wonders." One of Wimber's early ministry partners was the late Chuck Smith, who later parted ways with Wimber to start the Calvary Chapel church movement. Though Smith was not as extreme as Wimber when it came to an emphasis on the "sign gifts," he was still suspect in the minds of many mainstream evangelicals. In spite of that (and maybe because of that), Robertson invited Smith to come to CIU and speak to the student body every day for an entire week. Though I don't agree with everything Smith teaches, that was one of the best series of Bible messages I have ever heard.

In addition, while I was serving on the CIU Board, there arose a need to find a theology professor for CIU's seminary. A close friend of mine applied for the position. He was a CIU grad fully committed to CIU's core values, had earned his theological doctorate with distinction, had many years of proven church ministry and was a gifted teacher. I was thrilled. But CIU did not hire him. Why? Because my friend was strongly committed to Reformed theology. What's wrong with that? Nothing, except that the majority of the seminary's theology professors were also Reformed theologians, and Robertson felt that we needed someone from a different theological persuasion (e.g., dispensational or Wesleyan, etc.) to "round out" our faculty and demonstrate our commitment to interdenominational evangelical unity. So someone else was hired, demonstrating that CIU truly operates according to its core values and not just personal preferences.

Five Core Values for the Twenty-First Century

This subheading is the actual title of this entire chapter. You will notice that the first two subheadings deal with *CIU's* five core values. This final section will also talk about those same five core values, but not necessarily in connection with CIU. Why? Because these are five core values by which *any* Christian church, school, organization, group or family could, and I would submit, *should* operate. Certainly these are not the only core values that could be articulated and followed. Every effective Christian group needs to articulate a set of core values and operate according to those values. I would strongly submit, however, that the five values listed above are worthy of serious consideration and inclusion in anyone's list, especially as we move into the rapidly-changing, globalized culture of the twenty-first century.

Why are the five core values listed above relevant for living and operating in the twenty-first century? Because regardless of the period of human history in which we are living, human nature does not change, and the nature and character of our immutable God does not change either. Furthermore, the spiritual truths and disciplines contained in the five core values are universally applicable, independent of time or place. As such, they remain valid and valuable for any period of human history.

As we think about living and ministering with these core values in the world of the twenty-first century, I am both concerned and encouraged. I am concerned because if CIU (or any other Christian entity) seeks to operate in faithful adherence to these five core values, it will find itself more and more at odds with a godless world culture. The inerrancy, reliability and authority of Scripture are increasingly being questioned. Humanistic therapeutic behavioral sciences have no room for the possibility of a supernatural God indwelling a human life and giving victory over self, sin, addictions and other negative behaviors. The truths of the depravity of human nature and the exclusiveness of the Christian gospel as the only answer for human sin are now being branded as intolerant and bigoted. Management and marketing techniques, though not necessarily wrong in themselves, are tending to crowd out helpless dependence upon and prayer to the Lord. Ethnic and religious prejudice is increasingly rearing its head, dividing, not uniting people. We are fast approaching a time when official laws mandated by legitimate governments, even democratic governments, will go against some or all of these core values, and we will be compelled to say, with the early disciples of Jesus, "We must obey God rather than men"

(Acts 5:29) and face the consequences. Standing firm will come with a cost. Jesus never promised otherwise (see Matt. 24:9–14).

Yes, I am concerned, but I am also greatly encouraged. Why? Because living in faithful adherence to these five core values will cause us to "shine as lights in the world" in the midst of "a crooked and twisted generation" (Phil. 2:15). And when we do, people will recognize the authority inherent in the truth of Scripture as we proclaim it and obediently live under its teaching. People will crave the victory we have over sin and the power we have, through the Spirit of Christ, for right living and selfless serving. People will realize the truth of the gospel as we carry out the priority of preaching it, for the gospel of Jesus Christ is still "the power of God for salvation to everyone who believes" (Rom. 1:16). As we pray in belief and God answers, people will see the wisdom of trusting in an infinite God rather than in their own finite frailty. And as we lovingly unite with all those of like-minded faith, a watching world will know that we are Christ's disciples (see John 13:35). May the twenty-first century be a time of great spiritual harvesting for CIU and for all of God's children worldwide as we seek to demonstrate these (and other) biblical core values by the grace and to the glory of God!

Concise Timeline of J. Robertson McQuilkin

by Ron Barber Jr.

1927 Born September 7 to Robert Crawford and Marguerite Lambie McQuilkin in Columbia, SC

1944 Graduated Ben Lippen Boys School, Asheville, NC

1947 Graduated Columbia Bible College (BA), Columbia, SC

1948 Married Muriel Webendorfer

1950 Graduated Fuller Theological Seminary (MDiv), Pasadena, CA, in its first graduating class

1950–52 Taught at Columbia Bible College, Columbia, SC

1952–56 Headmaster, Ben Lippen School, Asheville, NC

1956–68 Church-planting missionary to Japan with The Evangelical Alliance Mission

1962–63 Interim President of Japan Christian College

1968–90 President and Professor, Columbia Bible College and Seminary, Columbia, SC

1978 Awarded Honorary Doctor of Law, Wheaton College, Wheaton, IL

1990 Resigned from Columbia Bible College and Seminary to care for Muriel

2003 Death of Muriel

2005 Married Deborah Jones Sink

2009 Awarded Honorary Doctor of Divinity, Columbia International University, Columbia, SC

2010 Awarded Lifetime of Service Award, Missio Nexus

2013 Retired from preaching and writing

Comprehensive Bibliography of J. Robertson McQuilkin

compiled by Ron Barber Jr. *

I. Books:

1973 *How Biblical Is the Church Growth Movement?* (Chicago, IL: Moody Publishers).

1974 *Measuring the Church Growth Movement: How Biblical Is It?*, 2nd, rev. ed. (Chicago, IL: Moody Publishers).

1983 *Understanding and Applying the Bible* (Chicago, IL: Moody Publishers).

1984 *The Great Omission: A Biblical Basis for World Evangelism* (Grand Rapids, MI: Baker).

1989 *An Introduction to Biblical Ethics* (Wheaton, IL; Tyndale House).

1992 *Understanding and Applying the Bible,* rev. ed. (Chicago, IL: Moody Publishers).

1995 *An Introduction to Biblical Ethics*, rev. ed. (Wheaton, IL; Tyndale House).

1995 *Living By Vows* (Columbia, SC: Columbia International University).

1997   Editor, *Free and Fulfilled: Victorious Living in the Twenty-First Century* (Nashville, TN: Thomas Nelson).

1997   *Life in the Spirit* (Nashville, TN: Lifeway Christian Resources).

1998   *A Promise Kept* (Wheaton, IL: Tyndale House).

2000   *Life in the Spirit* (repr., Nashville, TN: B&H).

2000   *Living the Life 1: Spiritual Maturity* (Rockville, VA: International Centre for Excellence in Leadership, International Mission Board, Southern Baptist Convention).

2001   *The Great Omission: A Biblical Basis for World Evangelism* (repr., Downers Grove, IL: IVP).

2002   *A Promise Kept* (repr., Wheaton, IL: Tyndale House).

2002   *The Great Omission: A Biblical Basis for World Evangelism*, rev. ed. (Waynesboro, GA: Authentic Media).

2007   *The Five Smooth Stones: Essential Principles for Biblical Ministry* (Nashville, TN: B&H).

2009   *Understanding and Applying the Bible: Revised and Expanded* (Chicago, IL: Moody Publishers).

2012   *The Great Omission: A Biblical Basis for World Evangelism* (repr., Downers Grove, IL: IVP).

2012   *Living the Life 2: God's Provision for Christian Living* (Rockville, VA: International Centre for Excellence in Leadership, International Mission Board, Southern Baptist Convention).

2014   Coauthor with Paul Copan, *An Introduction to Biblical Ethics: Walking in the Way of Wisdom*, 3rd. (Downers Grove, IL: IVP).

II. Articles and Chapters:

1954 "Born of the Spirit," in *Christian Life* 15/11 (March): 26–27, 86–87.

1956 "I Was an Embezzler," in *Moody Press Monthly* 56/2 (October): 34–35.

1956 "Marriage: Great Gift of God," in *Youth for Christ* magazine 14/5 (September): n.p.

1956 "This I Know," in *United Evangelical Action* 15/17 (November): 3–4, 6–7, 31.

1959 "Missionfields Aflame," in *Japan Harvest* 7/1 (February): 16–17.

1963–1964 "Total Mobilization," in *Japan Harvest* 13/1 (Winter): 6–9.

1964 "Total Mobilization: Manpower," in *Japan Harvest* 13/2(Spring): 12–14, 25.

1966–1967 "Communicating the Gospel or Why Aren't We Getting Through?" in *Japan Harvest* 16/1 (Winter): 6–8.

1967 "Bowling Blessings," in *TEAM Tegami* (January): 10–11

1967 "Japanese Values and Christian Mission," in the *Japan Christian Quarterly* 33/4 (Fall): 253–265.

1967 "The Mission of the Church in Japan Today," in *Eighth Hayama Missionary Seminar: The Mission of the Church* (Tokyo), 22–33.

1967 "Who's Biting?" in *Japan Harvest* 16/4 (Fall): 8–12.

1968 "The Modern Samurai in Japan," in *Horizons* (January-February): 38.

1968 "Too Much for Your Money," in *Japan Harvest* 17/3 (Summer): 9–10.

1970 "The Mission of the 70's" in 1970 *Annual Meeting Report, Interdenominational Foreign Mission Association* (Ridgefield Park, NJ:IFMA), 1–14.

1971 "High Theology Low," in *Christianity Today* 15/12 (March): 26.

1973 "How Biblical is Church Growth Thinking?" in *Church Growth Bulletin* 9/5 (May): 315–318.

1974 "An Evangelical Looks at Tongues," in *Logos Journal* 4/2(March-April): 22–26.

1974 "The Foreign Missionary—A Vanishing Breed?" in *Church/Mission Tensions Today* (Chicago, IL: Moody Press), 39–51.

1974 "Whatever Happened to Church Discipline?" in *Christianity Today* 18/13 (March): 22–26.

1974 "World Evangelization: God's Command," in *Today's Christian* 3/4 (April): 8.

1975–1976 "What About 'Church Growth'?" in *Japan Harvest* 25/1 (Winter): 14–15.

1976 "Church Growth and Selectivity," in *Japan Harvest* 26 (Summer): 27–30.

1976 "Living Water," in *Japan Harvest* 26 (Fall): 13–15.

1977 "Making the Numbers Count," in *Moody Press Monthly* 77/10 (June): 29–31.

1977 "Public Schools: Equal Time for Evangelicals," in *Christianity Today* 22/6 (December): 8–11.

1977 "The Behavioral Sciences Under the Authority of Scripture," in *Journal of the Evangelical Theological Society* 20/1 (March): 31–43.

1978 "The Crisis," in *Bulletin of Wheaton College* (July): 1–4.

1979 "The Future of the Church: The Essential Components of World Evangelization," in *An Evangelical Agenda: 1984 and Beyond* (Pasadena, CA: William Carey Library), 164–173.

1979 "When Is a Missionary Not a Missionary?" in *Christianity Today* 23/20 (August): 22–23.

1980 "Limits of Cultural Interpretation," in *Journal of the Evangelical Theological Society* 23/2 (March): 113–124.

1981 "Change," in *Family Life Today* 7/9 (September): 6–7.

1981 "Let Me Get Home Before Dark" (Columbia, SC: Columbia Bible College and Seminary).

1981 "Mission Invitation—Harvest Time," in *Seed of Promise* (Pasadena, CA: William Carey Library), 203–217.

1981 "The Narrow Way," in *Perspectives on the World Christian Movement* (Pasadena, CA: William Carey Library), 127–134.

1981–1982 "The Dark Half of the World," in *Japan Harvest* 31(4): 6–7.

1982 "Understanding Our Generation," in *Reaching Our Generation* (Pasadena, CA: William Carey Library), 20–37.

1983 "Be Strong and Do Exploits!" (Columbia, SC: Columbia Bible College and Seminary).

1983 "Looking at the Task Six Ways," in *Evangelical Missions Quarterly* 19/1 (January): 4–12.

1984   "God's Leader. Part 1," in *Increase* (July/August/September): 4–6.

1984   "Problems of Normativeness in Scripture: Cultural Versus Permanent," in *Hermeneutics, Inerrancy and the Bible* (Grand Rapids, MI: Zondervan), 217–253.

1984   "What Makes a Godly Leader? Part 2," in *Increase* (October/November/December): 4–6.

1984   "Who's Calling?" in F*aith & Fellowship* 51(5): 5–12.

1984   "World Missions: The Thread of Scripture, Parts I, II, III," in *Supporting World Missions in an Age of Change: Selected Addresses and Workshops Presented to the 1983 ACMC North American Conference* (Monrovia, CA: The Association of Church Missions Committees), 2–25.

1985   "Bible College Futures," in *Theological News* (July-September): 3–8.

1987   "Go for Life," in *Stepping Out: A Guide to Short Term Missions* (Monrovia, CA: Short-Term Missions Advocates, Inc.), 199–205.

1987   "Hermeneutics, Ethics and," in *Encyclopedia of Biblical and Christian Ethics* (Nashville, TN: Thomas Nelson), 177–178.

1987   "Materialism," ibid., 250–251.

1987   "Reformed Ethics," ibid., 346–348.

1987   "Worldliness," ibid., 444–445.

1987   "The Keswick Perspective," in *Five Views on Sanctification* (Grand Rapids, MI: Zondervan), 149–183.

1987   "Response to Dieter," ibid., 53–55.

1987 "Response to Hoekema," ibid., 98–99.

1987 "Response to Horton," ibid., 143–145.

1987 "Response to Walvoord," ibid., 236–237.

1990 "Living by Vows," in *Christianity Today* 40/2(October): 38–40.

1992 "Don't Let Expectations Get You Down," in *The Short-Term Mission Handbook* (Evanston, IN: Berry Publishing Services), 64–65.

1992 "Lost," in *Perspectives on the World Christian Movement,* 2nd ed. (Pasadena, CA: William Carey Library), A:148–155.

1992 "Understanding and Applying the Text," in *Leadership Handbooks of Practical Theology: Volume One: Word & Worship* (Grand Rapids, MI: Baker), 38–40.

1993 "A Bumper Crop," in *Moody Press Monthly* 93/11(July-August): 31, 33–34.

1993 "A Partner Speaks," in *65 Years* (Coral Gables, FL: World Team), n.p.

1993 "An Evangelical Assessment of Mission Theology of the Kingdom of God," in *The Good News of the Kingdom: Mission Theology for the Third Millennium* (Maryknoll, NY: Orbis), 172–178.

1993 "Best Friends," in *Moody Press Monthly* 93/10 (June): 35–36.

1993 "Cut it Out!" in *Moody Press Monthly* 93/9 (May): 34, 37–38.

1993 "Maximum Fulfillment," in *Moody Press Monthly* 93/6 (February): 39, 45.

1993 "Preparing for Full-Time Missionary Service," in *The 1993 Great Commission Handbook* (Evanston, IL: Berry Publishing Services, Inc.), 110–111.

1993 "Repaying a 40-year Debt," in *Marriage Partnership* 10/3 (Summer): 40.

1993 "The Big Connection," in *Moody Press Monthly* 93/8 (April): 40, 42–43.

1993 "The Insiders," in *Moody Press Monthly* 93/7 (March): 38, 40–41.

1993 "Why Hermeneutics?" in *Church Planter's Link* 4/2 (Second Quarter): 4–5.

1994 "Beyond Expectations," in *Moody Press Monthly* 94/2 (November): 13–14.

1994 "Canceling the Debt," in *Moody Press Monthly* 94/2 (November): 15–17.

1994 "Quest of the Nineties: Freedom and Fulfillment," in *Columbia Update* (February): 3–4.

1994 "Six Inflammatory Questions: Part 1," in *Evangelical Missions Quarterly* 30/2 (April): 130–134.

1994 "Six Inflammatory Questions: Part 2," in *Evangelical Missions Quarterly* 30/3 (July): 258–264.

1994 "When the Hurt Remains," in *Moody Press Monthly* 94/2 (November): 18–20.

1996 "Measuring Maturity: Jesus' Material Yardstick for Measuring Spiritual Maturity," in *Faithfulness* 1(1): 1–2.

1996 "Measuring Maturity: Jesus' Material Yardstick for Measuring Spiritual Maturity," in *Faithfulness* 1(2): 1–2.

1996 "Measuring Maturity: Jesus' Material Yardstick for Measuring Spiritual Maturity," in *Faithfulness* 1(3): 1–2.

1996 "Muriel's Blessing," in *Christianity Today* 40/2 (February): 32–34.

1996 "The Problem Isn't Success, It's Sticking Around Too Long," in *Evangelical Missions Quarterly* 32/1 (January): 27–28.

1996 "Use and Misuse of the Social Sciences," in *Missiology and the Social Sciences* (Pasadena, CA: William Carey Library), 165–183.

1997 "Imperfections: How Perfectionist is "Victorious Life" Teaching?" in *Free and Fulfilled: Victorious Living in the Twenty-First Century* (Nashville, TN: Thomas Nelson), 32–47.

1997 "Just As He Is," in *Christianity Today* 41/9 (August): 34–38.

1997 "On Wings of Praise," in *Decision* 38/11 (November): 8.

1997 "The Impact of Postmodern Thinking on Evangelical Hermeneutics," in *Journal of the Evangelical Theological Society* 40/1 (March): 69–82.

1997 "The Role of the Holy Spirit in Missions," in *The Holy Spirit and Mission Dynamics* (Pasadena, CA: William Carey Library), 22–35.

1997 "What's Your GCQ?" in *Trinity World Forum* (Winter): 1–3.

1998 "Preface," in *Mission in the New Testament: An Evangelical Approach* (Maryknoll, NY: Orbis).

1998 "What Is the Abundant Life?" in *Moody Press Monthly* 98/3 (January-February): 12–14.

1999 "But Thanks Be to God Who Gives Us the Victory!" in *CIU Connection* (Winter): 1–2.

1999 "Should We Stop Sending Missionaries?" in *Mission Frontiers* 21/1 (January-March): 38–41.

1999 "Stop Sending Money!" in *Christianity Today* 43/3 (March): 57–59.

1999 "Therapeutic Theology for Hurting People," in *Christian Counseling Today* 7(2): 20–24.

1999 "Tom Petty Prayer Warrior: At Rest," in *CIU Connection* (Winter): 3–4.

2000 "Commitment," in *Evangelical Dictionary of World Missions* (Grand Rapids, MI: Baker), 213–214.

2000 "Fads in Missions," ibid., 351.

2000 "Promotion of Missions," ibid., 792–793.

2000 "Ridderhof, Joy," ibid., 835.

2000 "Reached and Unreached Mission Fields," ibid., 808–809

2000 "The Missionary Task," ibid., 648–650.

2000 "Loving Muriel," in *Chicken Soup for the Golden Soul* (Deerfield Beach, FL: Health Communications Inc.), 141–144.

2000 "Reply to Chuck Bennett," in *Evangelical Missions Quarterly* 36/2 (April): 213–214.

2002 "What's Best for Muriel?" in *Moody Press Monthly* 103/1 (September/October): 24–28.

2003 "David H. Petty: An Anchor on the Board," in *CIU Connection* (Winter): 17–18.

2003   "McQuilkin Reflects on Student Impetus," in *CIU Connection* 3(3): 6.

2005   "In Sickness & in Health," in *Decision* 46/6 (June): 18–21.

2005   "The Year I Lost Christmas," in *Reach Out Columbia!* 1/4 (December): 14.

2006   "Lost Missions: Whatever Happened to the Idea of Rescuing People from Hell?" in *Christianity Today* 50/7 (July): 40–42.

2008   "Loving Muriel," in *Chicken Soup for the Soul: Older & Wiser* (Cos Cob, CT: Chicken Soup for the Soul Publishing), 56–59.

2008   "Prayer: Lifeblood of CIU," in *CIU Connection* 8/1 (Spring): 9.

2008   "Responses to Christopher Little's 'What Makes Mission Christian?'" in *International Journal of Frontier Missiology* 25/2 (Summer): 75.

2009   "Measuring Maturity," in *Lifestyle Giving* (December): 3.

2010   "Evangelical Unity at CIU: The Historical Perspective," in *CIU Connection* 10/1 (Spring): 10.

2010   "Why the Poor Harvest?" in *Evangelical Missions Quarterly* 46/3 (July): 298–301.

2011   "The Controversy at Lausanne III: Lausanne III: Win or Lose? It's a Question of Eternal Importance," in *CIU Connection* 11/1 (Spring): 19.

2012   "Exegeting the Audience," in *Trinity Journal* 33/2 (Fall): 199–207.

2012   "Foreword," in *Let Not Your Heart Be Troubled: John Fourteen: Chapter of Resurrection Life* (Columbia, SC: Columbia International University).

2012   "Saving Minds, Saving Bodies, Saving Souls: The Priorities of Uncle Tom Lambie," in *CIU Connection* 12/2 (Fall): 19.

2012   "Why This Sad Day?" in *Mature Living* 36/8 (May): 26–29.

n.d.   "The Two Sides of Forgiveness" (Columbia, SC: Columbia Bible College and Seminary).

*Note from Dr. Barber: This listing of published works is comprehensive from 1954 to 2014 but does not include translations of books or articles nor reprints of articles. It includes the preface to two volumes closely connected to CIU—*Mission in the New Testament,* written by CIU educators and graduates, and the foreword to Robert C. McQuilkin's *Let Not Your Heart Be Troubled*—but it does not include any of his other numerous forewords.

Notes

Chapter 1

1. Robertson McQuilkin, *Understanding and Applying the Bible: Revised and Expanded* (Chicago, IL: Moody Publishers, 2009), 241.

2. Robertson McQuilkin, *Life in the Spirit* (Nashville, TN: LifeWay Press, 1997).

3. Robertson McQuilkin, *Life in the Spirit,* reprint (Nashville, TN: Broadman & Holman, 2000).

4. You might begin with Robert C. McQuilkin, *Victory in Christ or Taking God At His Word, A Personal Testimony* (Columbia, SC: Columbia Bible College, 1939); *The Life of Victory and the Baptism of the Spirit* (Chicago, IL: Moody Publishers, 1953); *God's Law and God's Grace* (Grand Rapids, MI: Eerdmans, 1958); *John Fourteen: Chapter of Resurrected Life* (Columbia, SC: Columbia International University, 2012); and, by Robert C. McQuilkin's daughter, Marguerite McQuilkin, *Always in Triumph: The Life of Robert C. McQuilkin* (Columbia, SC: Bible College Bookstore, 1956).

5. Melvin E. Dieter et al., *Five Views on Sanctification* (Grand Rapids, MI: Zondervan, 1987), 236–237.

6. Ibid., 180.

7. Robertson McQuilkin, ed., *Free and Fulfilled: Victorious Living in the Twenty-First Century* (Nashville, TN: Thomas Nelson, 1997), xii.

8. Robertson McQuilkin, *An Introduction to Biblical Ethics* (Wheaton, IL: Tyndale House, 1995), 176–177.

9. Ibid., 200.

10. Ibid., 395.

11. Ibid., 121–122.

12. Robertson McQuilkin and Paul Copan, *An Introduction to Biblical Ethics: Walking in the Way of Wisdom,* 3rd ed. (Downers Grove, IL: IVP, 2014).

13. Republished as *Measuring the Church Growth Movement* (Chicago, IL: Moody Publishers, 1974).

14. Robertson McQuilkin and Bradford Mullen, "The Impact of Postmodern Thinking on Evangelical Hermeneutics," *Journal of the Evangelical Theological Society* 40/1(1997): 69–82.

15. Ibid., 70–71.

16. Robertson McQuilkin and Bradford Mullen, "The Behavioral Sciences under the Authority of Scripture," *Journal of the Evangelical Theological Society* 20/1(1977): 31–43.

17. McQuilkin, *Understanding and Applying the Bible*, 337.

18. Ibid., 342.

19. Robertson McQuilkin and Bradford Mullen, "Limits of Cultural Interpretation," *Journal of the Evangelical Theological Society* 23/2(1980): 113–124.

20. Earl Radmacher and Robert Preus, eds., *Hermeneutics, Inerrancy and the Bible* (Grand Rapids, MI: Zondervan, 1984), 217–253.

21. Robertson McQuilkin, *The Great Omission: A Biblical Basis for World Evangelism* (Grand Rapids, MI: Baker, 1984), 11.

22. Ibid., 12.

23. Ibid., 21.

24. Ibid., 49–50.

25. Robertson McQuilkin, *The Five Smooth Stones: Essential Principles for Biblical Ministry* (Nashville, TN: Broadman & Holman, 2007), vii.

26. Ibid., ix.

Chapter 2

1. Paul D. Stanley and J. Robert Clinton, *Connecting: The Mentoring Relationships You Need to Succeed in Life* (Colorado Springs, CO: NavPress, 1992), 42.

2. McQuilkin, *The Five Smooth Stones*, vii.

3. Ibid., 166–184.

4. Ibid., 119–127.

Chapter 3

1. McQuilkin, *Understanding and Applying the Bible: Revised and Expanded*, 8. This principle reads the same in all three editions of his book, which was originally written as a textbook for his class Introduction to Biblical Interpretation. It is still used today at CIU as one of the required texts.

2. Ibid., 95. Again, this statement is identical in all three editions.

3. Andreas Köstenberger and Richard Patterson, *Invitation to Biblical Interpretation: Exploring the Hermeneutical Triad of History, Literature, and Theology* (Grand Rapids, MI: Kregel, 2011), 58.

4. J. Scott Duvall and J. Daniel Hays, *Grasping God's Word: A Hands-On Approach to Reading, Interpreting, and Applying the Bible,* 3rd ed. (Grand Rapids, MI: Zondervan, 2012), 194–195.

5. Grant Osborne, *The Hermeneutical Spiral: A Comprehensive Introduction to Biblical Interpretation,* rev. and exp. ed. (Downers Grove, IL: IVP, 2006), 24–25.

6. Grant Osborne, "Literary Theory and Biblical Interpretation," *Words & the Word: Explorations in Biblical Interpretation & Literary Theory* (Downers Grove, IL: IVP, 2008), 23.

7. Jeannine K. Brown, *Scripture as Communication: Introducing Biblical Hermeneutics* (Grand Rapids, MI: Baker, 2007), 24.

8.   Carolyn J. Sharp, *Wrestling the Word: The Hebrew Scriptures and the Christian Believer* (Louisville, KY: WJK Press, 2010), 3.

9.   Kevin Vanhoozer, *Is There a Meaning in This Text? The Bible, the Reader, and the Morality of Literary Knowledge* (Grand Rapids, MI: Zondervan, 1998), 82.

10.   See the helpful summary of these, and many other approaches, in W. Randolph Tate, *Handbook for Biblical Interpretation: An Essential Guide to Methods, Terms, and Concepts,* 2nd ed. (Grand Rapids, MI: Baker, 2012). See also Kevin J. Vanhoozer, ed., *Dictionary for Theological Interpretation of the Bible* (Grand Rapids, MI: Baker, 2005); Stanley E. Porter, *Dictionary of Biblical Criticism and Interpretation* (New York, NY: Routledge, 2007); and Eryl W. Davies, *Biblical Criticism: A Guide for the Perplexed* (New York, NY: Bloomsbury, T&T Clark, 2013).

11.   For evangelical responses to the current hermeneutical morass, see, e.g., Stanley E. Porter and Beth M. Stovell, eds., *Biblical Hermeneutics: Five Views* (Downers Grove, IL: IVP, 2012); Eight volumes to date of the *Scripture and Hermeneutics Series* published by Zondervan with eds. Craig Bartholomew, Jonathan Chaplin, C. Stephen Evans, Joel B. Green, Colin Greene, Scott Hahn, Mary Healy, David Lyle Jeffrey, Karl Möller, Robin Parry, Murray Rae, Christopher Seitz, Robert Song, Anthony C. Thiselton and Al Wolters; Merold Westphal, *Whose Community? Which Interpretation?* (Grand Rapids, MI: Baker, 2009); James K. A. Smith, *The Fall of Interpretation: Philosophical Foundations for a Creational Hermeneutic* (Grand Rapids, MI: Baker, 2012); and D.A. Carson, *The Gagging of God* (Grand Rapids, MI: Zondervan, 1996), especially 57–137.

12.   I should here make clear that I am not endorsing canonical criticism as a method. I share many of the concerns of Carl F.H. Henry in "Canonical Theology: An Evangelical Appraisal," *Scottish Bulletin of Evangelical Theology* (1990): 76–108. I do not wish to be known as a

"canonical critic" but rather as an interpreter who incorporates some insights from canonical criticism into an author-centered hermeneutic. For further discussion critical of Henry's objections to Childs and canonical criticism, see Stephen B. Chapman, "Reclaiming Inspiration for the Bible," *Canon and Biblical Interpretation* (Grand Rapids, MI: Zondervan, 2006), 167–206.

13. For an excellent recent summary of scholarship on the Psalms, see J. Kenneth Kuntz, "Continuing the Engagement: Psalms Research Since the Early 1990s," *Currents in Biblical Research* 10(3): 321–378; and Andrew J. Schmutzer and David M. Howard Jr., *The Psalms: Language for All Seasons of the Soul* (Chicago, IL: Moody Publishers, 2013).

14. The best sources are: Gerald Wilson, *The Editing of the Hebrew Psalter* (Chico, CA: Scholar's Press, 1985); Interpretation 46/2(1992); J. Clinton McCann, *The Shape and Shaping of the Psalter* (Sheffield, England: Sheffield Academic Press, 1993); Norman Whybray, *Reading the Psalms as a Book* (Sheffield, England: Sheffield Academic Press, 1996); and David C. Mitchell, *The Message of the Psalter: An Eschatological Programme in the Book of Psalms*, (Sheffield, England: Sheffield Academic Press, 1997). The most recent full-length treatments are by Jean-Marie Auwers, *La Composition Littéraire du Psautier: Un État de la Question* (Paris: Gabalda, 2000) and Leslie McFall, "The Evidence for A Logical Arrangement of the Psalter," *Westminster Theological Journal* 62(2000): 223–56. See also more recent studies, such as Patrick D. Miller, *The Lord of the Psalms* (Louisville, KY: Westminster/John Knox Press, 2013) and Gordon J. Wenham, *Psalms as Torah: Reading Biblical Song Ethically* (Grand Rapids, MI: Baker, 2012), especially chapter 3, "The Psalter as an Anthology to be Memorized."

15. See especially chapters 2 and 3. For recent criticism of Wilson's ideas, see Yee Von Koh, "G. H. Wilson's Theories on the Organization of the Masoretic Psalter," *Genesis, Isaiah and Psalms: A Festschrift to Honour Professor John Emerton for His Eightieth Birthday* (VTSup 135; Boston, MA: Brill, 2010):177–192.

16. Patrick D. Miller, "The Beginning of the Psalter," *The Shape and Shaping*, 83–92; J.P. Brennan, "Psalms 1–8: Some Hidden Harmonies," *Biblical Theology Bulletin* 10(1980):25–29; and W. Brownlee, "Psalms 1–2 as a Coronation Liturgy," *Biblica* 52:321–336.

17. J. T. Willis, "Psalm 1–An Entity," *ZAW* 91(1979): 381–401.

18. Robert Cole has made a strong case for reading these psalms together in "An Integrated Reading of Psalms 1 and 2," *JSOT* 98(2002): 75–88; *Psalms 1–2: Gateway to the Psalter* (Sheffield, England: Sheffield Phoenix Press, 2012); and "Psalms 1 and 2: The Psalter's Introduction," *The Psalms: Language for All Seasons of the Soul* (Chicago, IL: Moody Publishers, 2013),183–195. He argues that Psalms 1–2 constitute an "integrated introduction" (*Psalms 1–2*, 193). Although I heartily endorse Cole's desire to read psalms together, I remain concerned that he has overinterpreted the relationship between Psalms 1 and 2. His reading, I suspect, will produce an overly narrow and flattened interpretation of the book of Psalms and its message. See my criticisms in *Psalms in Their Context: An Interpretation of Psalms 107–118* (Colorado Springs, CO: Paternoster Press, 2011), 58.

19. Brennan argues that the links between Psalms 2 and 148 (=MT 149) mean that a redactional process extends to the whole book (ibid., 28). See also, Tremper Longman III, "From Weeping to Rejoicing: Psalm 150 as the Conclusion to the Psalter," in *The Psalms: Language for All Seasons of the Soul*, ed. Andrew J. Schmutzer and David M. Howard J., 219-228.

20. Gerald Wilson, "The Use of Royal Psalms at the 'Seams' of the Hebrew Psalter," *JSOT* 35(1986):85–94.

21. See especially Brennan, ibid., 25–29, and "Some Hidden Harmonies in the Fifth Book of the Psalms," in *Essays in Honor of Joseph P. Brennan* (Rochester, NY: St Bernard's Seminary, 1976), 126–158. More recently, see David M. Howard, *The Structure of Psalms 93–100: Biblical and Judaic Studies,* vol. 5 (Winona Lake, IN: Eisenbrauns,

1997); Cole, *The Shape and Message of Book III, JSOT* 307 (Sheffield, England: Sheffield Academic Press, 2007)); Robert E. Wallace, *The Narrative Effect of Book IV of the Hebrew Psalter* (New York City: Peter Lang, 2007); and Crutchfield, *Psalms in their Context*.

22. I have dealt elsewhere with Whybray's objections in ibid., 59–61.

23. John Goldingay, *Psalms: Volume 1: Psalms 1–41, BCOTWP* (Grand Rapids, MI: Baker, 2006), 36–37. Robert Davidson, *The Vitality of Worship* (Grand Rapids, MI: Eerdmans, 1998), 7, also expresses doubt about finding an overarching purpose.

24. J. Kenneth Kuntz, "Continuing the Engagement: Psalms Research Since the Early 1990s," *Currents in Biblical Research* 10(3): 347–350.

25. Ibid., 57–97, and "The Redactional Agenda of the Book of Psalms," *HUCA* 74(2003): 21–47.

26. For a study of the relationship between the beginning of the book of Psalms (Psalms 1–2) and the end (Psalms 145–150), see Tim Undheim, "With Mace in Hand … and Praise in Throat: Comparisons and Contrasts in the Bookends of the Psalter," in *Windows to the Ancient World of the Hebrew Bible: Essays in Honor of Samuel Greengus* (Winona Lake, IN: Eisenbrauns, 2014), 187–199.

27. For a recent interpreter who holds to this view, see Goldingay, *Psalms, Volume 3: Psalms 90–150* (Grand Rapids, MI: Baker, 2008), 273–89.

28. The intro for Psalm 109 in the New International Version reads, "For the director of music. Of David. A psalm."

29. For the use of the Psalms in the New Testament, see Jean-Luc Vesco, *Le psautier de Jesus. Les citations des psaumes dans le Nouveau Testament. Volumes 1 and 2* (Paris: Cerf, 2012). For current more general discussions on the use of the Old Testament in the New, see G.K. Beale and D.A. Carson, eds., *Commentary on the New Testament Use of the Old Testament* (Grand Rapids, MI: Baker, 2007); Kenneth Berding and

Jonathan Lunde, eds., *Three Views on the New Testament Use of the Old Testament* (Grand Rapids, MI: Zondervan, 2008); and G.K. Beale, *Handbook on the New Testament Use of the Old Testament: Exegesis and Interpretation* (Grand Rapids, MI: Baker, 2012).

30. For more information on reading Psalms 109 and 110 together, see Jangpyo Jung, *A Study of Psalm 109: Its Meaning and Significance in the Context of the Psalter* (SBF Thesis ad Doctoratum in Theologia cum specializione Biblica 424; Jerusalem: Studium Biblicum Franciscanum, 2009).

31. For a study of the use of Psalms in Luke-Acts, see Joshua W. Jipp, "Luke's Scriptural Suffering Messiah: A Search for Precedent, A Search for Identity," in *Catholic Biblical Quarterly* 72(2010): 255–74.

32. Mitchell, *The Message of the Psalter*, 261–262.

33. In Matthew 27:39 and Mark 15:29, the Gospel writers allude to Psalm 109:25 to describe people mocking Jesus as He hung on the cross. This shows that the New Testament writers interpreted Jesus' experience using Psalm 109.

34. Craig L. Blomberg, "Matthew," in *Commentary on the New Testament Use of the Old Testament* (Grand Rapids, MI: Baker, 2007), 74.

35. See the discussion in W.D. Davies and Dale C. Allison, Jr., *International Critical Commentary: Matthew, Volume 3* (Edinburgh: T&T Clark, 1997), 111–131.

36. For a discussion of the genre of Psalm 119, see Will Soll, *Psalm 119: Matrix, Form, and Setting* (Washington, D.C.: The Catholic Biblical Association of America, 1991), especially Part Two; and David Noel Freedman, *Psalm 119: The Exaltation of Torah* (Winona Lake, IN: Eisenbrauns, 1999).

37. Jinkyu Kim has argued that "the editor(s) intended that all the Psalms in [Books IV-V] be understood eschatologically" ("The Strategic Arrangement of Royal Psalms in Books IV–V," *Westminster Theological Journal* 79[2008]: 157).

38. Wilson, *The Editing of the Hebrew Psalter*, 210–228.

39. For a recent discussion of the kingdom of God, see Joel B. Green, "Kingdom of God/Heaven," in *Dictionary of Jesus and the Gospels*, 2nd ed. (Downers Grove, IL: IVP, 2013), 468–481.

Chapter 4

1. McQuilkin, *Understanding and Applying the Bible: Revised and Expanded*, 13. The first edition was published in 1983. Throughout this chapter, references to pages in this third edition will be indicated in parentheses within the discussion rather than in endnotes.

2. Earl Radmacher and Robert Preuss, eds. "Problems of Normativeness in Scripture: Cultural versus Permanent," in *Hermeneutics, Inerrancy, and the Bible*, (Grand Rapids, MI: Zondervan, 1984), 219–240.

3. McQuilkin and Mullen, "Limits of Cultural Interpretation," 113–124.

4. It is worth noting that since the 1970s, the study of narrative as a distinct literary genre has grown in scope and influence. Representative works include: N.R. Petersen, *Literary Criticism for New Testament Critics* (Philadelphia, PA: Fortress, 1978); D. Rhoads and D. Michie, *Mark as Story: An Introduction to the Narrative of a Gospel* (Philadelphia, PA: Fortress, 1982); R.A. Culpepper, *Anatomy of the Fourth Gospel: A Study in Literary Design* (Philadelphia, PA: Fortress, 1983); J.D. Kingsbury, *Matthew as Story* (Philadelphia, PA: Fortress, 1986); R.C. Tannehill, *The Narrative of Luke-Acts: A Literary Interpretation. Vol. 1: The Gospel of Luke* (Minneapolis, MN: Fortress, 1986); M.A. Powell, *What Is Narrative Criticism? A New Approach to the Bible* (Minneapolis, MN: Augsburg, 1990); J.L. Resseguie, *Narrative Criticism of the New Testament* (Grand Rapids, MI: Baker, 2005).

5. The double work Luke-Acts in the NASB (see copyright page) will serve as the primary database for this study.

6. McQuilkin also includes the New Testament letters and the Old Testament Psalms in the same category as Jesus' teaching. The discussion below will explore whether a similar approach should be taken in dealing with the apostolic speeches in Acts.

7. McQuilkin states the overarching principle for chapters 15–18 in this way: "Since Scripture is God-breathed and true in all its parts, the unity of its teaching must be sought, and its supernatural elements recognized and understood" (233).

8. For the material that follows in this section and the next, I am heavily indebted to my former colleague and friend, Dr. William J. Larkin Jr., who worked with the text of Luke-Acts for more than forty years. His commitment to teaching meant that he developed many of his ideas about interpreting historical narrative in his course materials, although what he published on the topic is more limited. It was his work in this area that sparked the initial idea for this *Festschrift*, and he was originally recruited to write this chapter. Unfortunately, health concerns kept him from writing it. His book, *Culture and Biblical Hermeneutics: Interpreting and Applying the Authoritative Word in a Relativistic Age* (Grand Rapids, MI: Baker, 1988), includes a reflection on McQuilkin's hermeneutical approach (pages 118–125), and his commentary on Acts (IVP New Testament Commentary Series, Downers Grove, IL: IVP, 1995), seeks to apply his own approach to the authoritative application of material from historical narrative (see pages 15–17 for a concise discussion).

9. On the latter point, Lucian writes of Thucydides, "He brings in, too, the question of usefulness and what is, surely, the purpose of sound history: that if ever again men find themselves in a like situation they may be able, he says, from a consideration of the records of the past to handle rightly what now confronts them" (*Lucian, Volume VI* [Cambridge, MA: Harvard University Press, 1959], 57, 59).

10. I.H. Marshall, *Acts* (Grand Rapids, MI: Eerdmans, 1980), 39.

11. C.K. Barrett, *The Acts of the Apostles* (Edinburgh: T&T Clark, 1994), 132. Emphasis is in the original.

12. See, for example, his comment on Elihu's speech in Job (309).

13. If an inspired author is considered an authorized spokesperson for God, such a narrative clue would logically be considered in the same category as a positive evaluation of the teaching recorded.

14. D.G. Peterson, *The Acts of the Apostles* (Grand Rapids, MI: Eerdmans, 2009), 44.

15. Ibid., 43.

16. The same phrases occur four times (see 1:15, 41, 67; 4:14) and once (see 4:1) respectively in Luke's Gospel, twice in reference to Christ (see 4:1, 14).

17. For a more detailed discussion of Luke's use of these terms, see J.D. Harvey, *Anointed with the Spirit and Power* (Phillipsburg, NJ: P&R Publishing, 2008), 123–139.

18. I.H. Marshall, "How Does One Write a Theology on Acts?," in *Witness to the Gospel: Theology of Acts* (Grand Rapids, MI: Eerdmans, 1998), 13.

19. Peterson, *Acts of the Apostles*, 43.

20. This list is taken from C.S. Keener, *Acts: An Exegetical Commentary,* vol. 1 (Grand Rapids, MI: Eerdmans, 2012), 574. Keener suggests that the summary statements are best understood as marking the progress of the gospel among different groups. R.N. Longenecker focuses on six statements (6:7; 9:31; 12:24; 16:5; 19:20; 28:31) and suggests that each of the six concludes a "panel" of material within the book ("Acts," in *The Expositor's Bible Commentary*, vol. 9 (Grand Rapids, MI: Zondervan, 1981), 234).

21. Peterson, *Acts of the Apostles*, 42.

22. Larkin, *Acts*, 17.

23. Larkin, "Response to Benny C. Aker's 'Acts 2 as Paradigmatic for Luke's Theology of the Spirit,'" Paper presented at the annual meeting of the Evangelical Theological Society in Orlando, FL, November 21, 1998. See also a brief paragraph in Larkin, *Acts*, 50.

Chapter 5

1. The New King James Version is used exclusively in this chapter.

2. James Wilhoit, *Spiritual Formation as if the Church Mattered: Growing in Christ through Community* (Grand Rapids, MI: Baker Academic, 2008), 27.

3. Steven Barabas, *So Great Salvation: The History and Message of the Keswick Convention* (London: Marshall, Morgan & Scott, 1952), 69.

4. Wayne Grudem, *Bible Doctrine: Essential Teachings of the Christian Faith* (Grand Rapids, MI: Zondervan, 1999), 326.

5. Dallas Willard with Don Simpson, *Revolution of Character: Discovering Christ's Pattern for Spiritual Transformation* (Colorado Springs, CO: NavPress, 2005), 16.

6. *Westminster Shorter Catechism*, accessed April 4, 2014, http://opc.org/sc.html.

7. Columbia International University (CIU), *Student Handbook and Planner* (2013–2014), 4, accessed April 4, 2014, https://online.ciu.edu/ICS/icsfs/6396_2013-14_Student_Handbook_full_FINAL_low_res.pdf?target=939a45e9-8ec8-42cb-9fd8-c35e0bccb6ed.

8. Stephen and Mary Lowe, *Spiritual Formation in Theological Distance Education: An Ecosystems Model as Paradigm* (Paper presented for the National Consultation on Spiritual Formation in Theological Distance Education, Charlotte, NC, October 26–27, 2007), 35.

9. See the bibliography at the end of this volume for a complete list of McQuilkin's works, including his writing on the Holy Spirit and sanctification.

10. For more on McQuilkin's heritage and the foundation of CIU's emphasis on Victorious Christian Living, see *Free and Fulfilled: Victorious Living in the Twenty-First Century* (Nashville, TN: Thomas Nelson, 1997), chapters 1–5.

11. The five core values of CIU are: Authority of Scripture, Victorious Christian Living, World Evangelization, Prayer and Faith, and Evangelical Unity, accessed April 4, 2014, http://www.ciu.edu/discover-ciu/who-we-are/core-values. In a discussion of this chapter with the author, McQuilkin stated a personal preference for a phrase like "Life in the Spirit" rather than "Victorious Christian Living," partly because of misunderstanding related to the latter. He also said that there is no perfect term for the outworking of sanctification and that any term will require careful and repeated explanation.

12. Dieter et al., *Five Views on Sanctification*, 183.

13. McQuilkin, *Life in the Spirit* (Nashville, TN: LifeWay Press, 1997), 80.

14. Oswald Chambers, *My Utmost for His Highest* (New York, NY: Dodd, Mead & Company, 1935), 204.

15. John Piper, *I Love Jesus: An Unforgettable Moment in Seminary*, accessed on April, 4, 2014, http://www.desiringgod.org/articles/i-love-jesus-christ.

16. M. Robert Mulholland, "Spiritual Formation in Christ and Mission with Christ," *Journal of Spiritual Formation & Soul Care* 6/1(2013): 11, 17.

17. Robertson McQuilkin, *The Great Omission: A Biblical Basis for World Evangelism* (Grand Rapids, MI: Baker, 1990), 28–29.

18. The reader is invited to research the range of evangelical nuances in *Five Views on Sanctification* and McQuilkin's "Imperfections: How Perfectionist is 'Victorious Life' Teaching?," in *Free and Fulfilled*, 32–47.

19. McQuilkin, *Life in the Spirit*, 117 (emphasis added).

20. Peter K. Nelson, "Discipleship Dissonance: Toward a Theology of Imperfection Amidst the Pursuit of Holiness," *Journal of Spiritual Formation & Soul Care* 4/1(2011): 89.

21. Ibid., 44.

22. McQuilkin often told the story of how his mother taught him about the victorious life as a young person, telling him that the secret was in his two hands. Then she would spell out on her fingers Y-I-E-L-D and T-R-U-S-T, as seen in this video interview accessed April 29, 2014: https://www.youtube.com/watch?v=0IM307M9VgI.

23. Andrew Murray, *Absolute Surrender and other Addresses* (Chicago, IL: Moody Publishers, n.d.), 43.

24. A.W. Tozer, *The Pursuit of God: The Human Thirst for the Divine* (Camp Hill, PA: Christian Publications, 1993), 9.

25. Robert C. McQuilkin, *Joy and Victory* (Chicago, IL: Moody Publishers, 1953), 46.

26. Robertson McQuilkin, "Victorious Christian Living: A Biblical Exposition of Sanctification," accessed April, 4, 2014, http://www.ciu.edu/faculty-publications/article/victorious-christian-living-biblical-exposition-sanctification.

27. Ibid., 242.

Chapter 6

1. *Understanding and Applying the Bible* was first published by Moody Publishers in 1983.

2. McQuilkin, "The Keswick Perspective," in *Five Views on Sanctification,* ed. Stanley N. Gundry (Grand Rapids, MI: Zondervan, 1987), 151–183.

3. Robertson McQuilkin, *An Introduction to Biblical Ethics,* 2nd ed. (Carol Stream, IL: Tyndale House, 1995), 527.

4. McQuilkin, *The Five Smooth Stones*, 73ff.

5. McQuilkin, *Life in the Spirit* (Nashville, TN: Broadman & Holman, 2000).

6. Ibid., 12ff.

7. Unless otherwise noted, Scripture quotations are from the New American Standard Bible®, © 1960, 1962, 1963, 1968, 1971, 1972, 1973, 1975, 1977, 1995 by The Lockman Foundation. Used by permission.

8. For an exhaustive study of the Holy Spirit in Paul's letters, see G.D. Fee, *God's Empowering Presence: The Holy Spirit in the Letters of Paul* (Peabody, MA: Hendrickson, 1994).

9. E.g., "The grace of the Lord Jesus Christ be with your spirit" (Philem. 25).

10. E.g., "deceitful spirits" (1 Tim. 4:1).

11. For an extended discussion of Second Corinthians 3:1–18, see J.D. Harvey, *Anointed with the Spirit and Power* (Phillipsburg, NJ: P&R, 2008), 157–161.

12. For an extended discussion of First Corinthians 1:18–2:16, see ibid., 151–154.

13. McQuilkin highlights prayer both as a defensive strategy and as an offensive weapon in overcoming (see *Life in the Spirit*, 182, 187).

14. Harvey, *Anointed with the Spirit*, 164.

15. For an extended discussion of this passage, see ibid., 163–167.

16. McQuilkin, *Life in the Spirit*, 153–158.

17. Harvey, *Anointed with the Spirit*, 162.

18. For extended discussions of the fruit of the Spirit, see S. Briscoe, *The Fruit of the Spirit* (Wheaton, IL: Shaw, 1993), and J.W. Sanderson, *The Fruit of the Spirit* (Phillipsburg, NJ: P&R Publishing, 1999).

19. Harvey, *Anointed with the Spirit*, 103.

20. That is, Paul is confident that the Philippians' prayers and the Spirit's provision will ultimately deliver him from his imprisonment, whether by life or by death (see the immediate context of Phil. 1:12–20).

21. In the phrase "πνεῦμα . . . δυνάμεως καὶ ἀγάπης καὶ σωφρονισμοῦ" *pneuma . . . dunameos kai agapes kai sophronismou* (2 Tim. 1:7), the three genitives ("of power and of love and of sound judgment") should be understood as indicating what the Spirit produces. See Romans 8:15 ("Spirit of life") for a similar grammatical construction.

22. Compare the discussion of Ephesians 5:18–21 with the last two qualities.

23. Creating is absent, and Romans 8:16 appears to add an eleventh activity (see following discussion on 8:16 and 9:1).

24. See the discussion on Galatians 5:16–26.

25. C.E.B. Cranfield, *Romans* (Edinburgh: T&T Clark, 1975), 335–336.

26. See D.J. Moo, who suggests, "Paul is exhorting us to allow the Holy Spirit to 'set us on fire': to open ourselves to the Spirit as he seeks to excite us about the 'rational worship' to which the Lord has called us" (*Romans* [Grand Rapids, MI: Eerdmans, 1996], 778). The Greek participle (ζέοντες, *zeontes*) in this verse is imperatival (see D.B. Wallace, *Greek Grammar Beyond the Basics* [Grand Rapids, MI: Zondervan, 1996], 650–651).

27. "Love of the Spirit" (15:30) is best understood as love the Spirit produces (subjective genitive).

28. See also Harvey, *Anointed with the Spirit*, 156–157.

29. For a concise overview of Paul's theology and major themes in his letters, see J.D. Harvey, *Interpreting the Pauline Letters* (Grand Rapids, MI: Kregel, 2012), 79–100.

30. H.E. Burchett, *People Helping People* (Chicago, IL: Moody Publishers, 1979), 81.

31. "The law of the Spirit of life" is best taken as a reference to the Holy Spirit, with "law" understood as the authority the Spirit exercises on the believer and "life" understood as the product the Spirit's work brings into being (see Cranfield, *Romans*, 375–376).

32. The prepositional phrase "according to the Spirit" (κατὰ πνεῦμα, *kata pneuma*) denotes both control and standard (see Moo, *Romans*, 485).

33. The phrase "the things of the Spirit" (τά τῆς πνεύματος, *ta tes pneumatos*) describes the "outlook, assumption, values, desires and purposes . . . those who take the side of the Spirit share" (Cranfield, *Romans*, 386).

34. The verb Paul uses in verse 5 (φρονέω, *phroneo*) carries the idea of giving careful attention to something, with the nuance of orientation and attitude (see Phil. 2:5; 3:19).

35. Most commentators understand "τὸ πνεῦμα, *to pneuma*" in 8:10 as a reference to the Holy Spirit (e.g., T.R. Schreiner, *Romans* [Grand Rapids, MI: Baker, 1998], 415).

36. Although Calvin understood 8:11 to refer to the Spirit enhancing the life of those He indwells, most commentators understand it as a reference to the final resurrection (e.g., Cranfield, *Romans*, 391).

37. The combination of "so then" (ἄρα οὖν, *ara oun*) and "brethren" (ἀδέφοί, *adephoi*) signals a shift in the argument.

38. Moo understands "the deeds of the body" (τὰς πράξεις τοῦ σώματος, *tas praxeis tou somatos*) as "deeds worked out through the body under the influence of the flesh" (*Romans*, 495).

39. The phrases "spirit of slavery" (πνεῦμα δουλείας, *pneuma douleias*) and "spirit of adoption" (πνεῦμα υἱοθεσίας, *pneuma huiothesias*) should both be understood as rhetorical uses of πνεῦμα, *pneuma* that refer to

the Holy Spirit and contrast the result He does not produce with the one He does (see Schreiner, *Romans*, 424).

40. Although it is not one of the activities McQuilkin lists, Paul mentions the Spirit's testifying work twice in Romans (8:16; 9:1).

41. Συμμαρτυρεῖ τῷ πνεύματι ἡμῶν, *summarturei to penumati hemon* is best understood as "bears witness *with* our spirit" rather than ". . . to our spirit." See Moo, *Romans*, 504, footnote 40.

42. Ibid., 520, footnote 60.

43. Harvey, *Anointed with the Spirit*, 150.

Chapter 8

1. Robertson McQuilkin, "An Evangelical Assessment of Mission Theology of the Kingdom of God," in *The Good News of the Kingdom: Mission Theology for the Third Millennium* (Maryknoll, NY: Orbis Books, 1993), 177.

2. Robertson McQuilkin, "Lost Missions: Whatever Happened to the Idea of Rescuing People from Hell?" in *Christianity Today* 50/7(2006): 42.

3. McQuilkin, *An Introduction to Biblical Ethics,* 2nd ed. (Carol Stream, IL: Tyndale House, 1995), 467; see "Saving Minds, Saving Bodies, Saving Souls: The Priorities of Uncle Tom Lambie," CIU Connection 12/2(2012): 19.

4. To substantiate this claim, when *Evangelical Missions Quarterly* recently asked five different leaders to article their views regarding the relationship between proclamation and social action, only one presented a view approximating the prioritistic position (48/3(2012), 265–271).

5. A. Scott Moreau, *Contextualization in World Missions* (Grand Rapids, MI: Kregel, 2012), 318.

6. Ted Olsen, "Spotlight: The Way We Give Now," *Christianity Today* 57/3(2013): 11.

7. Donald McGavran, *Understanding Church Growth,* rev. ed. (Grand Rapids, MI: Eerdmans, 1980), 24.

8. C. René Padilla, "Holistic Mission," in *Dictionary of Mission Theology: Evangelical Foundations* (Downers Grove, IL: IVP, 2007), 158.

9. Of course, not all prioritists and holists would affirm everything in their represented columns, yet the evidence shows that these distinctions generally hold up.

10. E.g., Robert Woodberry observes that although colonial missionaries "perceived societal reform as a natural extension of their faith," they "viewed conversion as their primary goal" ("The Missionary Roots of Liberal Democracy," *American Political Science Review* 106/2(2012): 254–255).

11. Gary McGee, "Evangelical Movement," in *Evangelical Dictionary of Mission Theology* (Grand Rapids, MI: Baker, 2000), 337.

12. D.W. Bebbington, *Evangelicalism in Modern Britain* (New York, NY: Routledge, 1989), 5–14. Additionally, Garth Rosell defines evangelicalism as a movement centered on the cross with four additional convictions: "(1) a shared authority (the Bible); (2) a shared experience (conversion); (3) a shared mission (worldwide evangelization); and (4) a shared vision (the spiritual renewal of church and culture)," *The Surprising Work of God* (Grand Rapids, MI: Baker, 2008), 26.

13. Richard Lovelace, "A Call to Historic Roots and Conformity," in *The Orthodox Evangelicals* (Nashville, TN: Thomas Nelson, 1978), 47.

14. Carl Henry, while critiquing Fundamentalism's repudiation of social responsibility, still argued, as an evangelical, for the primacy of evangelism in the mission of the church (*The Uneasy Conscience of Modern Fundamentalism* [Grand Rapids, MI: Eerdmans, 1947], 88–89).

15. McGee, "Evangelical Movement," 339.

16. Wolfgang Günther and Guillermo Cook, "World Missionary Conferences," in *Dictionary of Mission* (Maryknoll, NY: Orbis, 1997), 503.

17. Paul Pierson, "International Missionary Council," in *Evangelical Dictionary of World Missions* (Grand Rapids, MI: Baker, 2000), 498–499.

18. Priscilla Pope-Levison, "Evangelism in the WCC: From New Delhi to Canberra," in *New Directions in Mission & Evangelization 2* (Maryknoll, NY: Orbis, 1994), 127.

19. Ibid., 130–131.

20. Accessed April 9, 2014, http://www.lausanne.org/en/documents/lausanne-covenant.html.

21. Accessed April 9, 2014, http://www.lausanne.org/en/documents/manila-manifesto.html.

22. Accessed April 9, 2014, http://www.lausanne.org/en/documents/ct-commitment.html,

23. Accessed April 9, 2014, http://www.lausanne.org/en/documents/lausanne-covenant.html.

24. Al Tizon, "Precursors and Tensions in Holistic Mission: An Historical Overview," in *Holistic Mission* (Eugene, OR: Wipf & Stock, 2010), 67–68.

25. Arthur Johnston, *The Battle for World Evangelism* (Wheaton, IL: Tyndale House, 1978), 329–330, 327.

26. Harold Lindsell, "Response," in *In Word and Deed* (Grand Rapids, MI: Eerdmans, 1985), 214.

27. Accessed April 9, 2014, http://www.lausanne.org/docs/2004forum/LOP33_IG4.pdf.

28. Accessed April 9, 2014, http://www.lausanne.org/en/documents/ct-commitment.html.

29. J. Andrew Kirk, *Mission Under Scrutiny* (Minneapolis, MN: Fortress Press, 2006), 47.

30. Christopher Wright, *The Mission of God* (Downers Grove, IL: IVP, 2006), 319.

31. Moreau, *Contextualization in World Missions*, 319.

32. Christopher R. Little, "What Makes Mission Christian?," *International Journal of Frontier Missiology* 25/2(2008): 67ff; "Breaking Bad Missiological Habits," in *Discovering the Mission of God* (Downers Grove, IL: IVP, 2012), 492ff; *Polemic Missiology for the 21st Century: In Memoriam of Roland Allen* (Amazon Kindle, 2013), 8ff.

33. Richard Stearns, *A Hole in Our Gospel* (Nashville, TN: Thomas Nelson, 2009), 3.

34. "Reflections of the Lausanne Theology Working Group," accessed April 9, 2014, http://www.lausanne.org/en/documents/all/twg/1177-twg-three-wholes.html.

35. Ibid.

36. "Micah Network Declaration on Integral Mission," accessed April 9, 2014, http://www.micahnetwork.org/sites/default/files/doc/page/mn_integral_mission_declaration_en.pdf.

37. Stephen Burris and Kendi Douglas, "Introduction," in *River of God: An Introduction to World Mission,* ed. Doug Priest and Stephen Burris(Eugene, OR: Wipf & Stock, 2012), 3.

38. Dean Flemming, *Recovering the Full Mission of God* (Downers Grove, IL: IVP, 2013), 18.

39. K. Ferdinando, "Gospel," in *Dictionary of Mission Theology* (Downers Grove, IL: IVP, 2007), 140–141.

40. R. Peace, "Evangelism," in *Dictionary of Mission Theology* (Downers Grove, IL: IVP, 2007), 115.

41. Scott McKnight, *The King Jesus Gospel* (Grand Rapids, MI: Zondervan, 2011), 46, 49–50.

42. Michael Horton, "Christ at the Center," *Christianity Today* 53/11(2009):48.

43. Michael Horton, *The Gospel-Driven Life: Being Good News People in a Bad News World* (Grand Rapids, MI: Baker, 2009), 127.

44. Duane Litfin, *Word Versus Deed: Resetting the Scales to a Biblical Balance* (Wheaton, IL: Crossway, 2012), 36, 45.

45. Michael Bird, *Evangelical Theology: A Biblical and Systematic Introduction* (Grand Rapids, MI: Zondervan, 2013), 53.

46. Litfin, *Word Versus Deed*, 55.

47. McKnight, *The King Jesus Gospel*, 133.

48. Arthur F. Glasser, *Announcing the Kingdom* (Grand Rapids, MI: Baker, 2003), 12.

49. Burris and Douglas, "Introduction," in *River of God*, 1.

50. Eric Swanson and Sam Williams, *To Transform a City* (Grand Rapids, MI: Zondervan, 2010), 81.

51. Bryant Myers, *Walking with the Poor: Principles and Practices of Transformational Development* (Maryknoll, NY: Orbis, 2002), 49.

52. Ken Eldred, *God Is at Work: Transforming People and Nations through Business* (Ventura, CA: Regal, 2005), 48, 71.

53. R. York Moore, *Making All Things New* (Downers Grove, IL: IVP, 2012), 152.

54. George Eldon Ladd, *The Presence of the Future,* rev. ed. (Grand Rapids, MI: Eerdmans, 1974), 265–266.

55. Glasser, *Announcing the Kingdom*, 358, 246.

56. I. Howard Marshall, *New Testament Theology: Many Witnesses, One Gospel* (Downers Grove, IL: IVP, 2004), 80.

57. Kirk, *Mission Under Scrutiny*, 94.

58. Tim Chester, *Good News to the Poor* (Wheaton, IL: Crossway, 2013), 90.

59. Litfin, *Word Versus Deed*, 121, emphasis added.

60. Kevin DeYoung and Greg Gilbert, *What Is the Mission of the Church? Making Sense of Social Justice, Shalom, and the Great Commission* (Wheaton, IL: Crossway, 2011), 112.

61. David J. Hesselgrave, "Evangelical Mission in 2001 and Beyond—Who Will Set the Agenda?" in *Trinity World Forum* Spring, 2001, 3.

62. Lowell Bliss, *Environmental Missions* (Pasadena, CA: William Carey Library, 2013), 17.

63. C. Neal Johnson, *Business as Mission* (Downers Grove, IL: IVP, 2009), 42.

64. Flemming, *Recovering the Full Mission of God*, 192.

65. Brian Woolnough, "Good News for the Poor—Setting the Scene," in *Holistic Mission*, 6.

66. Moore, *Making All Things New*, 159.

67. Carl Braaten, *The Apostolic Imperative* (Minneapolis, MN: Augsburg Publishing House, 1985), 11.

68. Stephen Neill, *Creative Tension* (London: Edinburgh House Press, 1959), 81.

69. Quoted by Charles Van Engen, *God's Missionary People* (Grand Rapids, MI: Baker, 1991), 28.

70. David Bosch, *Transforming Mission* (Maryknoll, NY: Orbis, 1991), 512.

71. Christopher Wright, *The Mission of God's People: A Biblical Theology of the Church's Mission* (Grand Rapids, MI: Zondervan, 2010), 26.

72. Timothy Tennent, *Invitation to World Missions* (Grand Rapids, MI: Kregel, 2010), 54.

73. McQuilkin, "Lost Missions", 42.

74. Augustine of Hippo, *The City of God* (New York, NY: Random House, 1950), 692.

75. John Piper, *Let the Nations Be Glad!* (Grand Rapids, MI: Baker, 2010), 130; See *A God-Entranced Vision of All Things* (Wheaton, IL: Crossway, 2004), 40.

76. Ben Witherington III, *Imminent Domain: The Story of the Kingdom of God and Its Celebration* (Grand Rapids, MI: Eerdmans, 2009), 25–26.

77. Todd Johnson and Peter Crossing, "Christianity 2014: Independent Christianity and Slum Dwellers," *International Bulletin of Missionary Research* 38/1(2014):29.

78. Samuel Moffett, "Evangelism: The Leading Partner," in *Perspectives on the World Christian Movement,* 4th ed. (Pasadena, CA: William Carey Library, 2009), 599–600.

79. David J. Hesselgrave, *Paradigms in Conflict: 10 Key Questions in Christian Mission Today* (Grand Rapids, MI: Kregel Academic & Professional, 2005), 144ff.

80. James Engel and William Dyrness, *Changing the Mind of Missions: Where Have We Gone Wrong?* (Downers Grove, IL: 2000), 23.

81. William Larkin Jr., "Mission in Luke," in *Mission in the New Testament: An Evangelical Approach* (Maryknoll, NY: Orbis, 1998), 158.

82. Harry Boer, *Pentecost and Missions* (Grand Rapids, MI: Eerdmans, 1961), 103–112, 205.

83. E.g., it is mentioned once in Wright's *The Mission of God*, 306, Wright's *The Mission of God's People*, 100, and in Burris and Douglas' *River of God*, 195. But it is not mentioned at all in "The Micah Network Declaration on Integral Mission" (accessed April 9, 2014,

http://www.micahnetwork.org/sites/default/files/doc/page/mn_integral_mission_declaration_en.pdf.), the Lausanne Occasional Paper on "Holistic Mission" (accessed April 9, 2014, http://www.lausanne.org/docs/2004forum/LOP33_IG4.pdf.), Myers' *Walking with the Poor* or Flemming's *Recovering the Full Mission of God.*

84. E.g., James Nkansah-Obrempong, "Holistic Gospel in a Developing Society: Biblical, Theological and Historical Backgrounds," Evangelical Review of Theology 33/3(2009): 202.

85. Thomas Nettles, "A Response to Hesselgrave," *Trinity World Forum* (Deerfield, IL: Trinity Evangelical Divinity School, Spring, 1990): 6.

86. Wright, *The Mission of God*, 439.

87. John Stott, "The Battle for World Evangelization," *Christianity Today* (Jan. 5, 1979): 34.

88. Roland Allen, *The Spontaneous Expansion of the Church* (Grand Rapids, MI: Eerdmans, 1962), 83.

89. Lesslie Newbigin, *The Gospel in a Pluralistic Society* (Grand Rapids, MI: Eerdmans, 1989), 137.

90. David J. Hesselgrave, "Redefining Holism," *Evangelical Missions Quarterly* 35/3(1999):281.

91. Hesselgrave, "Holes in 'Holistic Mission,'" *Trinity World Forum* (Deerfield, IL: Trinity Evangelical Divinity School, Spring, 1990): 4.

92. Hendrik Kraemer, *The Christian Message in a Non-Christian World* (Grand Rapids, MI: Kregel, 1963), 430.

93. Roland Allen, *The Ministry of the Spirit,* ed. David M. Paton (London: World Dominion Press, 1960), 99.

94. Donald McGavran, *How Churches Grow* (London: World Dominion Press, 1959), 12.

95. Mark Thomsen, in *Mission at the Dawn of the 21st Century: A Vision for the Church,* ed. Paul Varo Martinson (Minneapolis, MN: Kirk House Publishers, 1999), 261.

96. DeYoung and Gilbert, *What is the Mission of the Church?*, 176, 235.

Chapter 9

1. We want to thank Craig Ott, Harold Netland and James Plued-demann for feedback and advice on this paper.

2. See McQuilkin and Mullen, "The Behavioral Sciences Under the Authority of Scripture," 31-43; McQuilkin, *The Five Smooth Stones*, 9.

3. Robertson McQuilkin, "Exegeting the Audience," *Trinity Journal* 33/2(2012):200.

4. Ibid., 200; McQuilkin, *The Five Smooth Stones*, 26.

5. See McQuilkin's "Communicating the Gospel or Why Aren't We Getting Through?" *Japan Harvest* 16/1(1966-1967): 6–8; "Who's Biting?" *Japan Harvest* 16/4(1967): 8–12; "Japanese Values and Christian Mission," *The Japan Christian Quarterly* 33/4(1967):253–265; see also McQuilkin's "Use and Misuse of the Social Sciences," in *Missiology and the Social Sciences,* ed. Edward Rommen and Gary Corwin (Pasadena, CA: William Carey Library, 1996), 165–166.

6. McQuilkin, "An Evangelical Assessment of Mission Theology of the Kingdom of God," 172–178.

7. See McQuilkin's "Saving Minds, Saving Bodies, Saving Souls: The Priorities of Uncle Tom Lambie," 19; *The Five Smooth Stones*, 127–128.

8. McQuilkin, "Use and Misuse," 173; *The Five Smooth Stones*, 208.

9. McQuilkin, "Behavioral Sciences," 42.

10. Robert Priest, "'Experience-Near Theologizing' in Diverse Human Contexts," in *Globalizing Theology: Christian Belief and Practice in an Era of World Christianity* (Grand Rapids, MI: Baker, 2006), 180–195.

11. McQuilkin, "Exegeting the Audience," 199–207.

12. Robert Priest, "'Who Am I?' Theology and Identity for Children of the Dragon," in *After Imperialism: Christian Identity and the Global Evangelical Movement* (Eugene, OR: Pickwick Publications, 2013), 175–192.

13. McQuilkin devoted great attention to helping others work through this hermeneutical process. See especially his *Understanding and Applying the Bible: Revised and Expanded*, 304–347.

14. T. Nyasulu, "Moral Discipline in the Church of Central Africa Presbyterian (CCAP) Synod of Livingstonia, Malawi, 1995-2005," (PhD diss., Trinity Evangelical Divinity School, 2010).

15. Many of McQuilkin's writings focused on the importance of this point and what this should mean in practical terms. See, for example, "Behavioral Sciences"; "Use and Misuse"; *Understanding and Applying the Bible*; "Limits of Cultural Interpretation"; "Problems of Normativeness in Scripture: Cultural Versus Permanent," 217–253.

16. McQuilkin, "Use and Misuse," 172.

17. Robert J. Priest, "Missionary Elenctics: Conscience and Culture," *Missiology* 22(1994): 291–315; McQuilkin, "Use and Misuse," 171.

18. Robert J. Priest, "Cultural Factors in Victorious Living," in *Free and Fulfilled*, 128–142.

19. McQuilkin, "Use and Misuse," 173.

Chapter 10

1. E-mail to the author, June 26, 2009.

2. McQuilkin and Copan, *An Introduction to Biblical Ethics: Walking in the Way of Wisdom* (Downers Grove, IL: IVP, 2014).

3. McQuilkin, *An Introduction to Biblical Ethics* (Wheaton, IL: Tyndale House, 1995), 71.

4. Ibid., ix.

5. E-mail to the author, June 23, 2009.

6. E-mail to the author, September 5, 2012.

7. E-mail to the author, September 21, 2012.

8. McQuilkin, *An Introduction to Biblical Ethics*, 365–366.

9. Ibid., 439–443.

10. Ibid., 441.

11. "Statement from Wheaton College President Philip Ryken on Chapel Demonstration," in Wheaton College Media Center (February 10, 2014), accessed April 4, 2014, http://www.wheaton.edu/Media-Center/News/2014/02/Statement-from-Wheaton-College-President-Philip-Ryken-on-Chapel-Demonstration.

12. For a development of the views of both sides of the divide, see James Davison Hunter, *Culture Wars: The Struggle to Define America* (New York, NY: Basic Books, 1991).

13. McQuilkin, *An Introduction to Biblical Ethics*, 257.

14. See Alvin Schmidt, *How Christianity Changed the World* (Grand Rapids, MI: Zondervan, 2004); Rodney Stark, *The Victory of Reason* (New York, NY: Random House, 2005); Thom Wolf, *India Progress-Prone: Baliraja Proposal of Mahatma Phule* (New Delhi: University Institute, 2008); Vishal Mangalwadi, *The Book that Made Your World: How the Bible Created the Soul of Western Civilization* (Nashville, TN: Thomas Nelson, 2011); and Niall Ferguson, *Civilization: The West and the Rest* (New York, NY: Penguin, 2012).

15. Robert D. Woodberry, "The Missionary Roots of Liberal Democracy," *American Political Science Review* 106/2(2012): 244–274.

16. Ibid., 244–245.

17. Ibid., 254.

18. Andrea Palpant Dilley, "The World the Missionaries Made," *Christianity Today* 58/1(2014): 41.

19. For an extensive discussion on this and related topics, see Paul Copan and Kenneth Litwak, *The Gospel in the Marketplace of Ideas: Paul's Mars Hill Experience for Our Pluralistic World* (Downers Grove, IL: IVP Academic, 2014).

20. Rosaria Butterfield, *The Secrets Thoughts of an Unlikely Convert* (Pittsburgh, PA: Crown and Covenant, 2012).

21. Rosaria Butterfield, "My Train-Wreck Conversion," *Christianity Today* 57/1(2013): 112.

22. Robert Spitzer, "Can Some Gay Men and Lesbians Change Their Sexual Orientation? 200 Participants Reporting a Change from Homosexual to Heterosexual Orientation," *Archives of Sexual Behavior* 32/5(2003): 403.

23. Benedict Carey, "Psychiatry Giant Sorry for Backing Gay 'Cure'," *New York Times* (May 5, 2012).

24. Mark Yarhouse, "Two Changes, As It Were," accessed October 3, 2012, http://psychologyandchristianity.wordpress.com/2012/04/27/two-developments-as-it-were/.

25. Gerard van den Aardweg, "Frail and Aged, a Giant Apologizes," accessed October 3, 2012, http://www.mercatornet.com/articles/view/frail_and_aged_a_giant_apologizes.

26. For a defense of a number of these statements, see Joe Dallas and Nancy Heche, eds., *The Complete Christian Guide to Understanding Homosexuality: A Biblical and Compassionate Response to Same Sex Attraction* (Eugene, OR: Harvest House, 2010).

27. Dr. Elizabeth Moberly has observed a common pattern with same-sex attraction. For example, with males, the need for masculine love and affirmation that doesn't come in childhood may, with the onset of

sexual maturation, "be inappropriately eroticized—with a pre-adult developmental lack carried into adulthood and inappropriately met with sexual activity" ("Homosexuality and the Truth," *First Things* 71(1997): 32).

28. See Stanton Jones and Mark Yarhouse, *Ex-Gays? A Longitudinal Study of Religiously Mediated Change in Sexual Orientation* (Downers Grove, IL: IVP, 2007).

29. Mark Regnerus' peer-reviewed research findings challenge the 2005 official APA brief claiming that not "a single study has found children of lesbian or gay parents to be disadvantaged in any significant respect relative to children of heterosexual parents." ("How Different Are the Adult Children of Parents Who Have Same-Sex Relationships? Findings from the New Family Structures Study," accessed April 4, 2014, http://www.sciencedirect.com/science/article/pii/S0049089X12000610.). For more details, see www.familystructurestudies.com.

30. See Mark A. Yarhouse, *Understanding Sexual Identity: A Resource for Youth Ministry* (Grand Rapids, MI: Zondervan, 2013).

31. Ibid., 33.

Chapter 11

1. Richard John Neuhaus, *Freedom for Ministry* (Grand Rapids, MI: Eerdmans,1979), 3.

2. Neil Cole, *Church 3.0: Upgrades for the Future of the Church* (San Francisco, CA: Jossey-Bass, 2010), 28–42.

3. Margaret Wheatley, "Writings," accessed April 22, 2014, http://www.margaretwheatley.com/articles/leadershiplessons.html.

4. Alan Hirsch and Dave Ferguson, *On The Verge: A Journey into the Apostolic Future of the Church* (Grand Rapids, MI: Zondervan, 2011), 46.

5. Reggie McNeal, *Missional Renaissance: Changing the Scorecard for the Church* (San Francisco, CA: Jossey-Bass, 2011), 13–14.

6. These blessings in and by the Spirit will empower us to live a Christ-following lifestyle until Christ returns:

   a. His constant, personal and powerful indwelling presence (see John 14:16–18, 20, 23; 15:5, 8–9, 11, 16; 16:22–24; 17:15)

   b. Being marked by the Spirit, identified as God's children (see John 15:3, 19–21, 26–27; 16:1–3; 17:14)

   c. Being granted the authority to freely make requests of the Father in His name (see John 14:12–14; 15:7, 16, 21; 16:23–24, 26; 17:26)

   d. Going to the ends of the earth (see Acts 1:8) and yet quickly recognizing and bonding with other Christ followers in an unexplainable unity that is similar to the oneness of the Father, Son and Spirit (see John 13:34–35; 15:12–13, 17; 17:11–12, 18, 21–23)

   e. Sparks of creative illumination as humble followers seek His wisdom, involvement in and discernment to solve problems and face challenges (see John 14:26; 16:7–15, 33)

   f. A whole array of grace-fueled gifts entrusted to every believer, giving them a contribution to God's cause and to the welfare of their spiritual family (see John 16:14–15; Rom. 12:3–8; 1 Cor. 12–14; Eph. 4:11–12)

   g. A taste of the inheritance they can anticipate enjoying with Him at His return (see John 13:36; 14:1–3; 17:24; Eph. 1:3–14)

7. McNeal, *Missional Renaissance*, 4.

8. McQuilkin, *Life in the Spirit* (Nashville, TN: Broadman & Holman, 2000), 263–264.

9. Margaret Wheatley, "Living in the Age of Distraction," accessed April 22, 2014, http://www.margaretwheatley.com/articles/Wheatley-LivingInTheAgeOfDistraction.pdf.

10. Francis Chan, *Forgotten God: Reversing Our Tragic Neglect of the Holy Spirit* (Colorado Springs, CO: David C. Cook, 2009), 106.

11. Does the Bible say anything about God helping His people to navigate change? What does it look like for the Bible to be our functional authority in communicating change? I think the answer is obvious—it is on almost every page. The entire Bible is a record of God initiating and processing change. Creation, redemption and reconciliation are only a few of His changes. How does God guide us into change with clear, memorable and transferable communication? As I went through the Bible asking this question, here are a few of the things I observed:

   a. God uses *stories* (real history and parables): "Remember Abraham"(Exod. 32:13); "A farmer went out to sow his seed" (Mark 4:3, NIV).

   b. God uses *pictures/images* (in words and in objective learning tasks): "I am the true vine" (John 15:1, NIV); "Drink of [this cup]" (Matt. 26:27).

   c. God uses *proverbs* (distilled wisdom in memorable words)—they are God's bumper stickers! E.g., the ox, dirty stable and abundant crops referenced in Proverbs 14:4. Do I need to say more?.

   d. God uses *poetry* (the majority of poetry is set in musical form, which makes it memorable and transferable): "The Lord is my shepherd" (Ps. 23:1).

   e. God uses *consequences* (reaping from what is sown; "letting the chips fall"): See 1 Samuel 8 when God gives Israel a king.

   f. God uses *questions & dialogue* (some He asks, and some He lets people ask Him): "[Adam,] who told you that you were naked?" (Gen. 3:11); "Lord, how is it. . .?" (John 14:22). God listens as well as speaks.

   g. God uses *gifts/the blessing*: "It is your Father's good pleasure to give you…" (Luke 12:32).

h. God uses *correction/the curse*: "For the Lord disciplines the one he loves" (Heb. 12:6).

i. God uses *presence/being among*: "And the Word became flesh" (John 1:14).

I was a speech and drama major at university (back before the flood!). As I look over God's various ways of communicating truth and guiding His people through change, I realize that every great communicator I have studied uses many of the same forms. I try to really clarify what I want others to take home and apply. I then think through this list and try to use three or more of these forms in getting the one idea across.

12. Paul Stanley and J. Robert Clinton offer a constellation model of mentoring that may be helpful for Christ followers and leaders: "Mentoring is a relational experience in which one person empowers another by sharing God-given resources. . . . A lifetime constellation affirms that God, in His typically wild and unpredictable manner, will touch our lives with a variety of people. They will serve in a variety of roles (discipler, spiritual guide, coach, counselor, teacher, sponsor and hero [contemporary and historical]) who touch us for various lengths of time and with a broad range of depth of engagement" (*Connecting: The Mentoring Relationships You Need to Succeed in Life*, 33, 41–42).

13. Gordon MacKenzie, *Orbiting the Giant Hairball: A Corporate Fool's Guide to Surviving with Grace* (New York, NY: Viking Penguin Inc., 1988), 159.

14. E-mail to the author, June 2013.

15. McQuilkin, *The Five Smooth Stones*, 176.

16. See John 14:12, 17; 17:13–24; Rom. 8:6; 2 Cor. 3:18; Eph. 2:8–10.

Conclusion

1. McQuilkin, *Understanding and Applying the Bible: Revised and Expanded*, 241.

PUBLICATIONS
Fort Washington, PA 19034

This book is published by CLC Publications, an outreach of CLC Ministries International. The purpose of CLC is to make evangelical Christian literature available to all nations so that people may come to faith and maturity in the Lord Jesus Christ. We hope this book has been life changing and has enriched your walk with God through the work of the Holy Spirit. If you would like to know more about CLC, we invite you to visit our website:

www.clcusa.org

To know more about the remarkable story of the founding of CLC International we encourage you to read

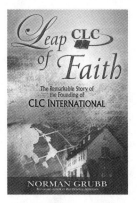

LEAP OF FAITH

Norman Grubb

Paperback
Size 5¹/₄ x 8, Pages 248
ISBN: 978-0-87508-650-7
ISBN (*e-book*): 978-1-61958-055-8